IMAGES
of America

MONONGAHELA CITY

On the Cover: Monongahela was a thriving city back in 1908, thanks in part to the arrival of immigrants from all over the world, who labored in the mines and industries in town. This photograph depicts the Old Home Week Celebration, September 6–13, 1908. The patriotic banners, bunting, and welcoming signs throughout the city displayed Monongahela's sincere effort and pride as it welcomed its native sons and daughters home once again. (Courtesy scrapbook of Potente Zanardelli.)

IMAGES
of America

MONONGAHELA CITY

Susan M. Bowers and Laura M. Magone

ARCADIA
PUBLISHING

ISBN 978-0-7385-7635-0

Published by Arcadia Publishing
Charleston, South Carolina

Printed in the United States of America

Library of Congress Control Number: 2011925434

For all general information, please contact Arcadia Publishing:
Telephone 843-853-2070
Fax 843-853-0044
E-mail sales@arcadiapublishing.com
For customer service and orders:
Toll-Free 1-888-313-2665

Visit us on the Internet at www.arcadiapublishing.com

We dedicate this publication to the great people who built Monongahela City, to those who work each and every day to make it a better place, and to those who follow, hoping they will treasure the rich history as we do. Our thanks are given to our combined eight Italian-American grandparents, who labored tirelessly and selflessly, preparing the path for our parents, for us, and for future generations. Noi vi vogliamo bene.

Giuseppe and Assunta (Ferriello) Albero
Francesco and Domenica (Belasi) Corbelli
John and Mary (Zanardelli) Previtali
Joseph and Caroline (Mandarino) Magnone

Contents

Foreword

We would like to thank Susan and Laura for taking on this project about our hometown, of which we are so very proud. Laura has already put Monongahela on the map with her documentary *One Extraordinary Street*, which tells the story of Park Avenue. Park Avenue is indeed an extraordinary neighborhood, but then, why shouldn't it be when it is just one small part of a very special city? Susan and Laura have shown how extraordinary Monongahela truly is in this pictorial history.

We have always thought the best place to live and raise a family is in a community lining the banks of the Monongahela River Valley, such as we did with our children Bruce and Toni Jo. Monongahela is a beautiful city with the river on one side and, opposite, a vista of homes as fine as one would find in a place such as Colonial Williamsburg. A true community where neighbors know and help each other, Monongahela demonstrates the best qualities of a small town. In its heyday, the business district, which spans between First and Fifth Streets, had eight grocery stores, six meat markets, two produce stores, four bakeries, six ice cream parlors, 10 restaurants, two soda manufacturing plants, five shoe stores, two furniture stores, four appliance stores, two five-and-dimes, three hardware stores, four jewelers, three paint and wallpaper stores, three florists, two funeral homes, six bars, six barbershops, four tailor shops, five shoemakers, six car agencies, four real estate offices, two news and magazine offices, one newspaper, two printing shops, five gas stations, two bowling lanes, three hotels, six social clubs, two lumberyards, and two blacksmiths. Most were owned and operated by local people.

We believe one of the most relaxing things to do in life is to take the time to get out the family photograph album and bring back wonderful memories as we reminisce about the past. We are sure this book will offer a similar experience, helping us to enjoy our rich traditions and preserving our collective heritage for future generations.

—Aldo and Joan Bartolotta
April 2011

Acknowledgments

The authors would like to extend their gratitude to all those who contributed photographs and information for the preparation of this publication. A community truly rallied when asked to participate. Photographs came in by person, mail, and email from all around the country. The authors would also like to thank their friends and family members who helped with proofreading, technical support, typing, and answering history questions.

A special mention must be made of two of the most prolific keepers of photographic community history. Monongahela is fortunate enough to have two individuals who worked diligently to preserve local history. Both scrapbooks were located in places where townspeople could contribute to them, and contribute they did—photographs, clippings, poems, and other memorabilia. Dr. W.P. Taylor was a dentist in Monongahela, and he compiled 42 scrapbooks that document community treasures from the period of the 1800s through the mid-1900s. Dr. Taylor's scrapbooks not only document Monongahela and American history, they also depict the life of an educated person who was cultured and well traveled. His scrapbooks have been entrusted to the Monongahela Area Historical Society, which is in the process of archiving and digitizing them.

Several photographs were taken from a scrapbook compiled by Potente "Pot" Zanardelli, born of Italian immigrants. His scrapbook depicts the immigrants' working-class experience. After Pot's untimely death, the scrapbook was preserved by William and Dora Zanardelli Turri, his brother-in-law and sister, and passed on to Bernard and Dolores Turri Zanardelli, their son-in-law and daughter. The scrapbook has now been entrusted to Laura M. Magone.

Unless otherwise noted, all images are from the archives of the Monongahela Area Historical Society.

The city of Monongahela is doubly blessed, not only by its immense rich history, but also by the vast number of people who cared and still care so much to preserve it. In Dr. Taylor's scrapbook, there is a personal account from Mary B. Collins that she typed in July 1936. It is entitled "Thoughts after the Markell Sale." Speaking to her Monongahela treasures and memories, she says, "So care for them tenderly, as I would were I here. They have caused me much joy and many a sad tear." And so we shall care tenderly.

INTRODUCTION

Nestled in the Middle Monongahela Valley region along the Monongahela River in southwestern Pennsylvania, the city of Monongahela had its beginning in the late 1700s. Abraham Decker originally claimed land based on a Virginia entry, confirmed by patent No. 3783, bearing the date of August 26, 1769. Because of a dispute between Virginia and Pennsylvania, both claiming it as part of their states, the Board of Property finally declared Decker's Pennsylvania title to be valid. In 1770, the Parkison family arrived from the east. Joseph, one of five brothers, built a cabin near Pigeon Creek. He ran a ferry on the south side of the river, while the Devour family's ferry, already in operation prior to Parkison's, ran one on the north side.

During this early time, the value of the river was overlooked because of fear of the Indians who lived along its banks. Joseph Parkison had no fear of them and entered into business to succeed. The transporting of goods and people on the river gave him the incentive to lay out a new town in 1782 in the upper region near Pigeon Creek extending to what became Third Street, and call it Parkison's Ferry, which was later changed to Williamsport, after his son.

A separate plot of land was sold to Adam Wickerham by Paul Froman in 1792. In 1807, Wickerham laid out another town on the lower part, beginning at what became Third Street; he called it Georgetown after his son. There were two towns until 1816. Upon the urging of city lot holders to make Georgetown a part of Williamsport, Wickerham declared it so in the paper on February 23, 1816, after a vote was taken, thus creating the one town of Williamsport. On April 1, 1837, it took the present name of Monongahela City.

Monongahela's part in the Whiskey Insurrection is commemorated by a plaque erected near the spot where the angry farmers met. After the Revolutionary War, whiskey (viewed as distilled grain) was the best money crop to transport across the mountains in exchange for iron and salt. The farmers thought it unfair to tax them for "drinking our grain instead of eating it!" Whiskey Point, the bluff at Main Street and Park Avenue, was the site of a meeting of 226 irate farmers on August 14, 1794. It was also where Albert Gallatin's eloquent speech turned the tide, resulting in the peaceful ending of the Whiskey Insurrection, thus cementing Monongahela's place in American history forever. (It has been explained that people on the western side of the Allegheny Mountains use the term "Whiskey Insurrection" instead of "Rebellion," because it was the farmers' legal right to oppose what they viewed as an unfair tax.)

The city's historical significance did not end with the Whiskey Insurrection. There were other contributors. Too numerous to name them all, their contributions built a community and, in many ways, changed the world. Some noteworthy inventors and their inventions include Edward G. Acheson, Carborundum; brothers George, John, and Christopher Anton, the Anton miner lamps; and Fred Cox, the Nerf football. All lived and worked in Monongahela at various times. Locals contend that the first foot-long hotdog had its beginning in Monongahela, being served at Frankie's Place, a hotdog stand near Pigeon Creek Bridge, by its creator, Frankie. John Blythe, a prominent architect of the late 1800s, is attributed with changing the look of the city by designing several of the churches and early homes. His prominence was noted in several newspapers, including a Pittsburgh periodical of that time. Early on, there were numerous factories, businesses, a racetrack, an opera house, two movie theaters, macaroni and glass factories, and much more. Monongahela also has one of the largest Native American burial grounds ever excavated in the United States. It is where the Mounds Park is currently located. The ancient Adena people, who once lived along the river, built the burial mounds centuries ago. A collection of Native American artifacts from Monongahela, consisting of arrowheads, tools, utensils, and more, is now housed in "America's Attic," the Smithsonian Institution in Washington, DC.

Monongahela today has continued to fulfill the dream of the early settlers. There are many churches, social organizations, civic groups, specialty shops, businesses, and even a river museum. The city also has an active chamber of commerce, a progressive city government, a library, a volunteer fire department, an effective police department, and a world-class, ever-growing hospital. The city can also boast of its unique Aquatorium (an extensive stage with seats built jetting out on the river.) The Monongahela Cemetery is one of the largest and most beautiful in the area and is listed in the National Register of Historic Places for its design and landscaping. But the heart of the city has always been and will always be its residents—inventive, good-willed, and charitable—who form a welcoming and cohesive community.

The cover depicts the city's first 100-year homecoming, welcoming its residents' return to the place of their birth. The tradition has continued throughout the years, including its bicentennial, Fourth of July celebrations, and especially Kennywood Day, on which many Monongahelans still return each year. The elements were all there at the beginning to develop Monongahela into a thriving city and are still present today for its continued success. The residents continue to embrace its ongoing potential, and by doing so, they honor the man who braved the wilderness so many years ago and laid out those first lots along the river. And that man was named Joseph Parkison—first permanent settler, town founder, first postmaster, ferry master, innkeeper, and patriot.

The following poem, "The River Mon," written by Susan M. Bowers, best exemplifies what makes this area so special.

Ever-flowing past the city's banks
As it once did along the Indians' paths
Swelling at times with might to flood
Rolling peacefully, raging north
Bringing so many to its door
Settlers with their visions intact
The Great Mon, the Deliverer
Glistening waters, winding through valleys
Ever-flowing, ever-present still

One

The Founding

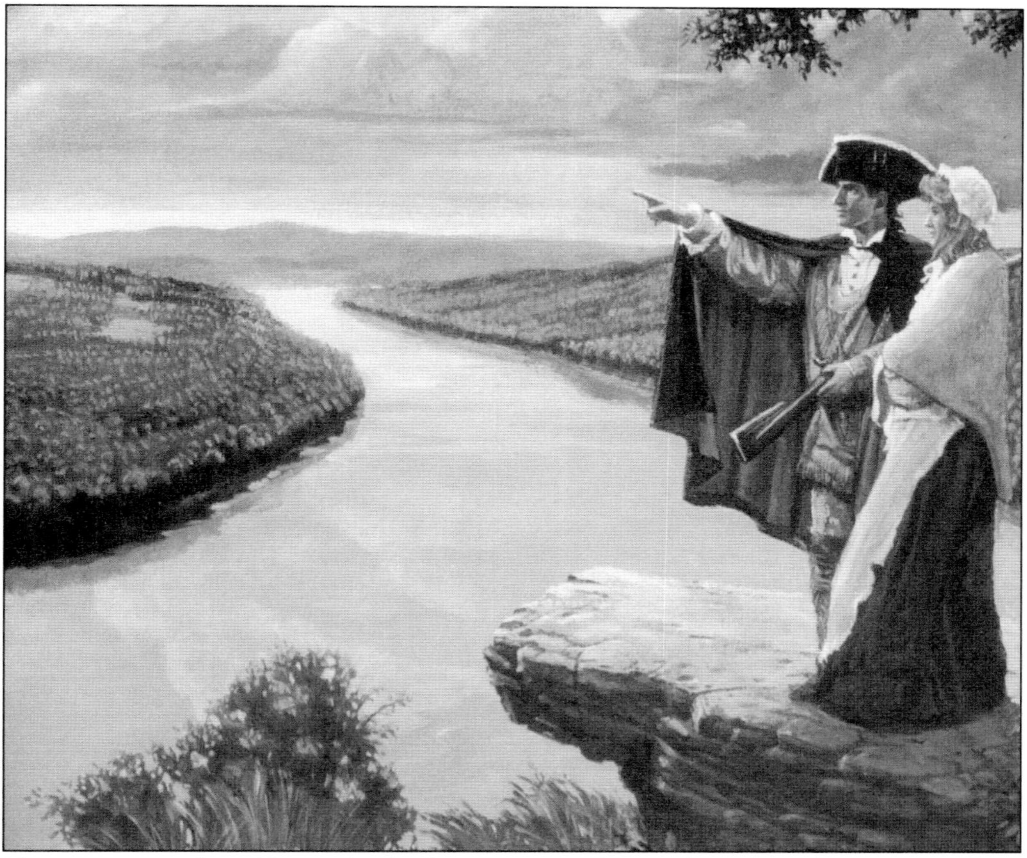

Upon arriving in the wilderness lands of western Pennsylvania, the early settlers must have been filled with awe when seeing, for the first time, the virgin land of rolling hills covered with forests along a winding river. Everything was there—lumber, fish, wild game, flowers, and fruit—making it a paradise for those brave enough to tame it. And so the story began. (Courtesy Mon Valley Progress Council.)

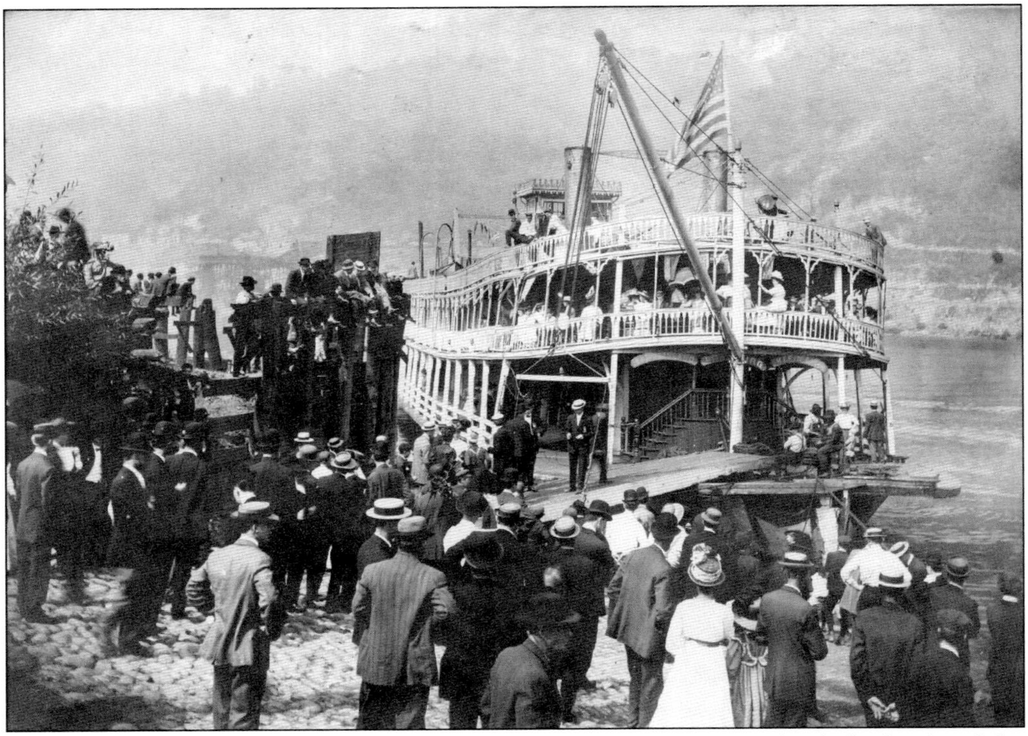

At the arrival of a Pittsburgh excursion boat at the Second Street wharf, the banks of the Monongahela River are bustling with excitement as people are welcomed home during the Old Home Week celebration of 1908. Men, women, and children appear in their Sunday best, donning a derby, straw hat, or a frilly bonnet. Anticipation filled the air as former town residents returned to participate in the grand festivities.

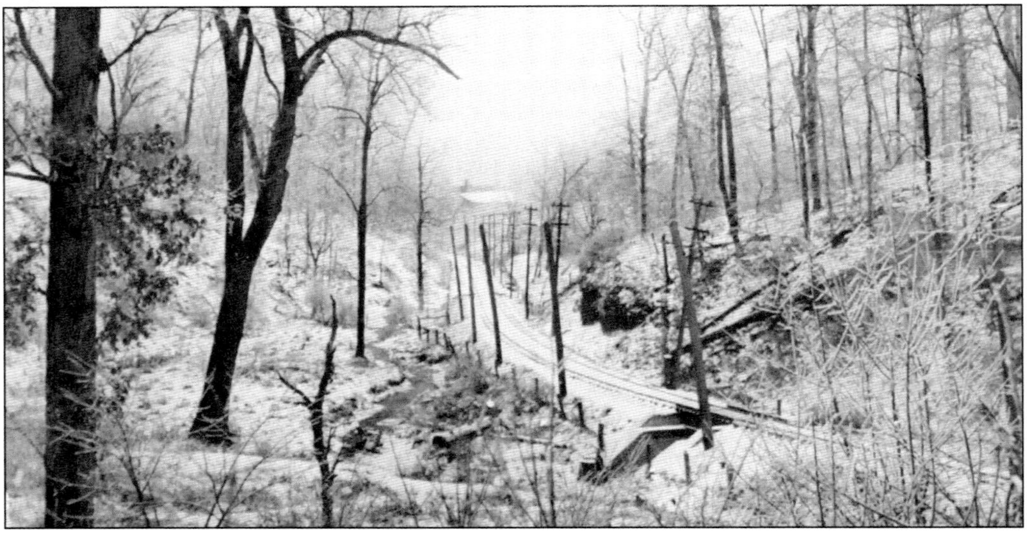

During the 1700s, an idea was born near the mouth of Pigeon Creek. The man was Joseph Parkison. His dream began with the purchase of land from Abraham Decker. Parkison laid out lots, established a village, and named it Parkison's Ferry. During his 94 years, he watched it grow into a flourishing town called Williamsport. Pigeon Creek flows through Monongahela City, ever present, ever near. (Courtesy scrapbook of Potente Zanardelli.)

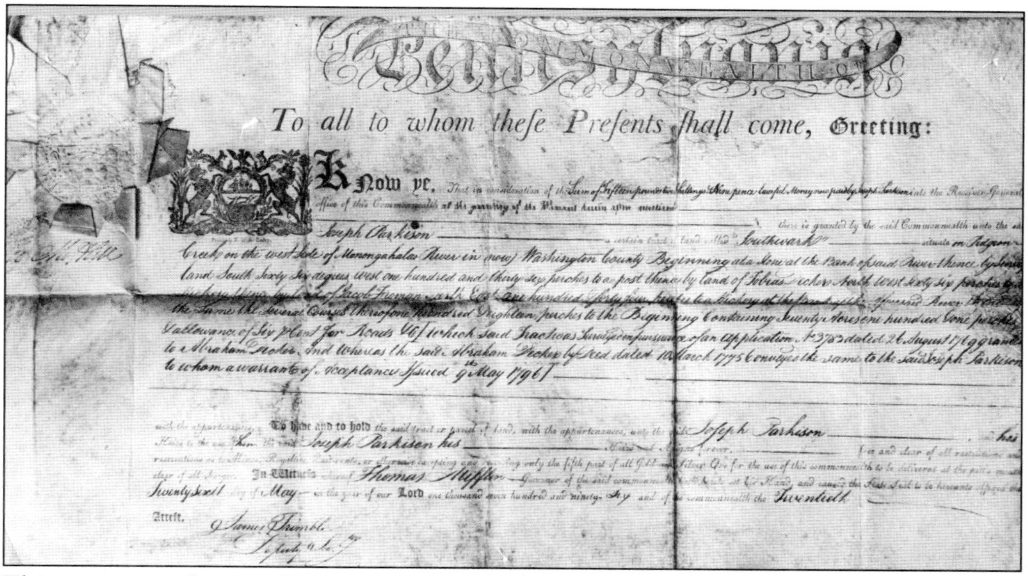
To all to whom these Presents shall come, Greeting:

Know ye, That in consideration of the Sum of ... Joseph Parkison ... Southwark ... Creek on the west side of Monongahala River in (now) Washington County ... Abraham Decker ... Joseph Parkison ... In Witness ... Thomas Mifflin ... Twenty sixth day of May in the year of our Lord one thousand seven hundred and ninety-six ... Twentieth

Attest.

This patent was the one that was given to Abraham Decker on August 26, 1769, and was held by him until it came into the possession of Joseph Parkison. Patent No. 3783 was given to Joseph Parkison on May 11, 1796, entitling him to all the land from Pigeon Creek to what is today Third Street. The dividing line ran between the Crall and Meredith buildings on Main Street.

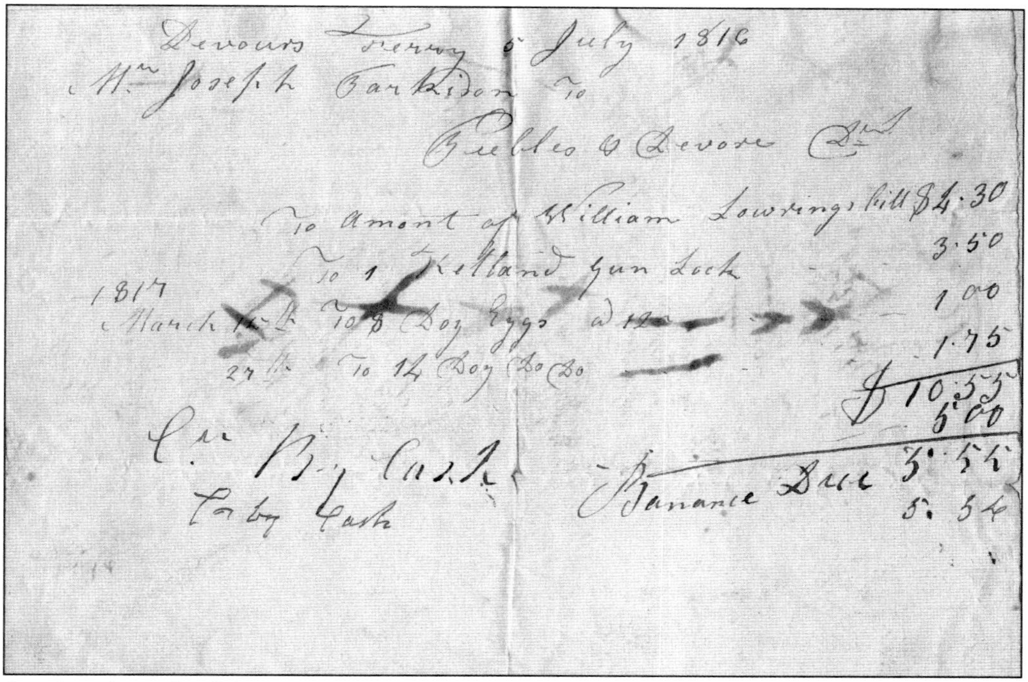
Devours Ferry 6 July 1816

Mr Joseph Parkison To

Peebles & Devore Dr

To Amont of William Lowring bill $4.30

To 1 Killand gun Lock 3.50

1817 March ... To 8 Doz Eggs at ... 1.00

27th To 14 Doz Do Do 1.75

$10.55

5.00

Cr By Cash Banance Due 5.55

Cr by Cash 5.54

On the other side of the river, Devour's Ferry (later spelled DeVore) was established in 1771. The ferry ran before Parkison built his on this side of the river. The arrangement between the two competitors was that anyone coming from east to west used Devour's, and those going from west to east used Parkison's. The receipt above illustrates the need for Devour and Parkison to use each other's ferry from time to time.

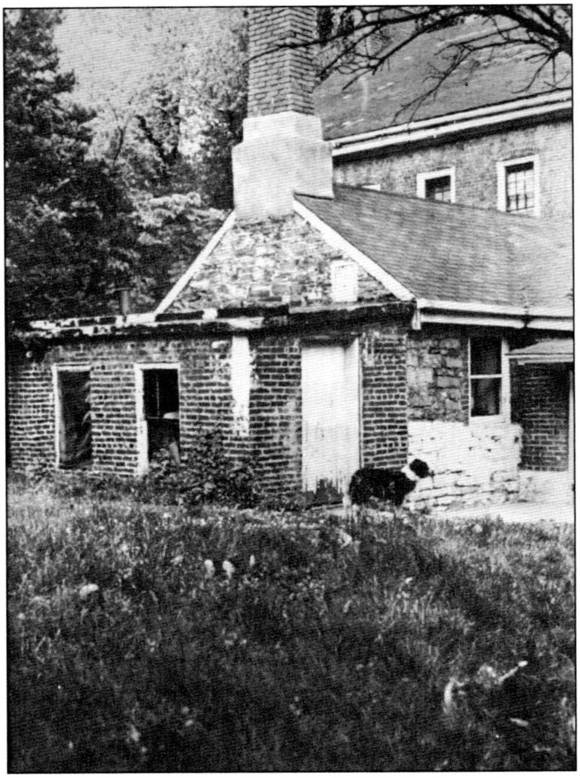

Abraham Decker was the only one of the early landowners who started a homestead. He built his cabin along Route 481, above the spring and in front of what is now the VanVoorhis House. Parkison and his wife, Margaret, were sheltered here on their arrival in 1770. The remains of the original cabin are shown at left. It is the part between the brick house and the shed.

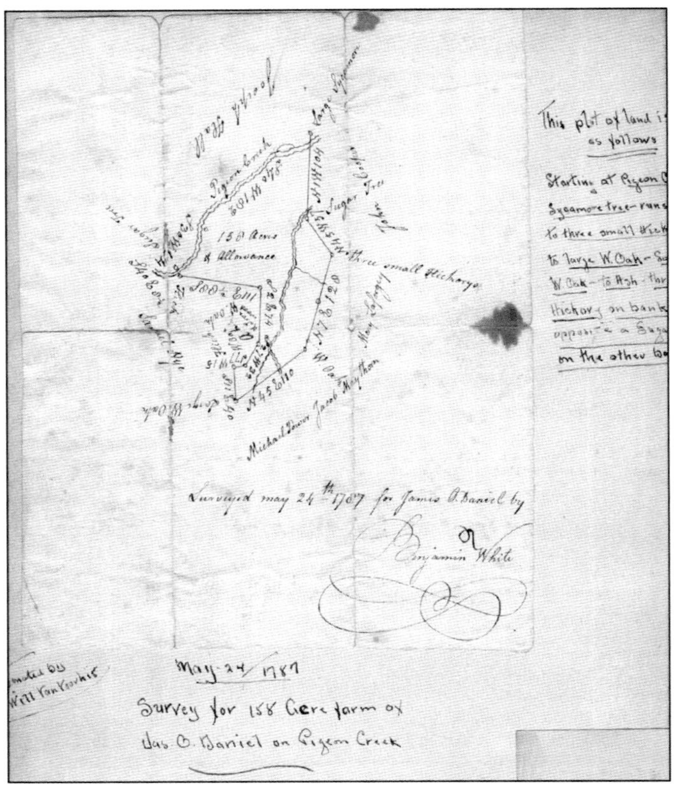

The May 24, 1787, survey is for the 158-acre farm of James B. Daniel of Pigeon Creek. It was laid out as follows: "Start at Pigeon Creek at a large Sycamore tree—runs North to Sugar tree to three Hickorys—to White Oak—to large White Oak—South to Hickory—to White Oak—to Ash—thru small woods—to Hickory on bank opposite Sugar Tree on other bank."

Elizabeth Black Bentley was the first baby born in Parkison's Ferry, on July 5, 1797. She was the firstborn of Samuel Black, who moved to the village in 1795. He operated a store and built a flour mill on Pigeon Creek and a glass factory and mill at Dry Run. Elizabeth grew up in the "Red House," on lot No. 1. She married William Bentley in 1825 and lived a long life.

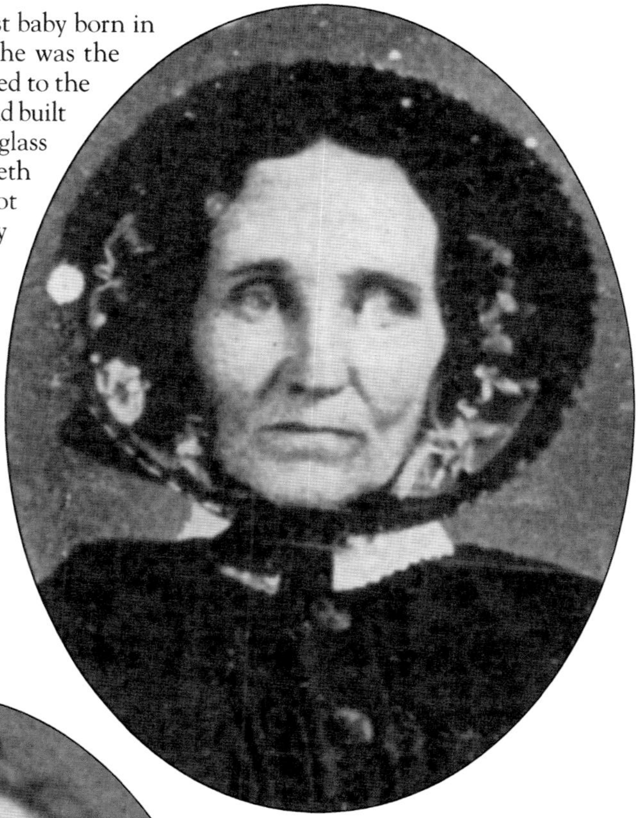

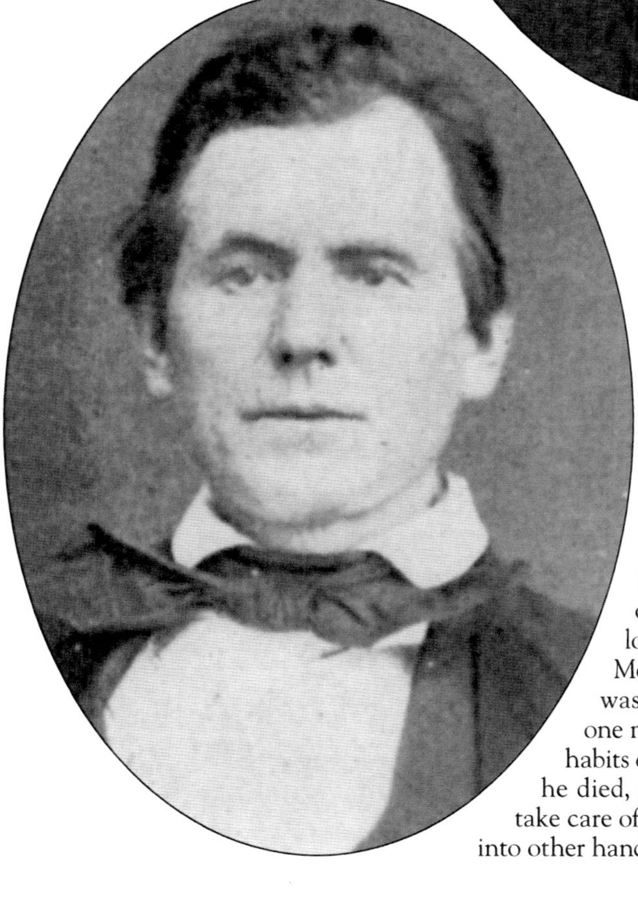

Cyrus Black was one of 12 children of Samuel Black, a first purchaser of lots for Parkison's Ferry. Cyrus was a Methodist revivalist. His father, Samuel, was a remarkable man, but he made one mistake. He did not train his sons in habits of thrift and business sense, so when he died, none, including Cyrus, were fit to take care of his numerous properties, which fell into other hands.

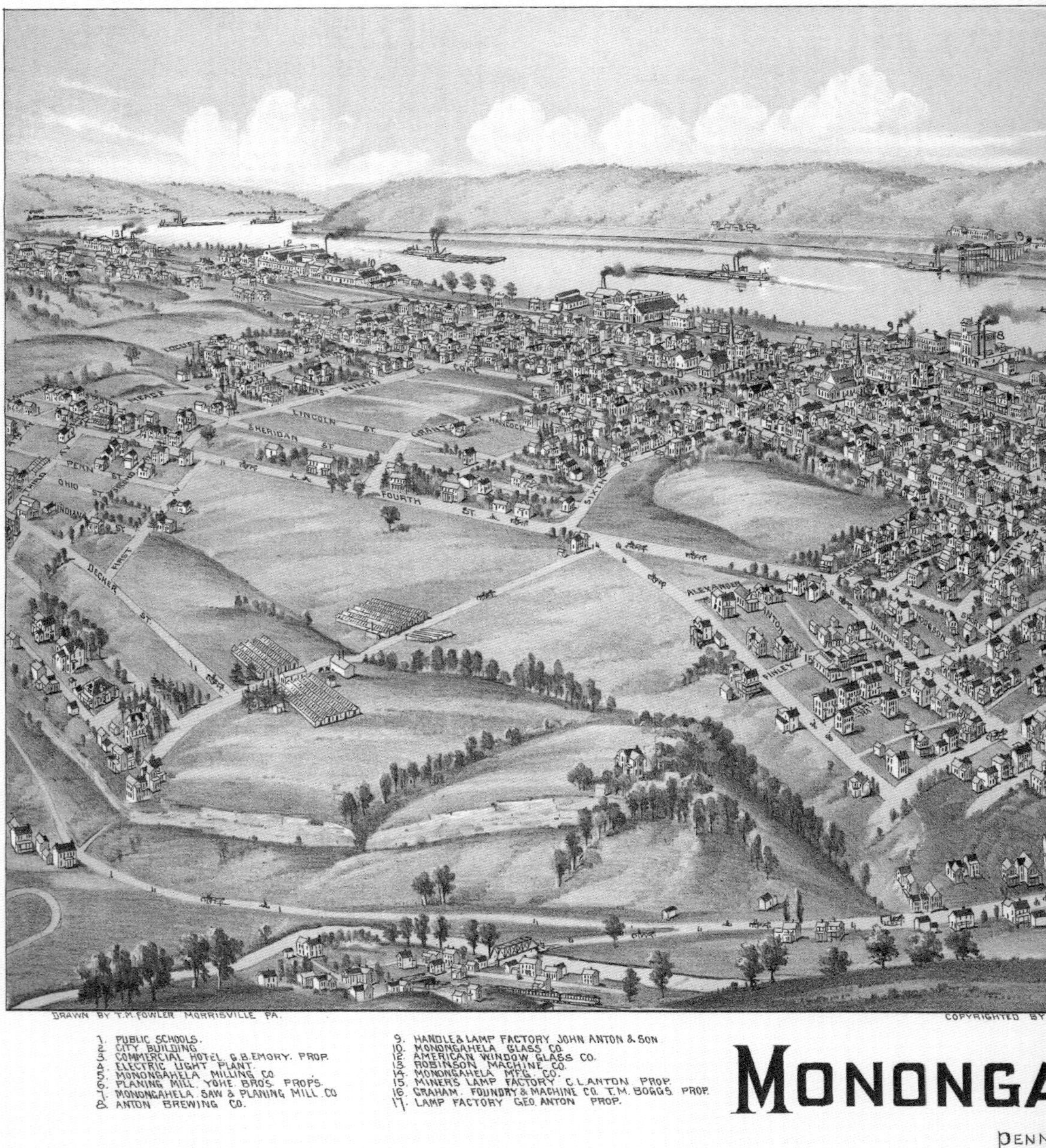

This bird's-eye-view lithograph of Monongahela City was hand-drawn in 1902 by Thaddeus Mortimer Fowler of Morrisville, Pennsylvania, who signed his work "T.M. Fowler." He and other artists made very accurate and detailed panoramic maps of various towns around the United

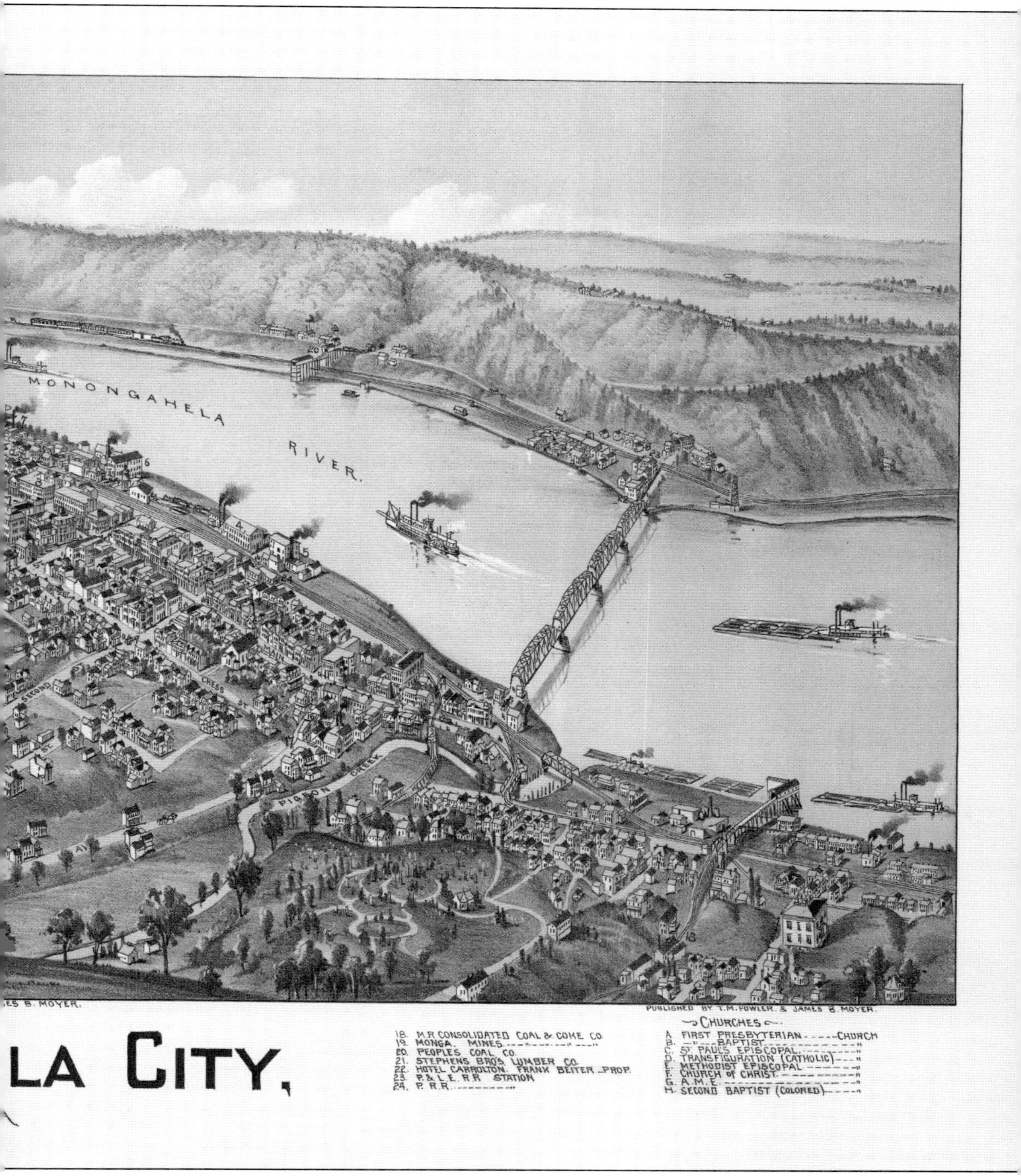

States. This drawing of Monongahela City, when enlarged, shows details of individual houses, schools, churches, and businesses, complete with horses and buggies, river traffic, and individual street names. Fowler completed drawings of nearly 250 views of Pennsylvania communities.

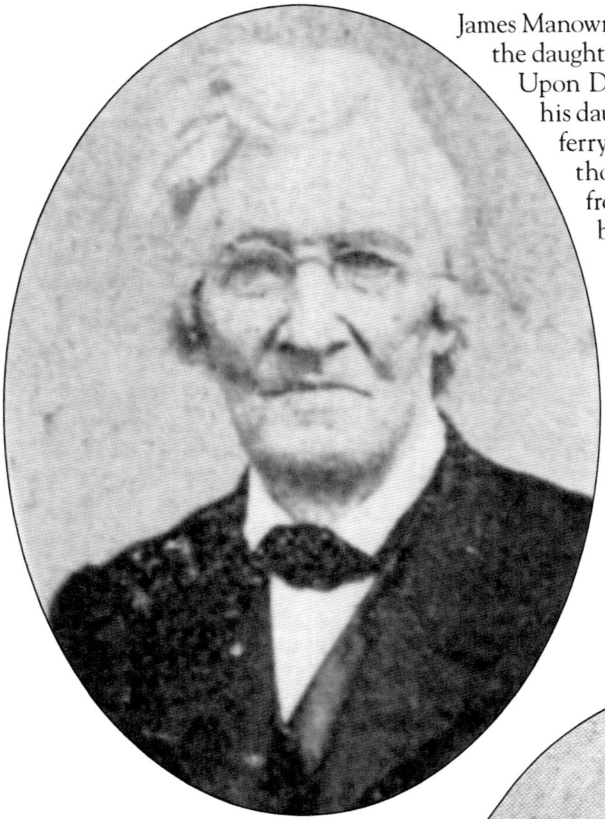

James Manown arrived in America in 1798; he married the daughter of ferry owner David Devour in 1808. Upon Devour's death, all his property went to his daughter. Manown continued running the ferry with Parkison, who received tolls from those going east. Manown received tolls from all persons going west. Manown then bought Parkison's failing business and ran the ferry until the covered bridge was built. He died at age 94.

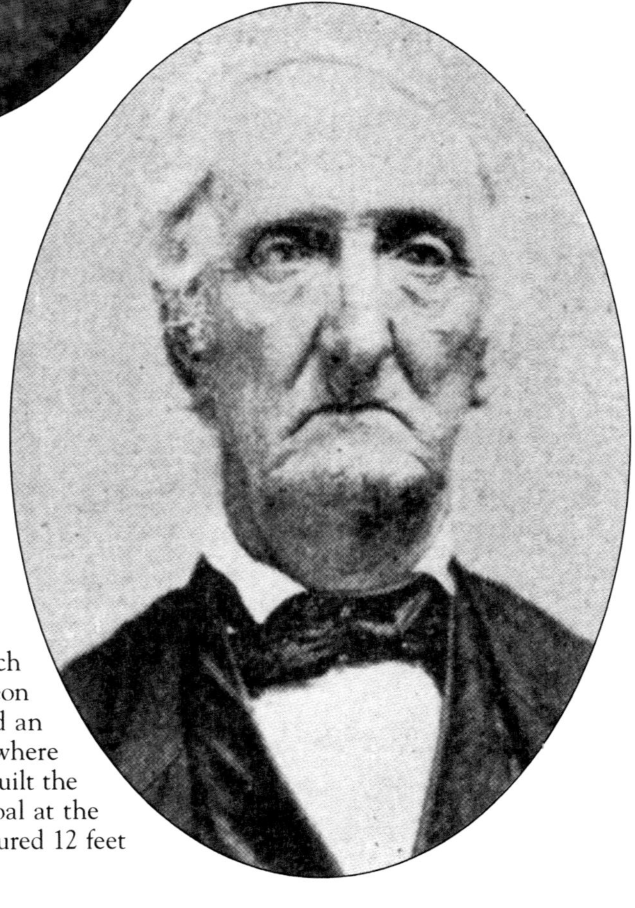

Isaac VanVoorhis was born on March 15, 1794. He built his home on Pigeon Creek. In 1836, Isaac was ordained an elder of the Presbyterian church, where he was a member for 50 years. He built the first coal boat to be loaded with coal at the Williamsport wharf; the boat measured 12 feet wide and 40 feet long.

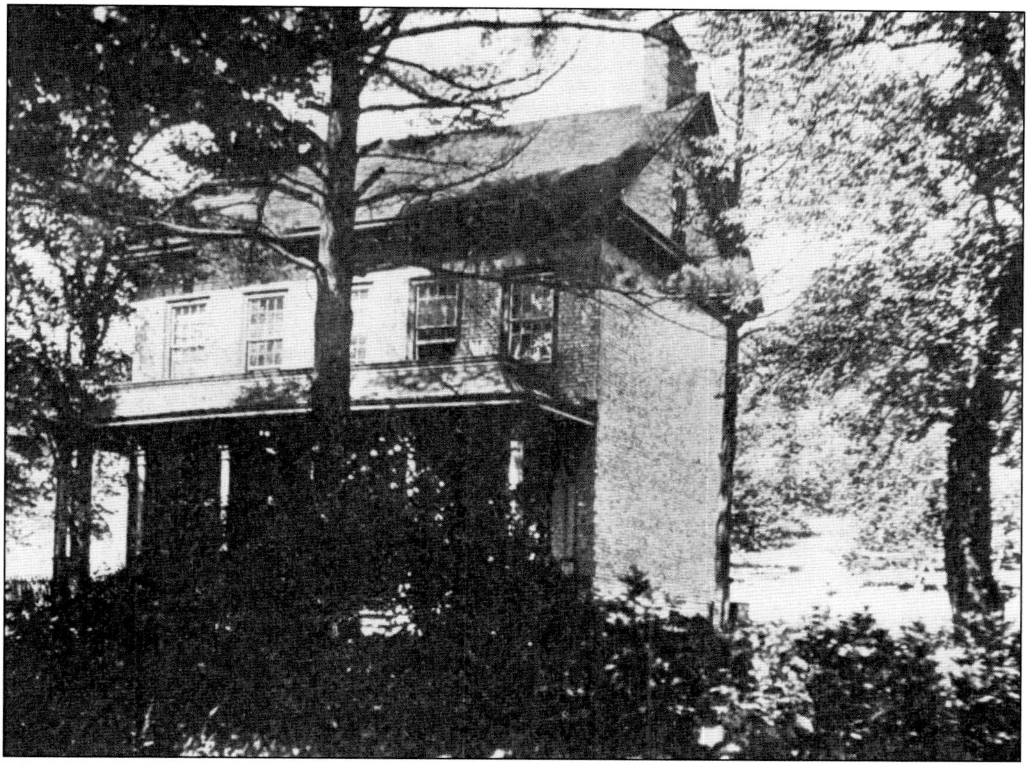

The VanVoorhis House is surrounded by controversy as to who built it and when. The original tract of land was bought by Abraham Decker of Virginia in 1769, and Parkison was granted it from Pennsylvania in 1770. Legend says that he built part of it, but some historians attribute the still-standing home on Route 481 as being built by the VanVoorhis family. Its distinctive features are indeed extraordinary.

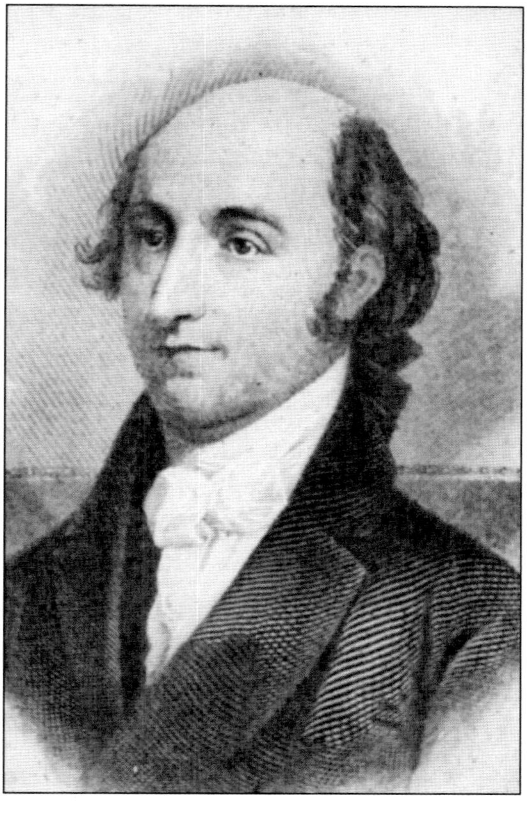

Albert Gallatin was a delegate summoned to a meeting on a bluff overlooking Monongahela later called Whiskey Point. He gave a speech urging the angry farmers to adhere to the law about the tax on whiskey, because the government was bound to vindicate its laws and would surely send an overwhelming force against them. His eloquent speech finally turned the tide and brought about a peaceful ending to the insurrection.

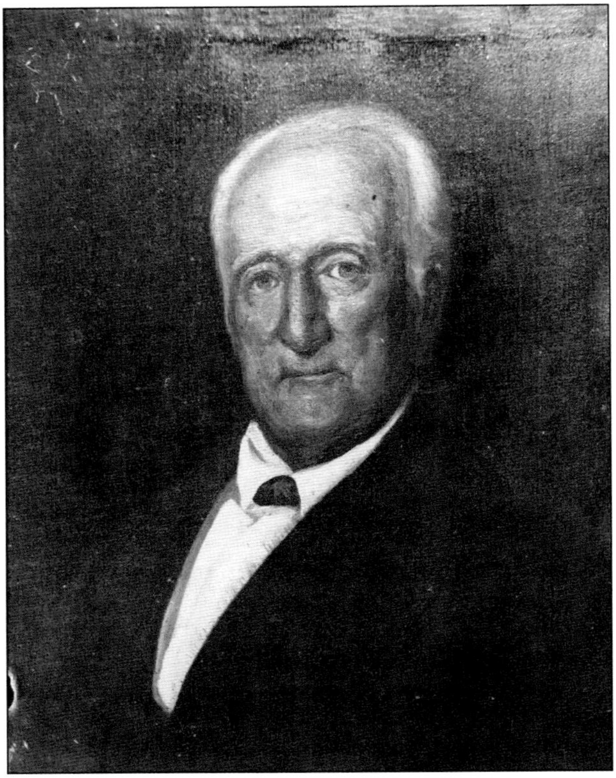

Benjamin Parkison, a nephew of the Benjamin Parkison who held the land patent, was an active participant in the Whiskey Insurrection. He erected the river mills opposite Mingo and married Olivia Rodgers in 1796. He was accustomed to making annual trips carrying flour to New Orleans. When making these trips by flatboat, he took a horse to ride home, a distance of 1,200–1,500 miles. He died in 1851.

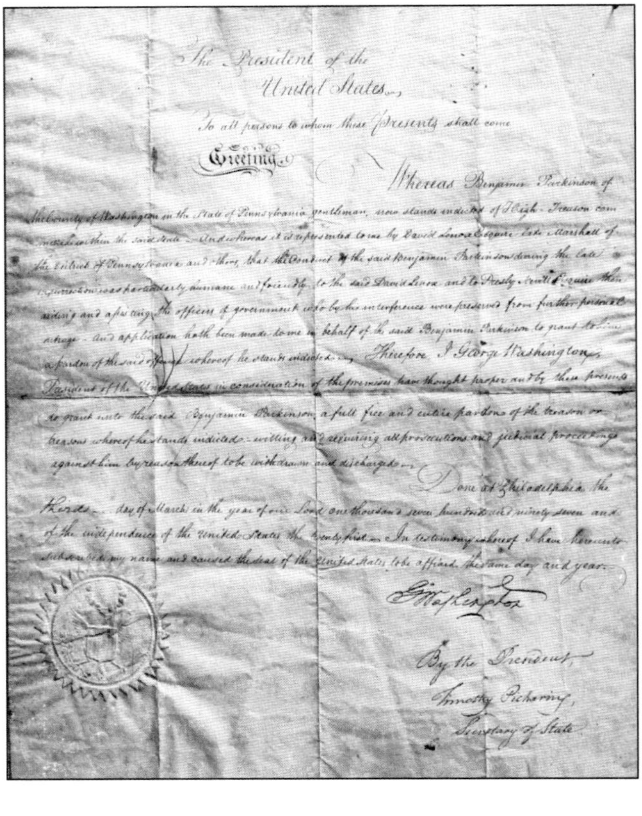

The President of the United States,

To all persons to whom these Presents shall come

Greeting.

Whereas Benjamin Parkinson of the County of Washington in the State of Pennsylvania gentleman, now stands indicted of High Treason committed within the said State — And whereas it is represented to me by David Lenox Esquire late Marshall of the District of Pennsylvania and others, that the conduct of the said Benjamin Parkinson during the late insurrection was particularly humane and friendly to the said David Lenox and to Presly Neville Esquire then aiding and assisting the officers of government, who by his interference were preserved from further personal outrage — And application hath been made to me in behalf of the said Benjamin Parkinson to grant to him a pardon of the said offence whereof he stands indicted — Therefore I George Washington, President of the United States in consideration of the premises have thought proper and by these presents to grant unto the said Benjamin Parkinson a full free and entire pardon of the treason or treasons whereof he stands indicted — willing and requiring all prosecutions and judicial proceedings against him by reason thereof to be withdrawn and discharged —

Done at Philadelphia the third day of March in the year of our Lord one thousand seven hundred and ninety seven and of the independence of the United States the twenty first — In testimony whereof I have hereunto subscribed my name and caused the Seal of the United States to be affixed the same day and year.

G^o Washington

By the President,
Timothy Pickering,
Secretary of State

After the Whiskey Insurrection subsided, Gen. Henry Lee issued a proclamation of amnesty and pardon to all participants in the surrounding counties except for Benjamin Parkison and 32 others, too numerous to mention. Some of those not pardoned were taken to Pittsburgh and tried, while others, such as Parkison, were marched to Philadelphia, kept in prison six months, tried, and then discharged. A part of Benjamin Parkison's pardon is given here.

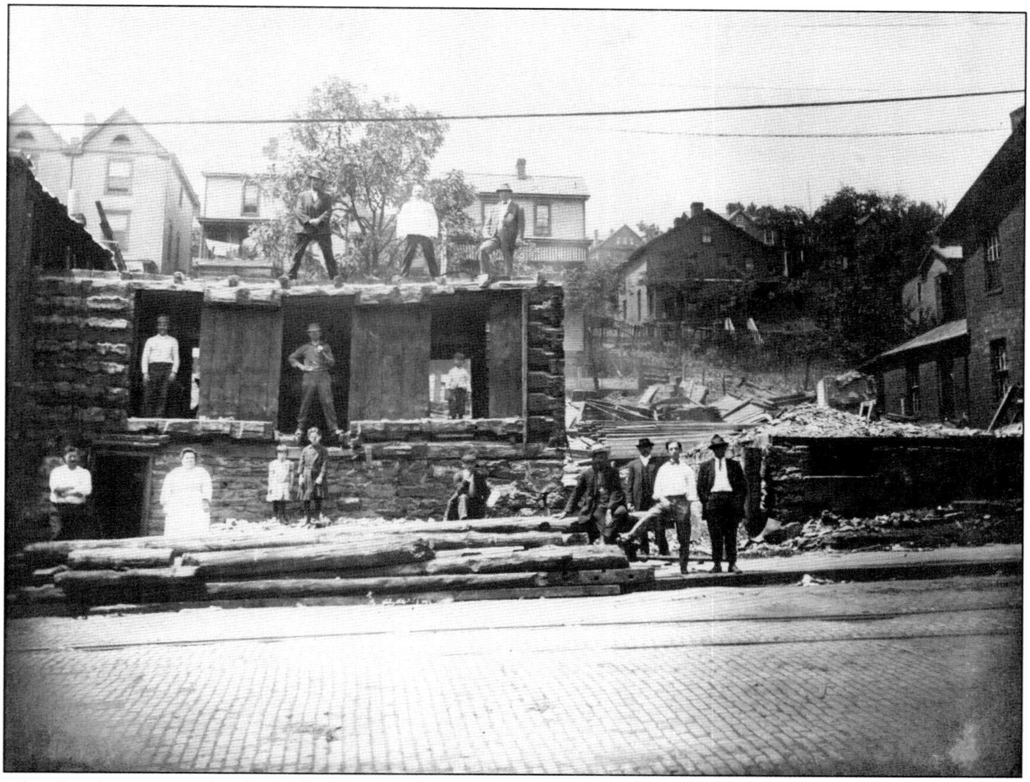

This log house was built in the late 1700s and was used as a general store, post office, and private residence. In this building, the resolutions ending the Whiskey Insurrection were drawn to present to Pres. George Washington. The photograph shows the razing of the Old Bentley House, on Main Street, to make way for the Bentley Theatre.

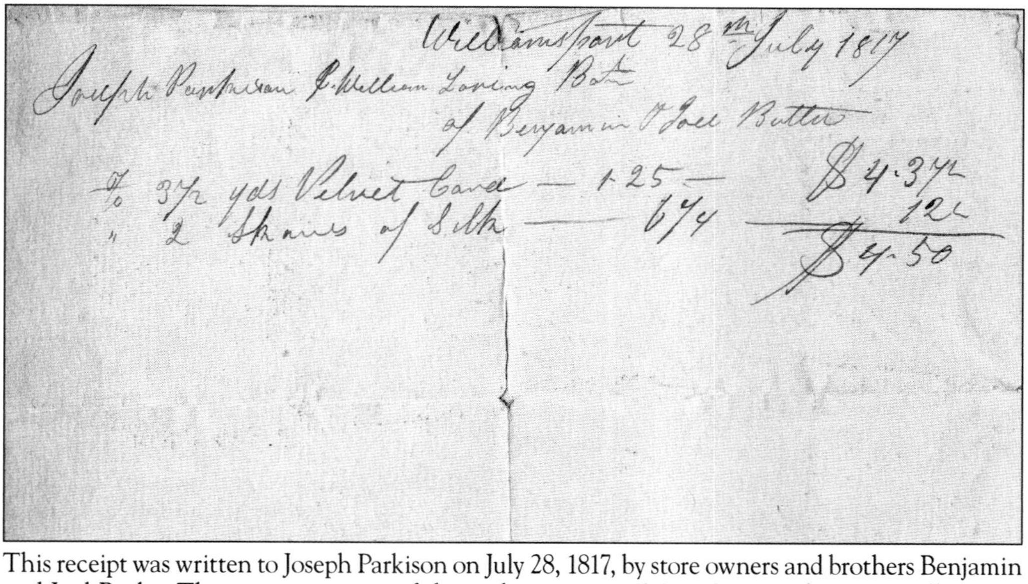

Williamsport 28th July 1817
Joseph Parkison & William Loving Bot
of Benjamin & Joel Butler
To 3½ yds Velvet Card — 1.25 — $4.37½
" 2 Skeins of Silk — 6¼ 12½
$4.50

This receipt was written to Joseph Parkison on July 28, 1817, by store owners and brothers Benjamin and Joel Butler. Their store was one of the earliest ones on Main Street. The receipt illustrates the second name of Parkison's Ferry, which was Williamsport. The purchase was for velvet and silk, luxury items in that era.

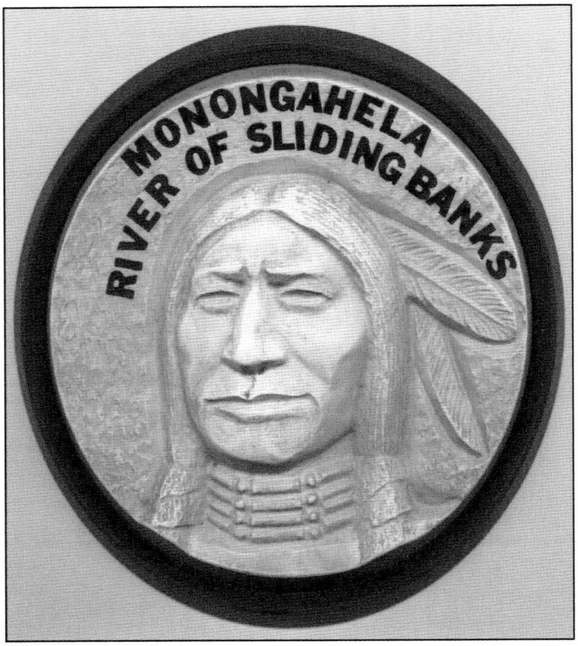

The pictured medallion's title states the meaning of the city's name. Monongahela means "River of Sliding Banks." It was taken from the language of the Adena, the Native Americans who lived along the Monongahela River over 2,000 years ago. The Adena lived here and built the mounds atop the hills.

MONONGAHELA

"The Oldest Settlement in the Valley"
"The Original Home of Carborundum"
"The Present Home of the Pennsylvania State Little League Champions"

¶ We sure have heard some very comic ways of pronouncing it—by Strangers, Radio Announcers, and the larger majority of our Own Home Town Citizens.

¶ Here are some of them:-

Mongah-hay-lah
Mungah-hay-lah
Mon-ah-guh-hay-lah
Mon-ah-gay-hay-lah
Monon-gay-hay-lah

¶ And of course, some folks and some newspapers very often use **"Mon City"**

Monon-gay-he'-lah

¶ Is the proper name of our city, and also the famous river, upon the banks of which it is situated

This tidbit was found in one of Dr. Taylor's scrapbooks, and what a treasure it is! Throughout the years, the townsfolk have had to pronounce and spell Monongahela for out-of-towners more times than can be counted. Even today, three variations of the pronunciation of the fourth syllable exist: "he," "hay," and "hel." When all else fails, "Mon City" will do just fine.

Two

Scenes about Town

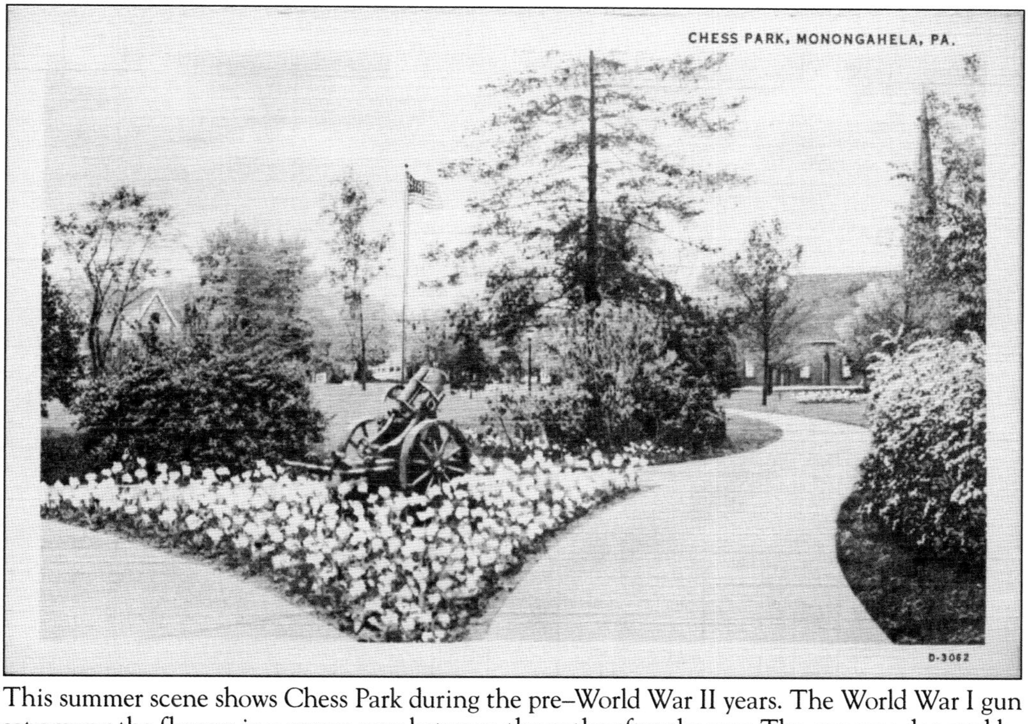

This summer scene shows Chess Park during the pre–World War II years. The World War I gun sat among the flowers in a grassy area between the paths after the war. The gun was donated by Monongahela City to be used for scrap metal for the World War II effort. People everywhere did their part to ensure a victory for the country.

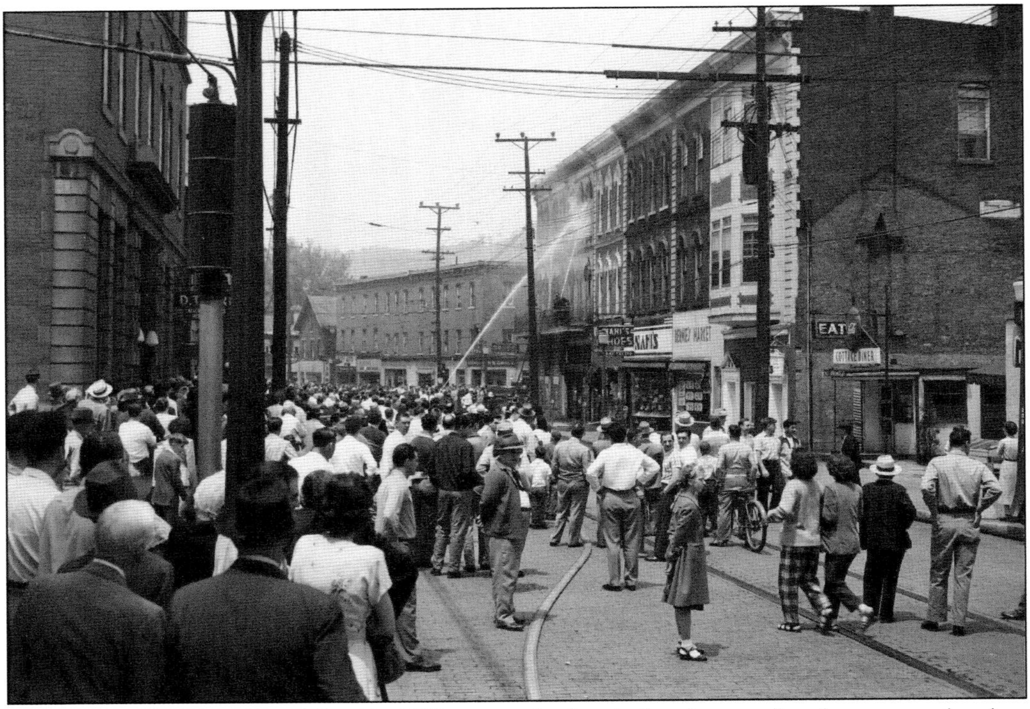

A huge crowd gathered on May 28, 1950, to watch the city's volunteer fire department battle a blaze at the Byers Building on the corner of Fourth and Main Streets. Both building owners and businesspeople were anxiously waiting in hopes that the fire would not spread and that other structures would be spared.

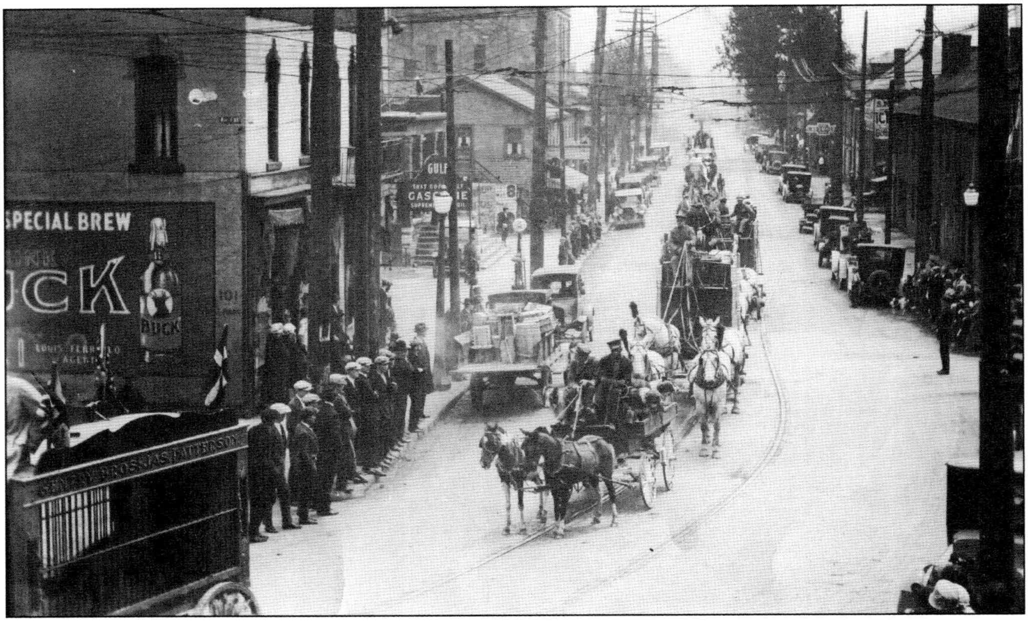

Excitement filled the air in the early 1900s when the circus came to town. It is parading through the city near First Street and Park Avenue. The Gentry Brothers and James Patterson's Circuses had horses, wagons, entertainers, and exotic animals, such as the caged tiger in the passing wagon. (Courtesy scrapbook of Potente Zanardelli.)

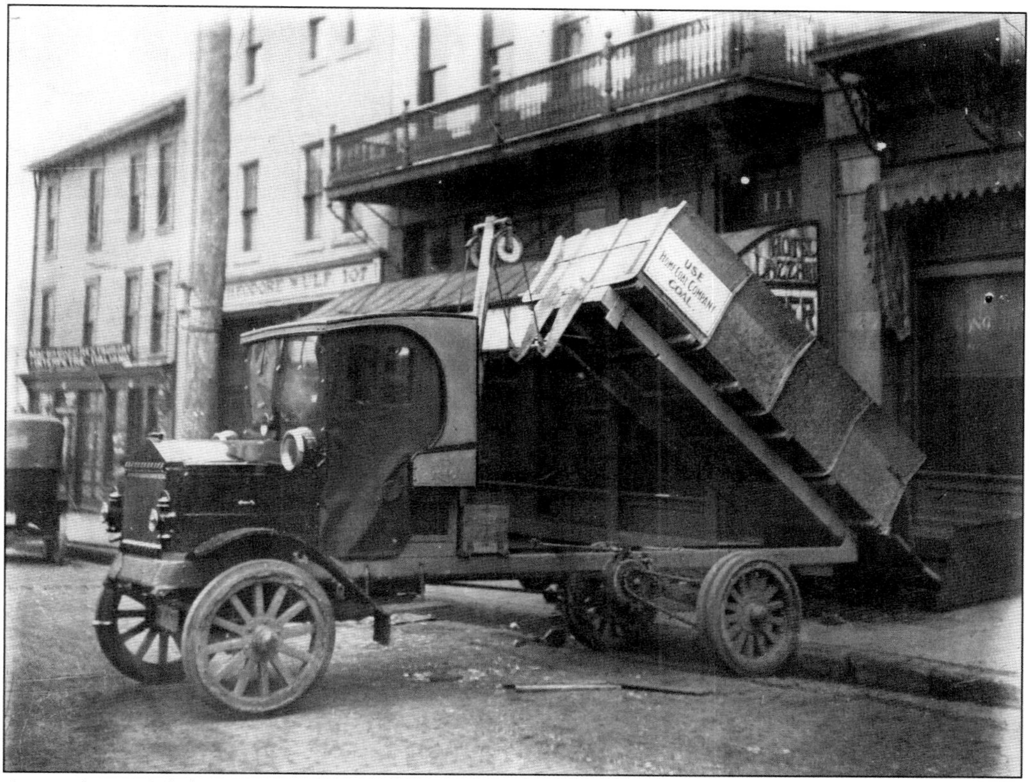

An early-model dump truck is making its delivery of coal down the coal shoot of one of the businesses in town, which was located at Second and Railroad Streets. The Hotel Lazzari is to the left of the truck. Home Coal Company, through its advertising on the side of the truck, is urging everyone to "Use 'Home Coal Company' Coal." (Courtesy scrapbook of Potente Zanardelli.)

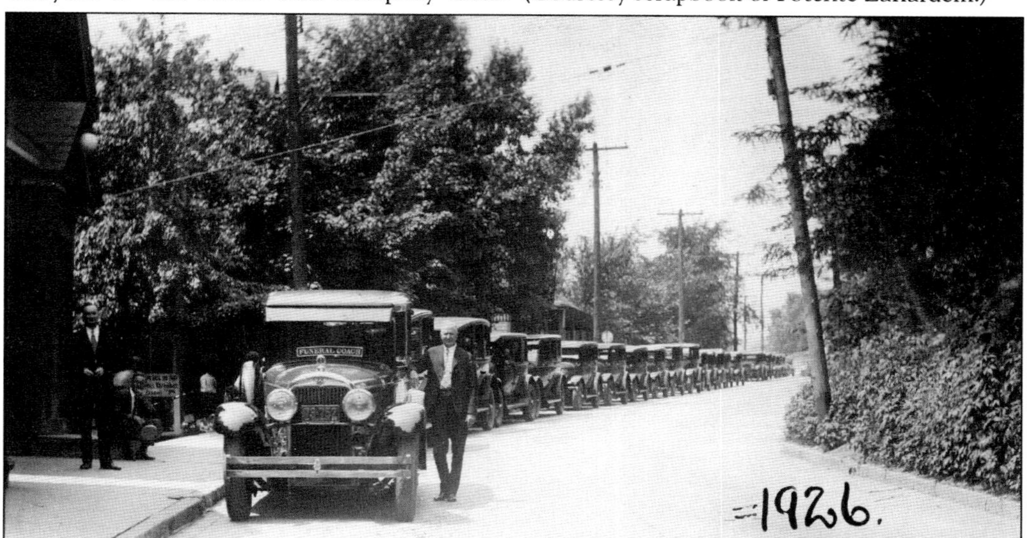

The line of cars is part of the funeral procession of Guy Turri of Monongahela, who died in 1926. The cars are parked in front of the original St. Anthony's Church on Park Avenue. On either side of the funeral coach are the funeral directors, C. Patterson (left) and F. Bebout. (Courtesy scrapbook of Potente Zanardelli.)

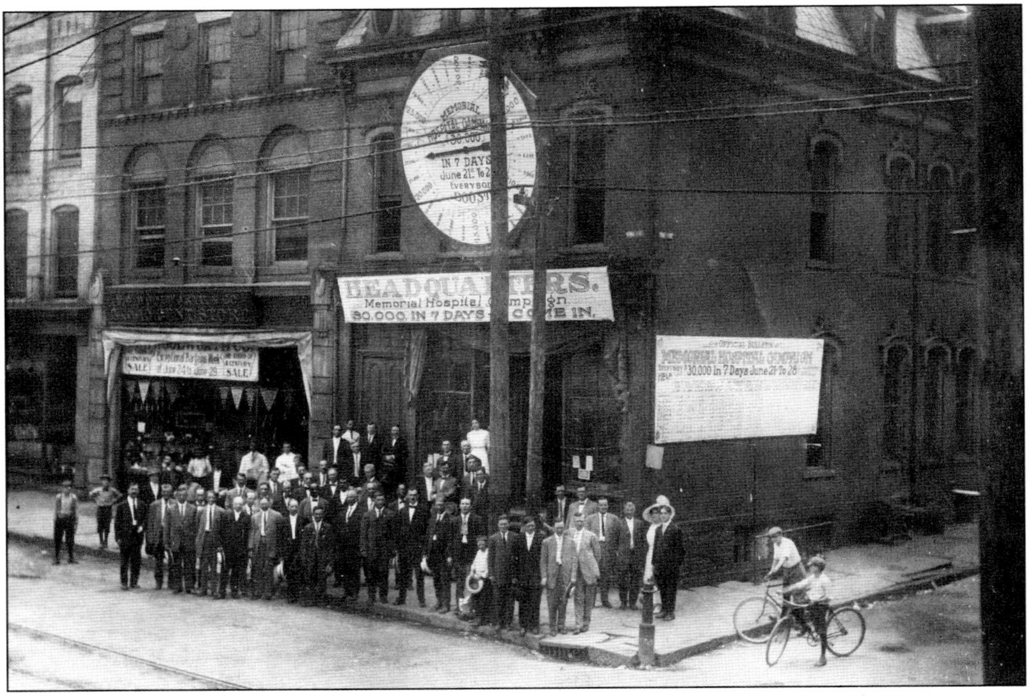

The year was 1928 and a great undertaking was taking place in the old hometown. This building housed the headquarters of the drive to raise $30,000 for Memorial Hospital in just seven days. The fundraiser ran from June 21 to June 28. What an enormous effort it must have been to have just seven days to complete such a task.

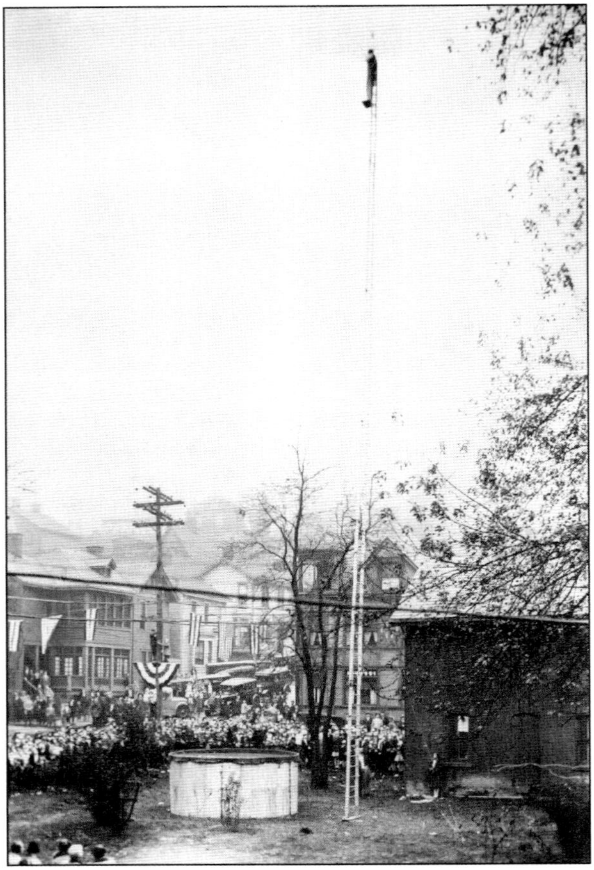

Daredevils were alive and well in Monongahela throughout the years. Proof of this shows a man atop a tall ladder, preparing to dive into a small pool below. This feat took place on the corner of Third and Chess Streets, in the rear of the Alexander Bank Building. It seems that only a "before" photograph was taken, because no "after" photograph was found. One can only wonder why.

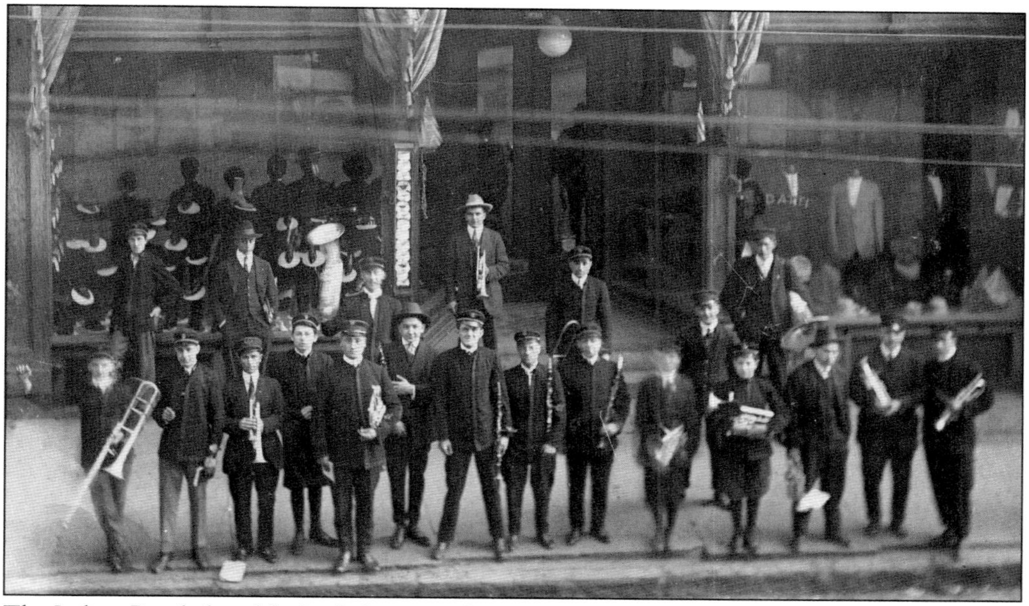

The Italian Band played for both festive and somber occasions. This photograph shows the band standing on the day of Mrs. Nick Pizzica's funeral as the funeral procession passed on the street. It was particularly sad, because it occurred on Mother's Day. Members shown include, in no particular order, A.K. Turri, Mr. Inserra, Mr. Cerutti, Mr. Bova, D. Turri, L. Nagy, Mr. Parenti, Mr. Antoniello, W. Turri, Mr. La Scala, Mr. Ramsini, and J. Pezzoni. (Courtesy scrapbook of Potente Zanardelli.)

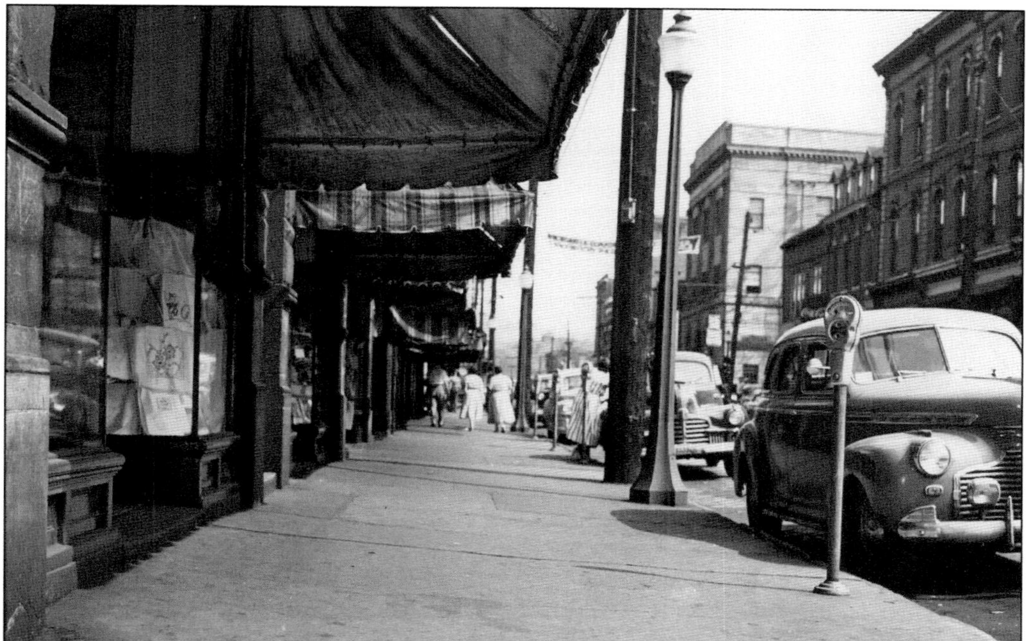

Summer is definitely visible at the sight of the McCrory's Five and Ten Store's striped awning, providing shade to the two women passersby. The photograph shows Main Street facing Third Street. In the distance, a banner stretches across the street announcing the upcoming Kennywood Day, a yearly community event held on the first Wednesday in August.

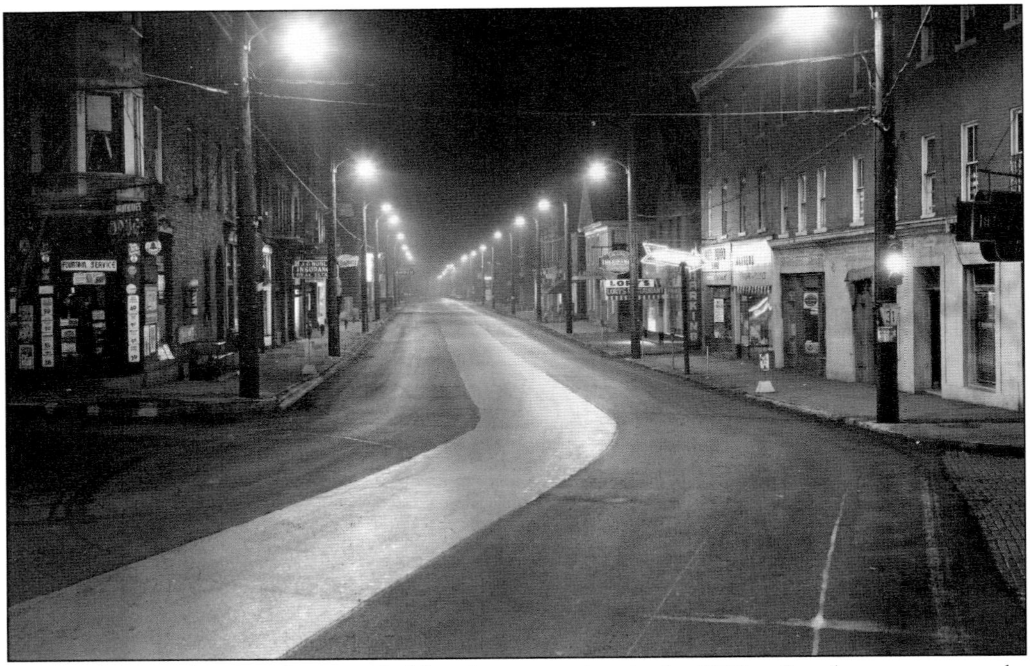

This nighttime photograph was probably taken some time in the 1950s, after the streetcar tracks were removed. The shot looking down Fourth Street shows several businesses from days gone by, such as Hawthorne's Drugstore (located in the Yohe Building, on the corner of Fourth Street), the Blue Goose, Alfred's, Key Auto, several insurance companies, and Lory's Restaurant. An Amoco sign is farther down.

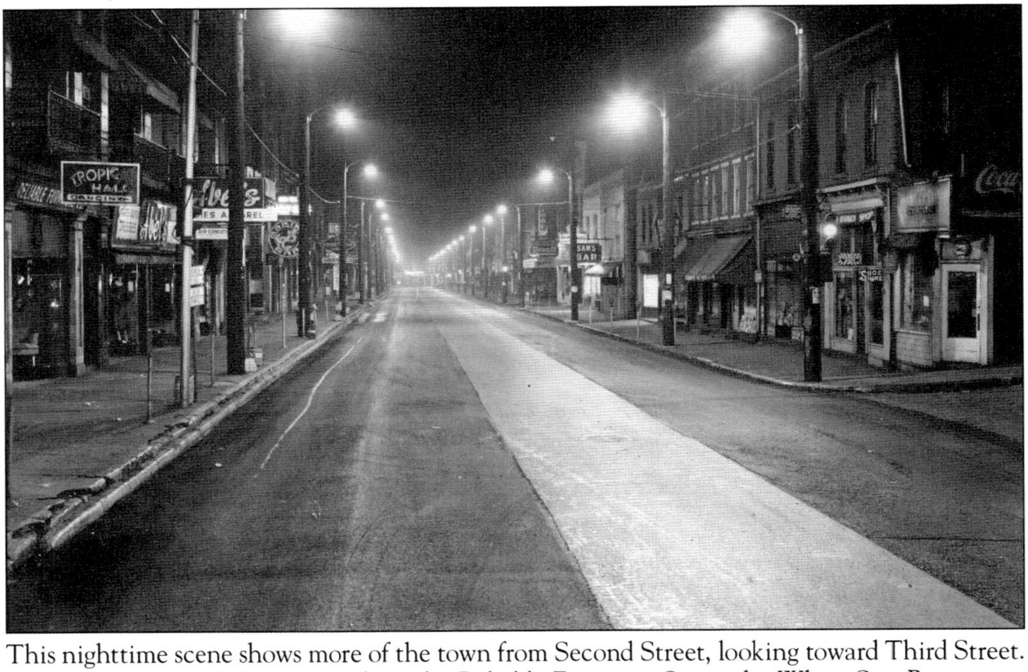

This nighttime scene shows more of the town from Second Street, looking toward Third Street. Seen here are establishments such as the Reliable Furniture Store, the White Star Restaurant at the bridge entrance, the Tropic Dance Hall, Abel's Clothing, Marine Bar, and the Lantern Grille. It seems odd that no cars or people are in the picture.

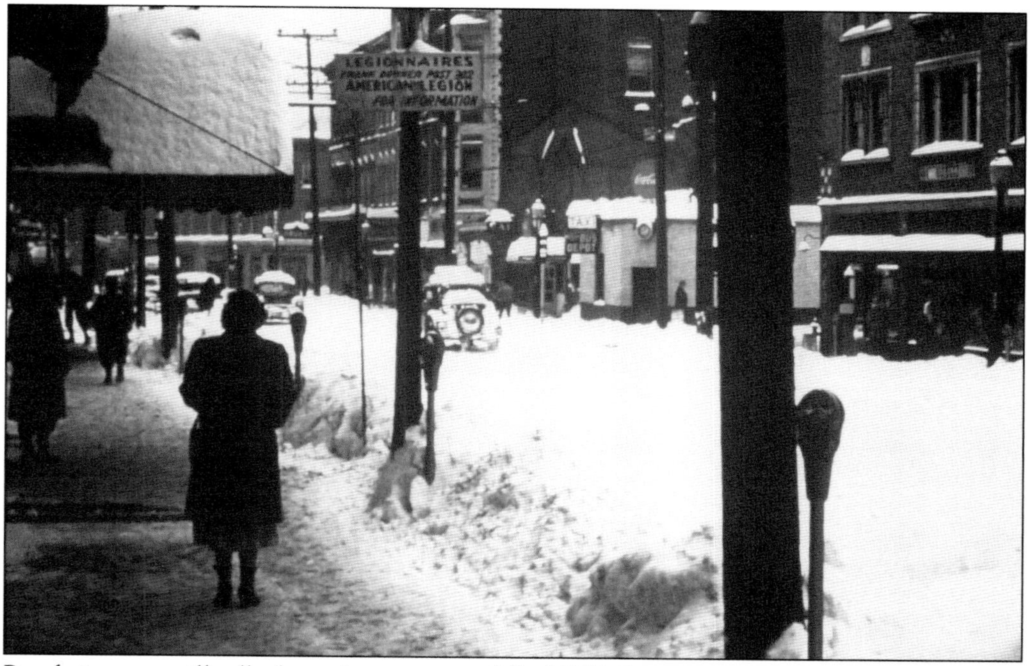

People in town still talk about the great snowfall of 1950. It is easy to see why, as Main Street is so snow-covered that it was very difficult for cars to maneuver. The snow may have stopped cars and taxis from venturing out, but the people shown are going about their daily business, snow or no snow!

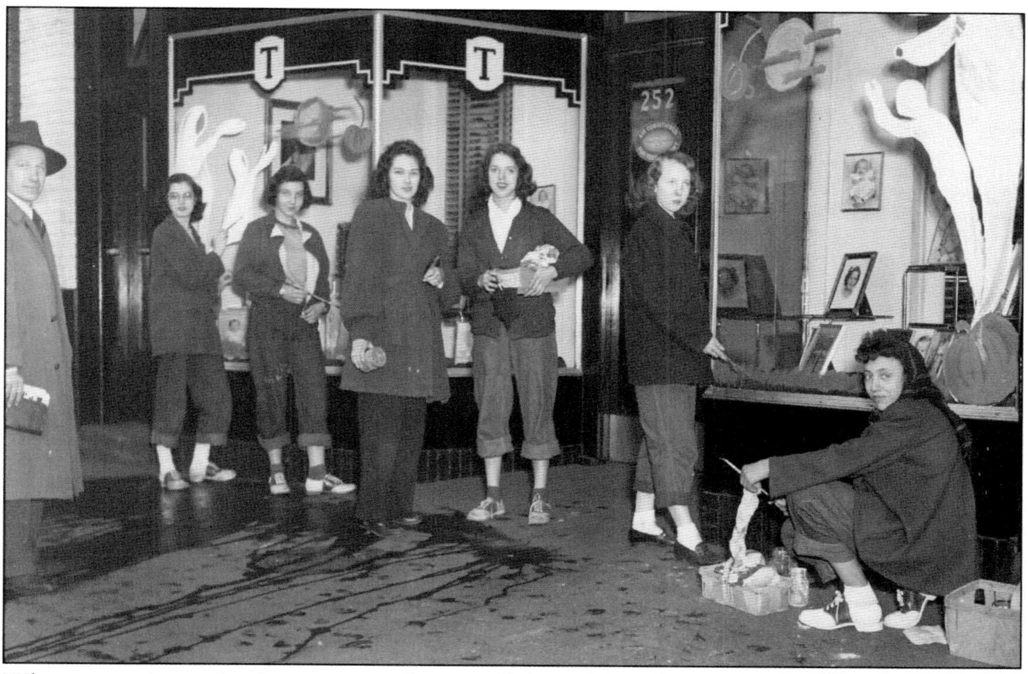

What a treat it was for the townspeople to stroll down Main Street every Halloween and see all the wonderful window paintings done by the high school art students. Prizes were always given to the winners after the entries were judged. Some of the girls shown in the 1949 photograph are, in no particular order, Barbara Holdy, Betty Pigford, Virginia Staffen, and Betty Wenzel.

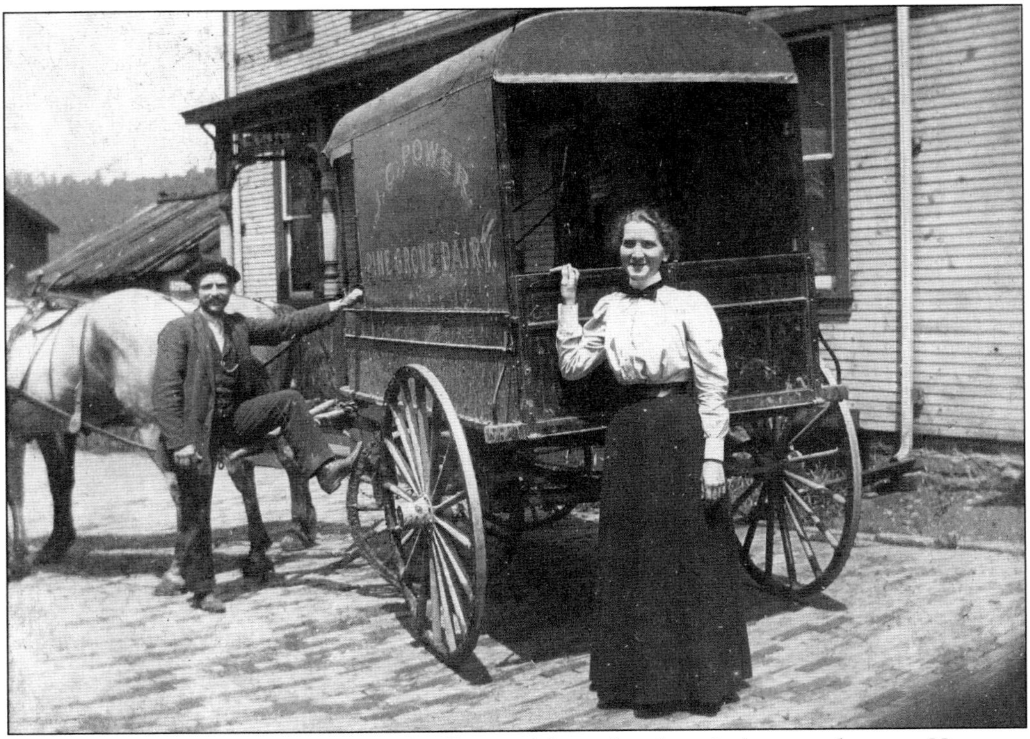

Gone are the days when glass bottles of milk were delivered to doors by horse and wagon. However, in 1898, Bell and Joe Power, of the Power Milk Wagon, were a familiar sight in town as they delivered fresh milk daily through the cobblestone streets and alleys to their customers.

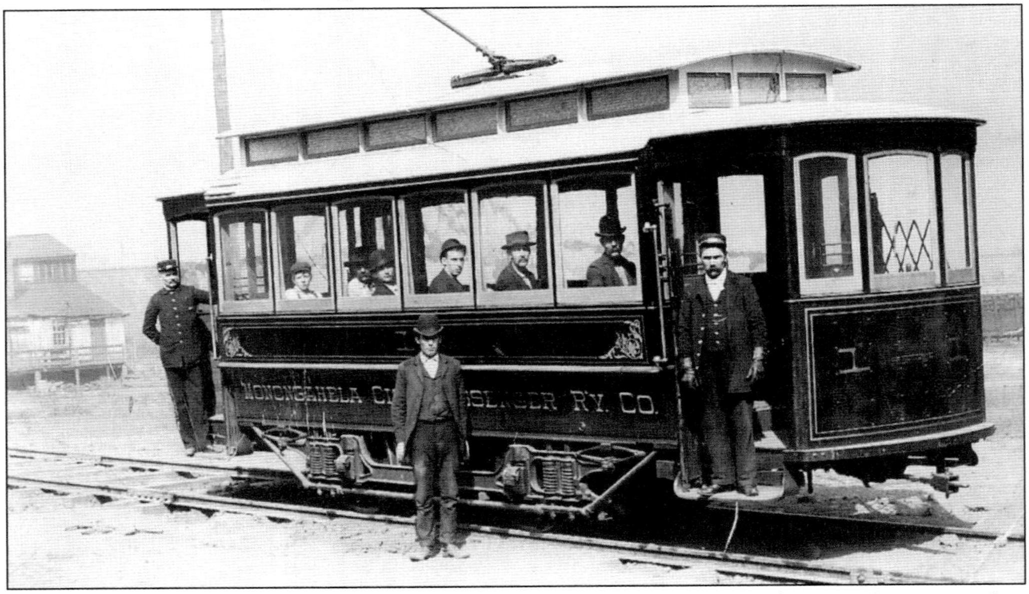

The year is 1895, and Monongahela streetcar No. 1 has made its usual run and is stopped at the New Eagle end of the track. The streetcar, part of the Passenger Railing Company, has "Monongahela City" painted on its side. The passengers, five men and one boy, look delighted with their mode of transportation. They are accompanied by two workers and one passenger, looking eager to get on board.

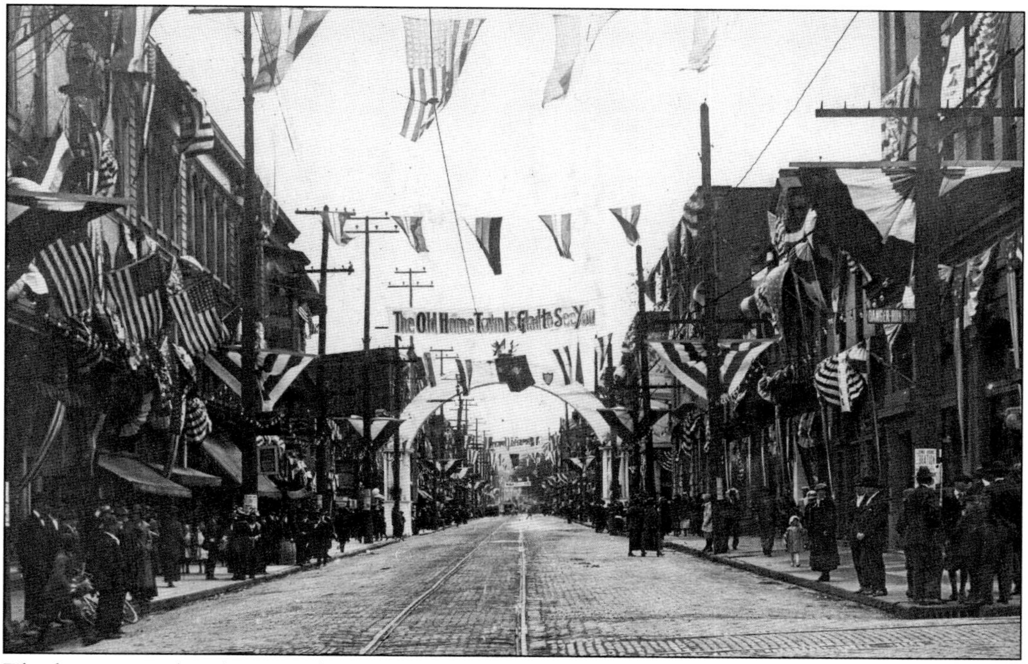

The banner in the photograph, which shows Monongahela dressed for Old Home Week in 1908, reads, "The Old Town is Glad to See You!" It was hung one block down from the welcome arch erected at Third Street. Those returning home could not help but feel heartened when seeing all the effort that was made to welcome them.

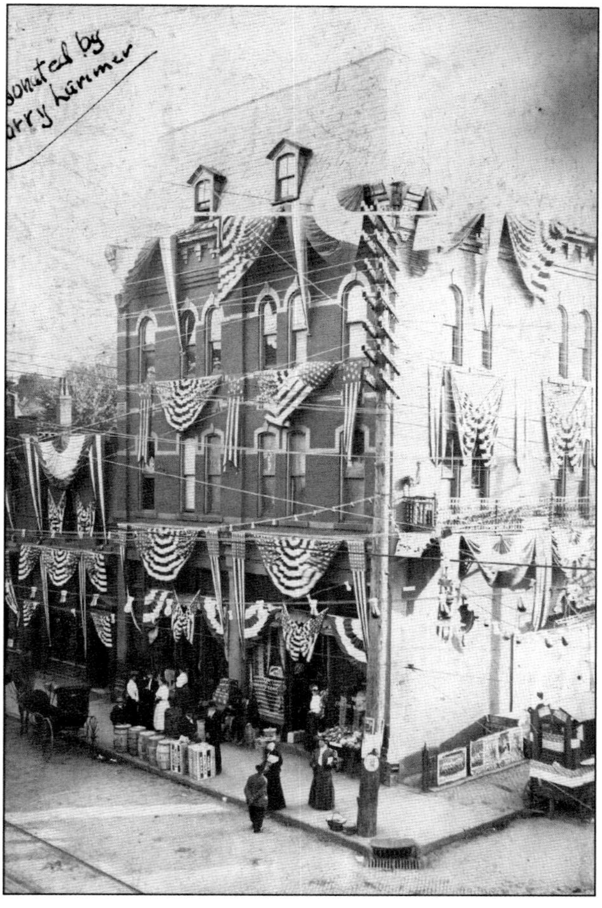

How lucky Monongahelans were to have Gamble's Opera House in town. Many renowned opera singers performed in lavish productions there. The building is dressed for a parade during Old Home Week in 1908. The photograph shows the Bogg family's horse and buggy. The caption identifies a few people in the photograph as Mrs. William Bogg, on left of photograph with her back to the street; Bella Bogg, wearing white; and Dr. VanVoorhis standing on the right with his back to the photographer, facing Mrs. Grant to his right.

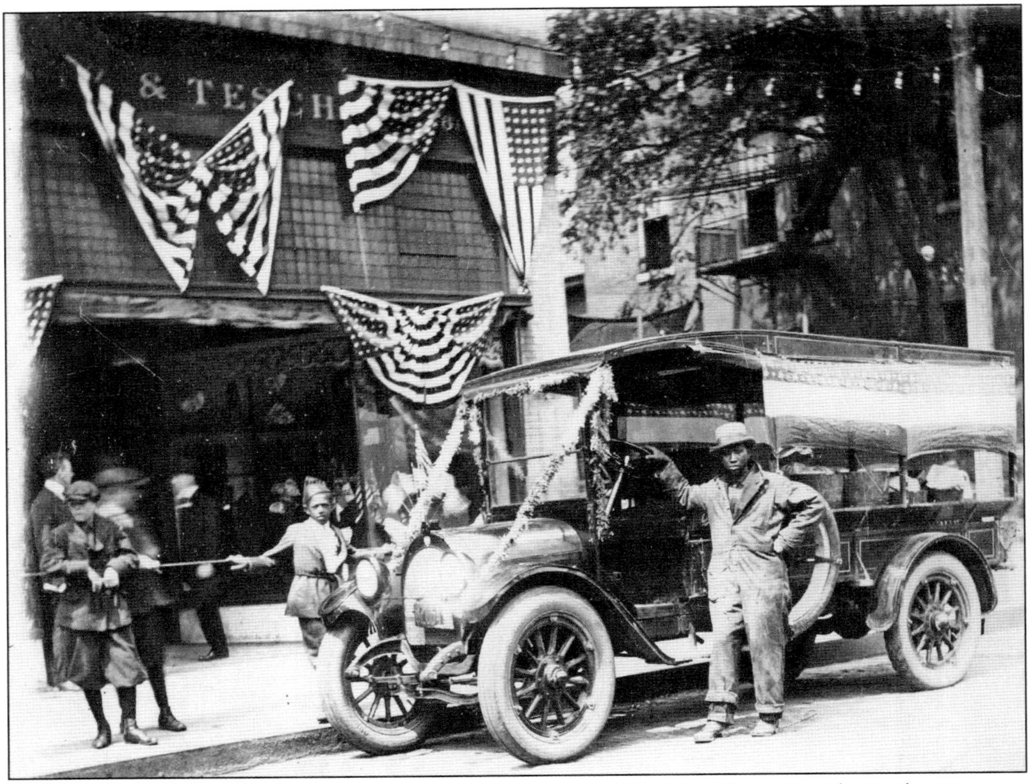

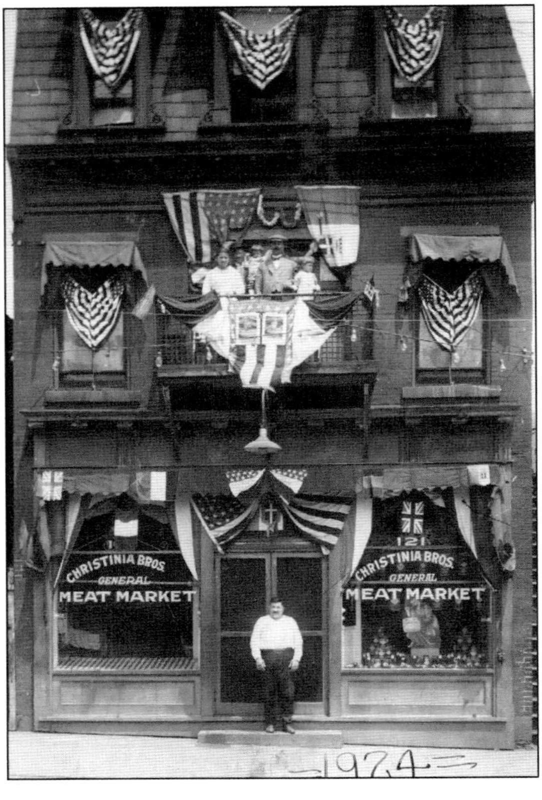

Mr. Waverly Clanton is shown here in a photograph taken in 1917 at the corner of Third and Main Streets. Clanton's vehicle and the town are decorated for a grand parade. A big crowd is expected, as evidenced by the way the sidewalk is cordoned off, and it looks like the boys will have front-row spots.

The Christina Brothers General Meat Market, on Main Street, was all decked out for a parade in 1924. Owner Nick Christina, affectionately called "Chicken Man" by locals, stands proudly in front. Above, a group of onlookers are watching from the balcony among the many buntings. They are, from left to right, Albina and Tony Paterlini and Evelyn, Angelo, and Linda Lazzari.

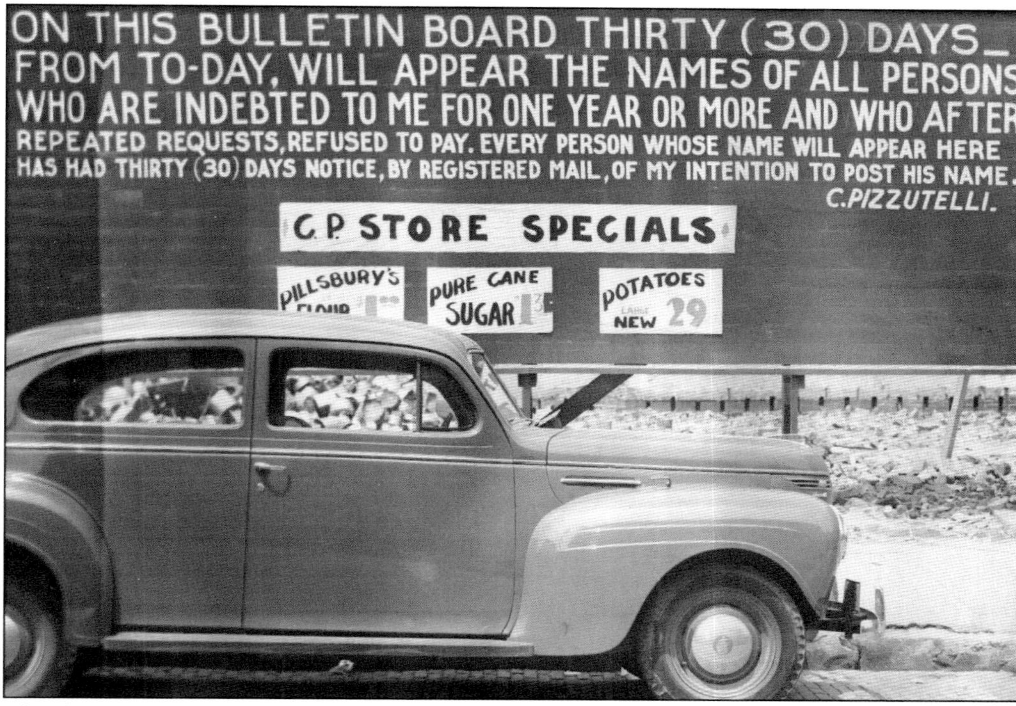

The threat of unwanted publicity, intended to expose the names of debtors on a public billboard by grocer Clem Pizzutelli, caused quite a stir in 1941. He saw his chain of 19 groceries dwindle to just one on Third Street from having thousands of dollars of uncollected funds dating back to the Great Depression. Pizzutelli had "carried" his unemployed customers in hard times. Now he wanted to be repaid.

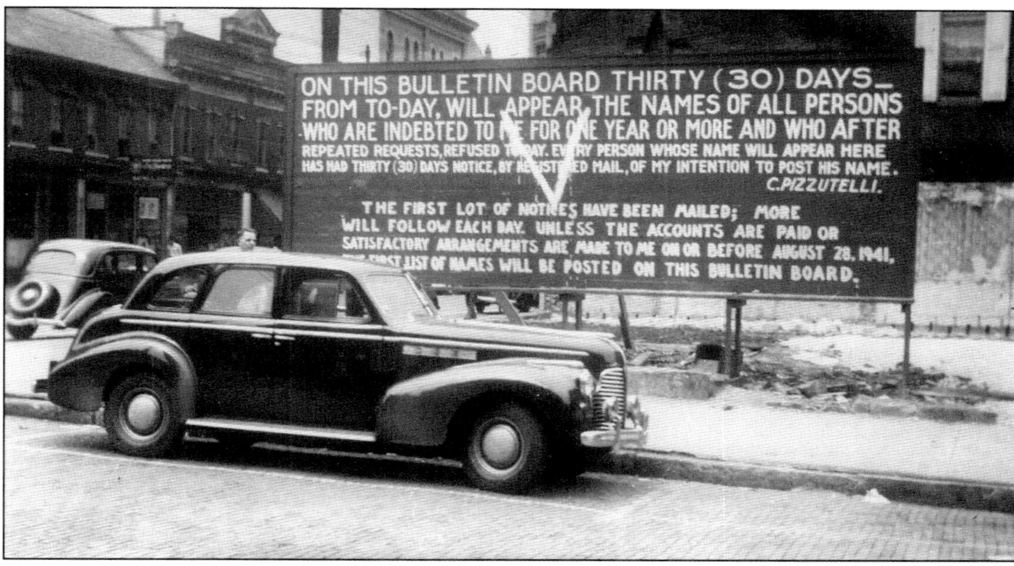

Clem Pizzutelli and his "Famous Billboard" generated its own publicity and made the newspapers, magazines, and even the radio back in 1941. An hour after the sign had been painted, his phone started to ring. A man paid one dollar on a four-year old bill. Another paid off a $19 account dating from 1928. Dozens arranged to pay in installments. Clem's strategy worked, as shown by the *V* for victory, painted after only 30 days.

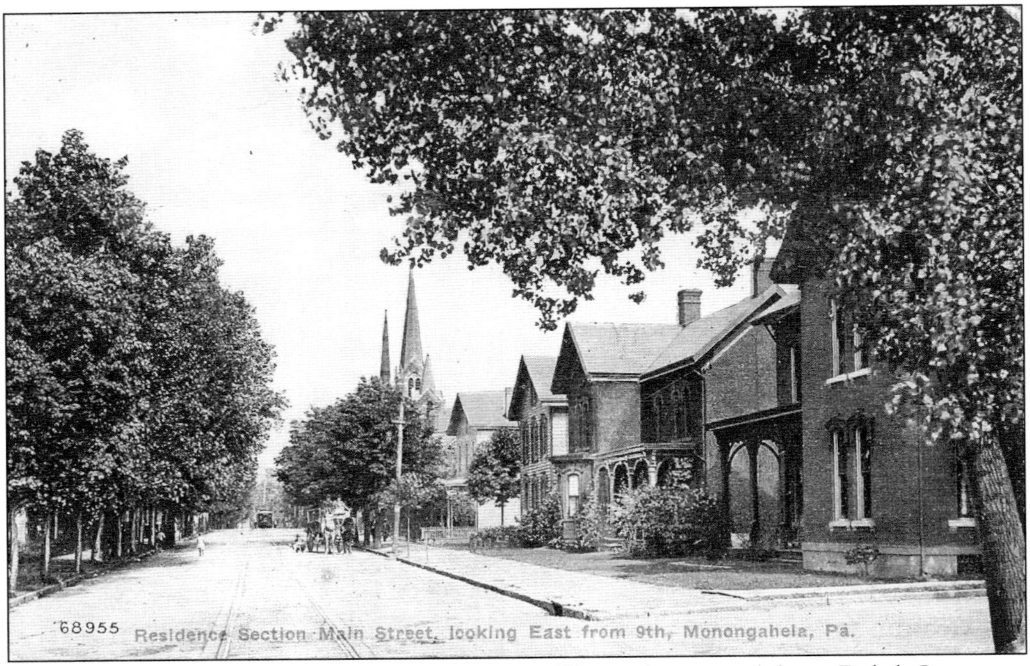

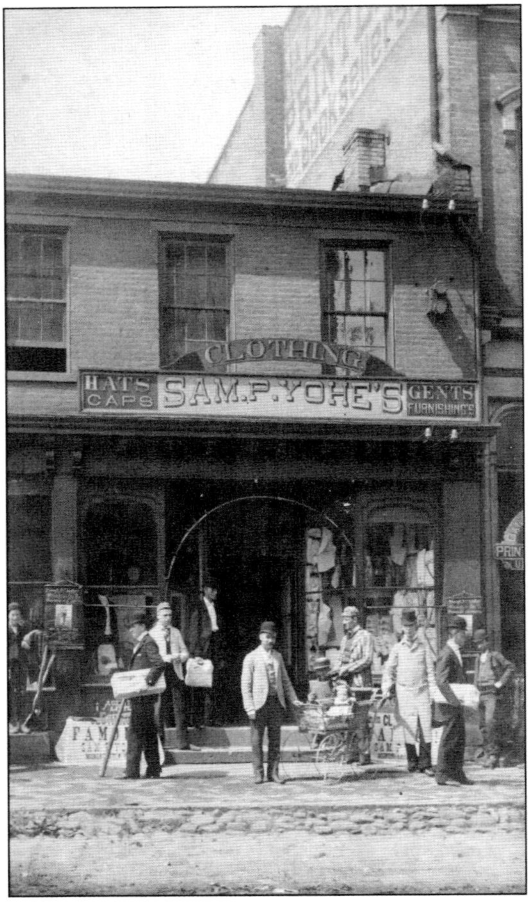

This early postcard shows Eighth Street looking toward town. The homes of brothers John and James Blythe are showcased on the right. John Blythe, a prominent architect in the 1800s, designed several of the beautiful churches and homes in Monongahela, such as the Bethel AME Church and the Longwell House, to name a few. He and his brother James, who supervised much of the building, were business partners.

The Sam P. Yohe Clothing Store was a busy place on Main Street during the early 1900s. As the storefront says, the store sold "gent's furnishings," such as hats, caps, and all other articles of clothing necessary to be a well-dressed gentleman. It seemed that men took great care to be impeccably stylish as they walked about town. The baby in the carriage must surely be a boy.

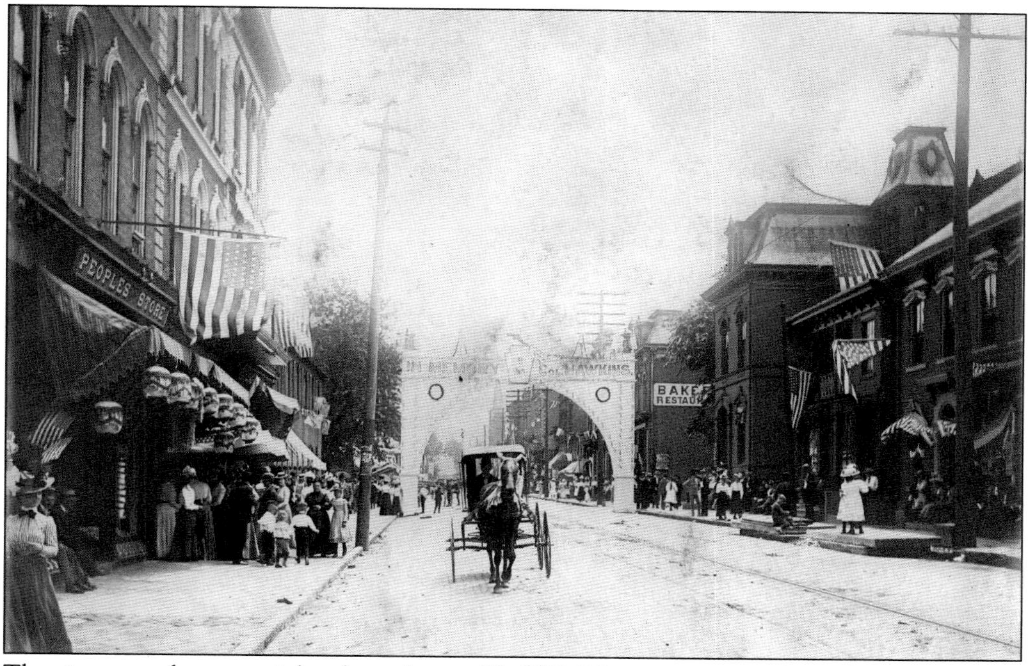

The city erected a memorial arch on August 30, 1899. The impressive arch was located at Third and Main Streets. Its grand appearance stretching across the street was a welcome sight as the soldiers of Company A returned home for a huge reception in town that was well attended by patriotic residents.

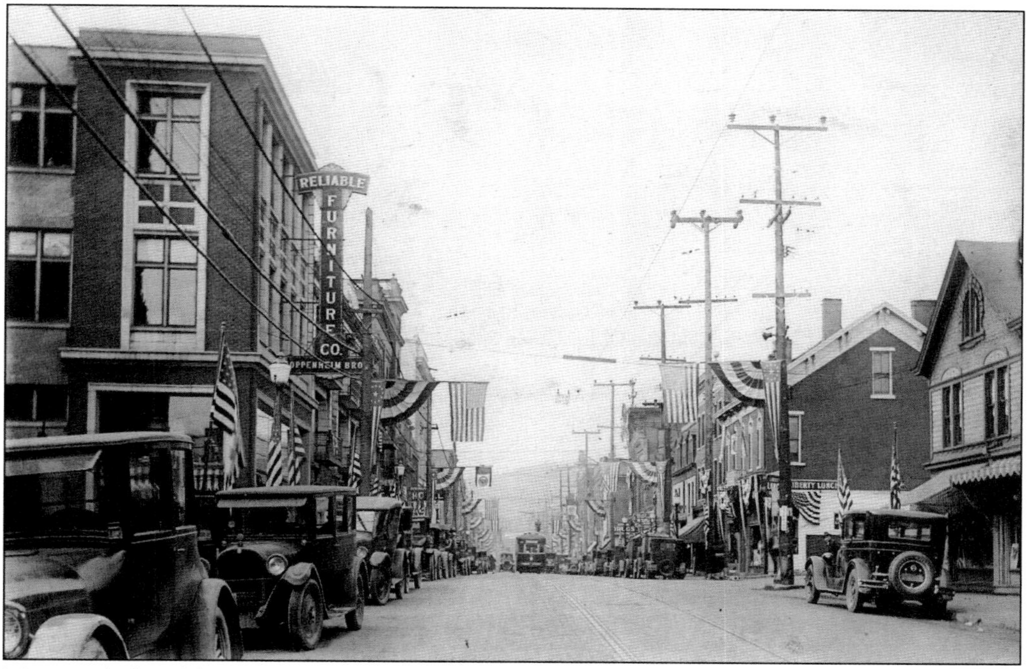

Monongahela celebrated Victory Week in 1928. This scene is looking toward downtown from the entrance of the bridge. The signs of several businesses are visible, including the Reliable Furniture Store, on the left, and the Liberty Lunch, on the right. Automobiles were coming into their own, and are seen parked on both sides between First and Second Streets.

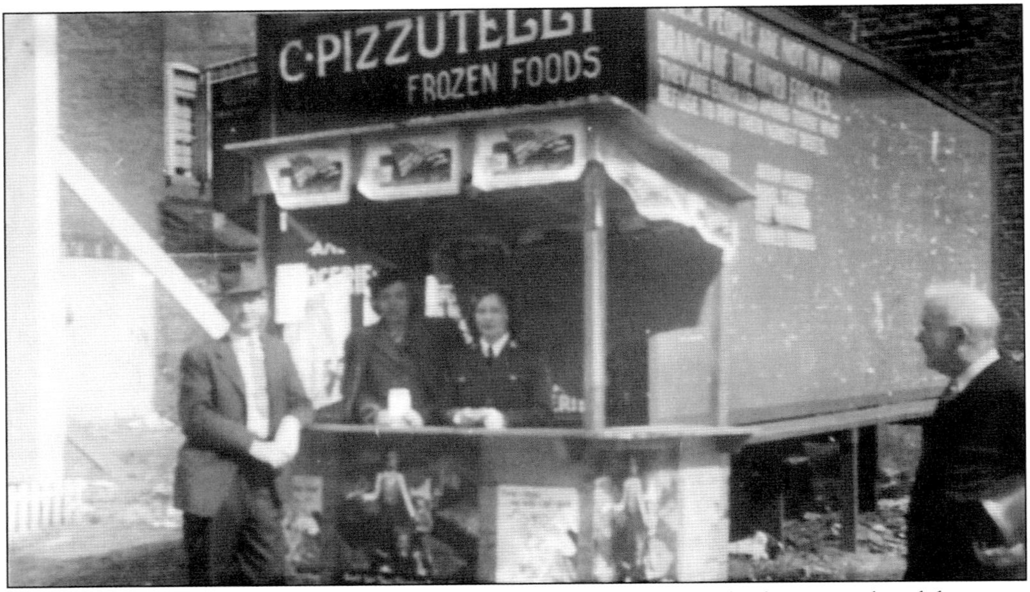

The sale of war bonds was a common practice during World War II. The first major bond drive was held on September 28, 1942. A booth was set up on Third and Main Streets at Clem Pizzutelli's Frozen Foods. The two men in the photograph are William Gray (left) and William Graham. The important role of women helping the war effort is evidenced by the two women selling the bonds, one in uniform.

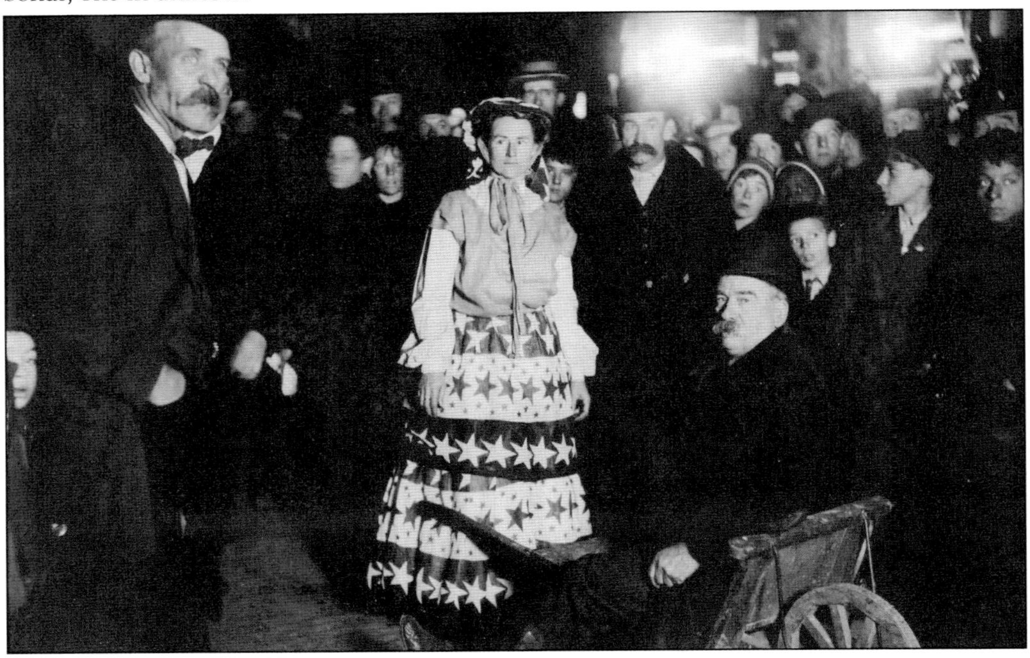

People did not lose their sense of humor during election time. Mrs. Joseph Coatsworth lost a presidential election bet to Henry Loutitt in 1909. On February 14, she had to wheel him from Ideal Theatre to Fourth Street and back. Her costume was made by Mrs. William Isaac. The saying "We've come a long way baby" is a reflection from this photograph's era, when women were not allowed to vote, to the present day, in which women can now run for the highest offices (even if there is no female US president as of 2011.)

Three

Treasures

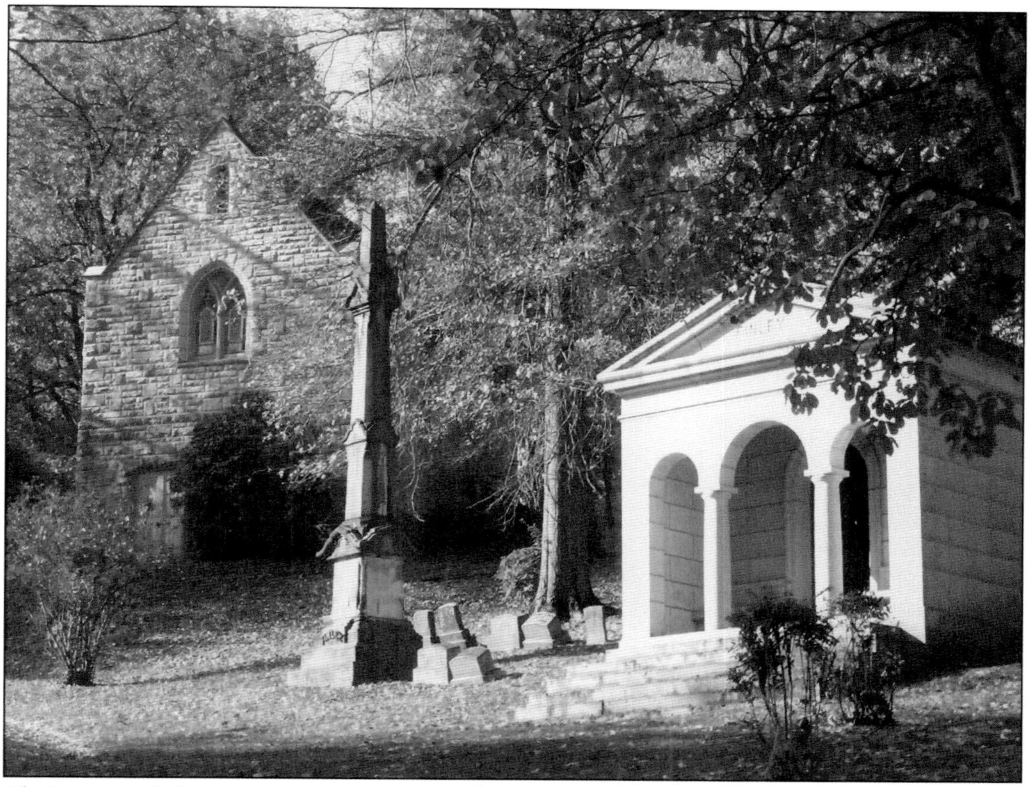

The Monongahela Cemetery is one of Pennsylvania's most beautifully landscaped areas. Residents purchased a parcel of land from local farmer William McClure to create a final resting place for Civil War soldiers in 1863. This picture shows the chapel, built with a receiving vault in 1894 at a cost of $3,525.98, and the Finley Mausoleum. Hare & Hare, 19th-century landscape artists of national repute, designed the cemetery grounds, and the architecture is Gothic Revival. The cemetery was listed on the National Register of Historic Places in 2001, and popular community tours were conducted over the years by Monongahela historian Charles Talbert.

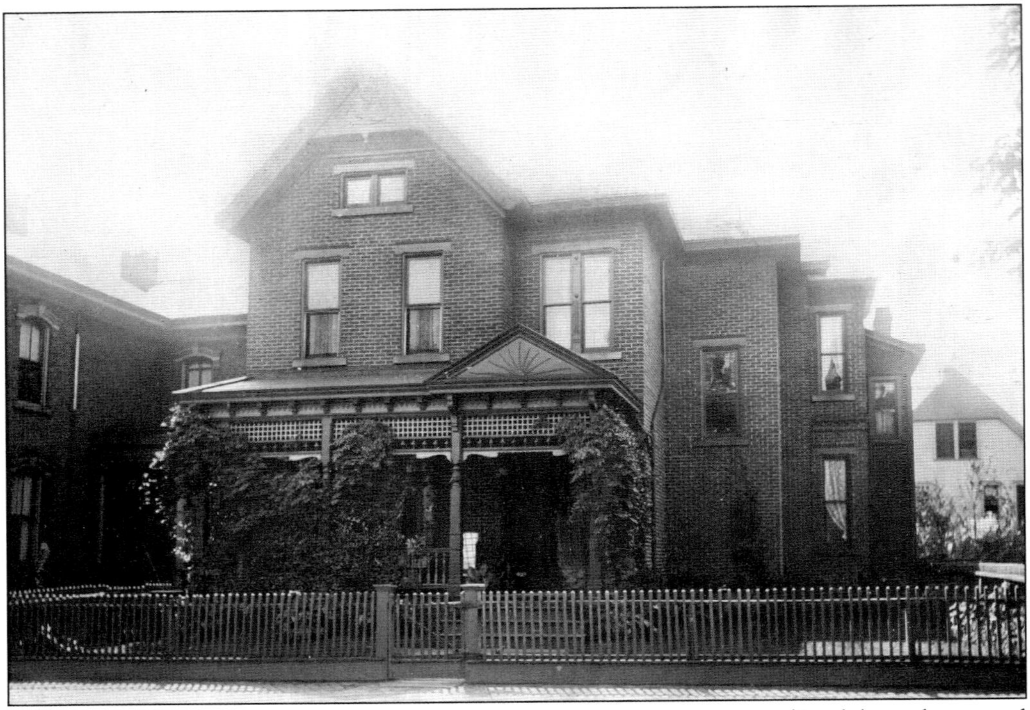

The Acheson House was built in 1884 and demonstrates the Queen Anne/Eastlake architectural style. In 1976, Congress chose "Homes of American Inventors" as its theme for historic sites to be nominated as National Historic Landmarks. Because it was one of the homes of Edward Acheson, inventor of Carborundum, it was chosen. This National Historic Landmark is truly one of the jewels of the city.

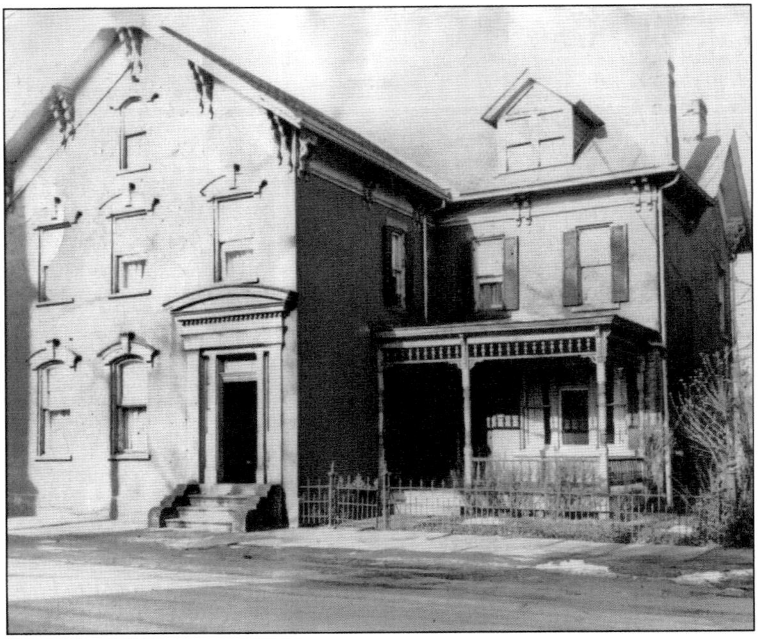

The Anawalt-Taylor House was built in 1854 with additions added in 1890. It is a Greek Revival house remodeled in the Italianate style. The house was built during the peak of the boat-building era throughout the Mon Valley. J.B. Taylor, the owner, was also a true abolitionist. The house was a stop on the Underground Railroad; enslaved people on the path to freedom were hidden in the barn behind the house.

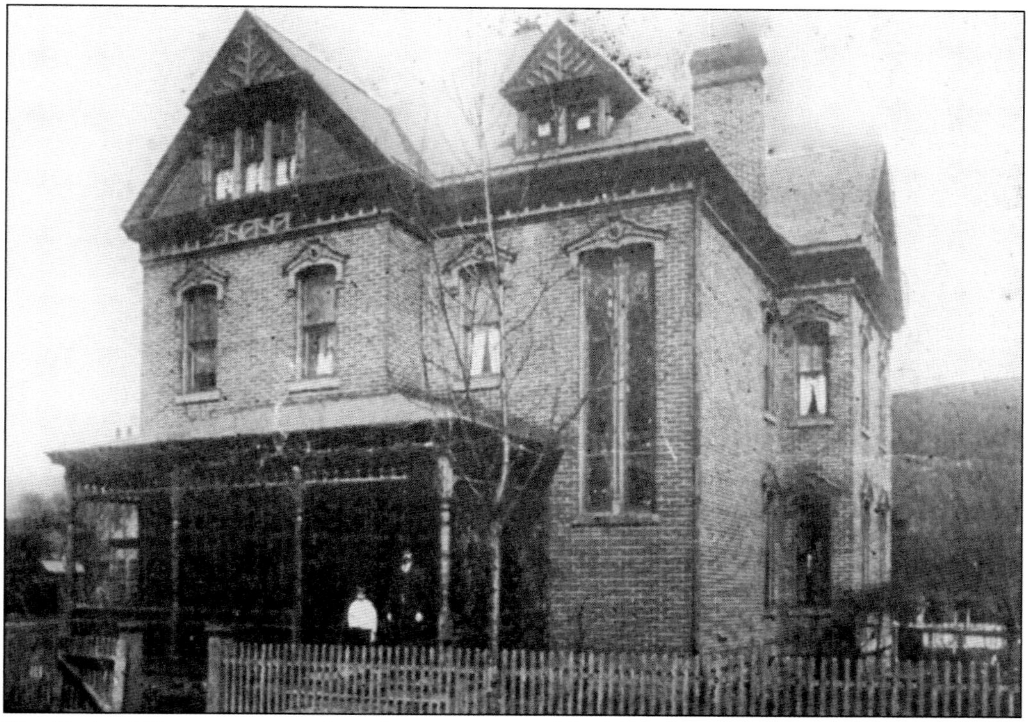

The Borland House once stood on the present site of the Monongahela Area Library. It was built in 1860 by Mark Borland, who along with his sons owned several stores spanning the Fourth Street block in town. The house's most distinguishing features were the elongated stained-glass windows facing Main Street. Town residents also recall the fragrant wisteria bushes that enveloped the house.

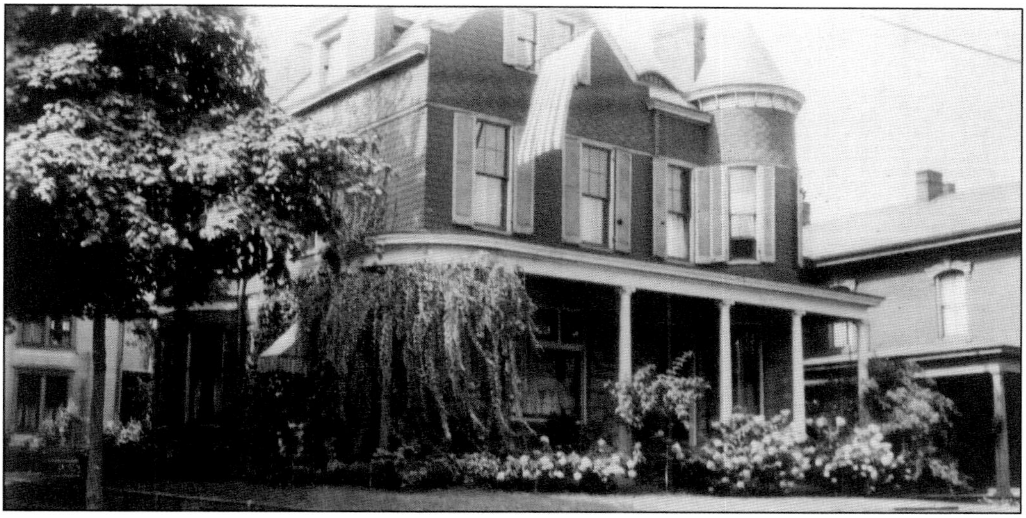

This was the former home of the Theodore M. and Agnes Byers family. Mr. Byers opened the Byers Dry Goods Store on April 5, 1880. The family bequeathed its home to the city to be used as a library. The first library association was created on May 7, 1902, and met in the Mellvain Building on Main Street. The Byers Memorial Library began with a donation of 150 books, and Flora Jones was the first librarian. The library remained at this location until the mid-1970s, when a newer library was built across Main Street.

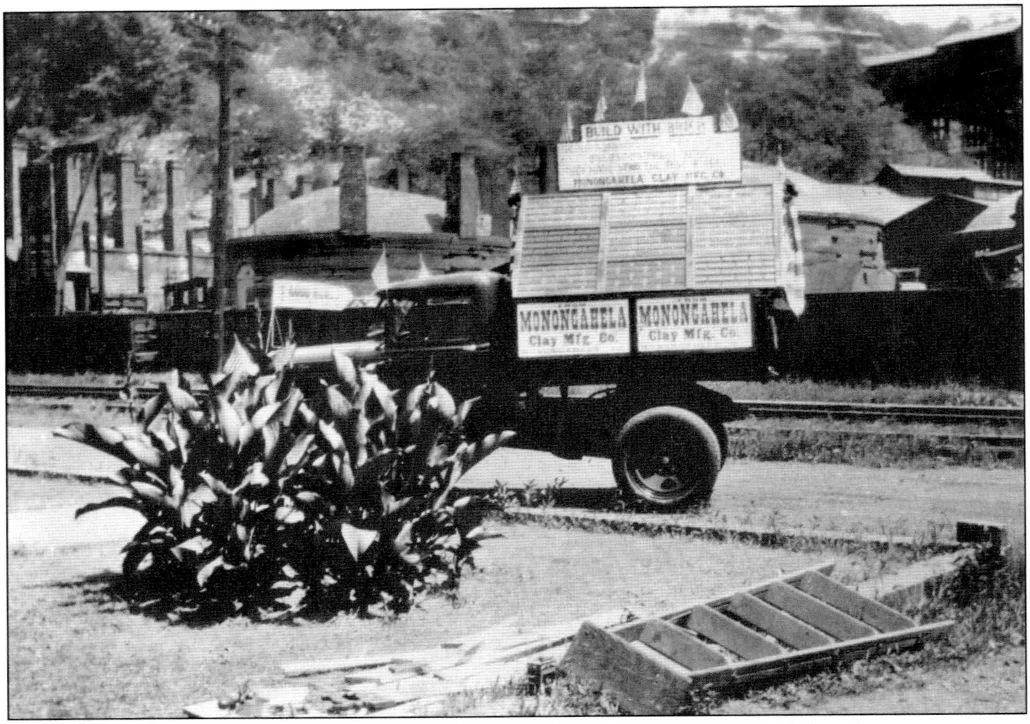

The Monongahela Clay Manufacturing Company was built in 1902 and was located on Pigeon Creek behind Cox Grocery store on Park Avenue. The plant had both square and round kilns, and each held 90,000 bricks. It made mostly red bricks, and most went into the construction of homes, businesses, and industries in the Monongahela Valley. It closed between 1958 and 1959.

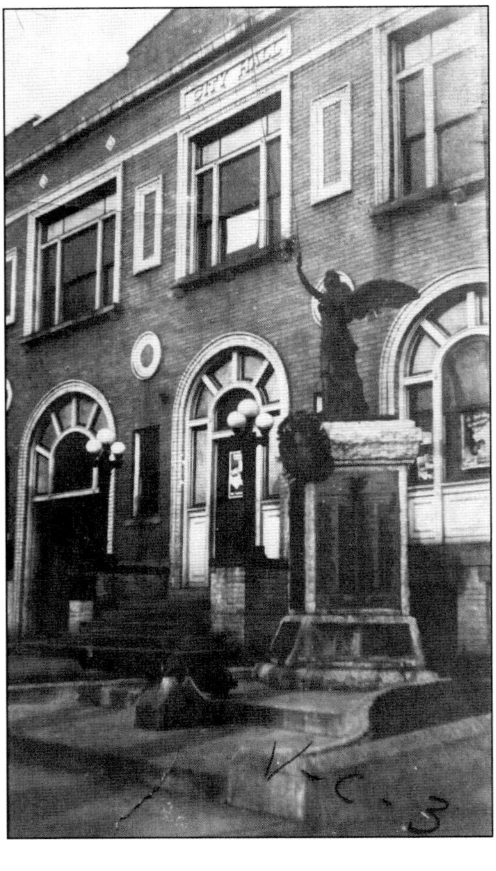

The old city hall stood on Main Street in the Fifth Street block. It was constructed in 1915 and modernized in 1955. The municipal building was demolished to make way for the present-day structure, which also houses the police and fire departments. The antique globe light fixtures from the old city hall now adorn the walls in the present council chambers.

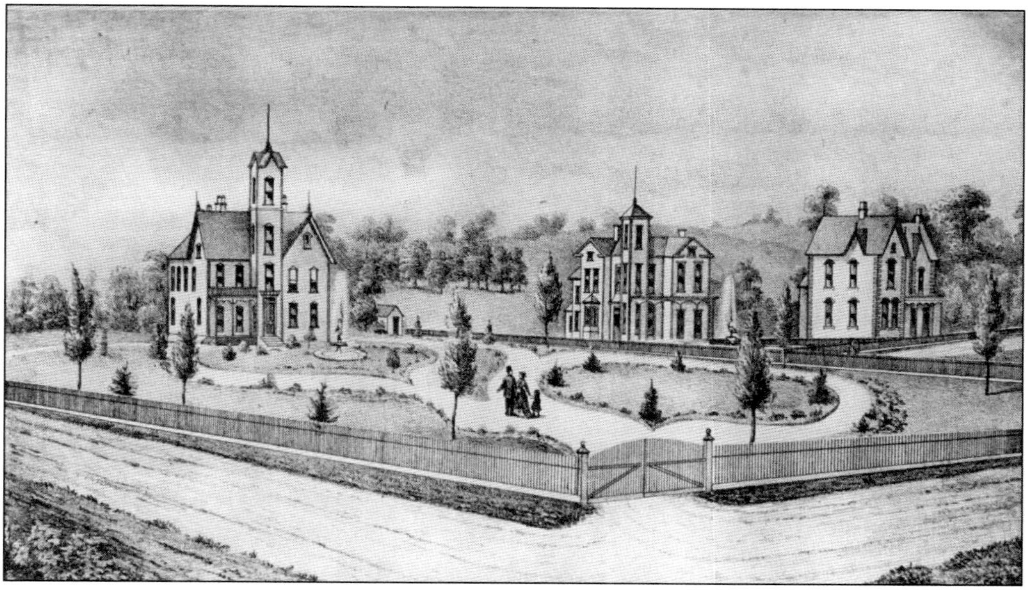

The sketch above shows the one-time residence of Isaac Shelby Crall. Crall was a florist and horticulturist in town. The mounds of the Adena people of 2,000 years ago were discovered on his property, located off Fourth Street. While excavating the foundation walls, workers unearthed skeletons and other artifacts. Crall had a greenhouse on his farm and established his floral business in 1867.

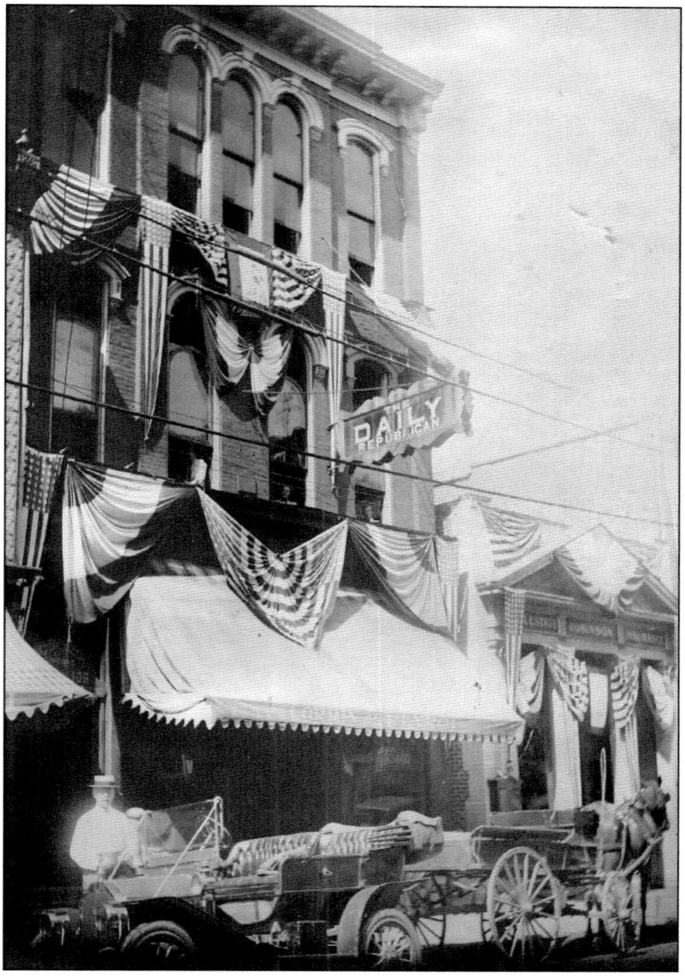

The *Daily Republican* newspaper was established in 1881, and the first publisher was Chill W. Hazzard. The first issue was published on Monday, May 23, 1881, and the cost was 2¢. In 1968, the *Daily Republican* merged with Donora's *Herald American*, becoming the *Daily Herald*. Both publications had been owned by Monongahela resident Robert H. Robinson and then by his sons John and William Robinson.

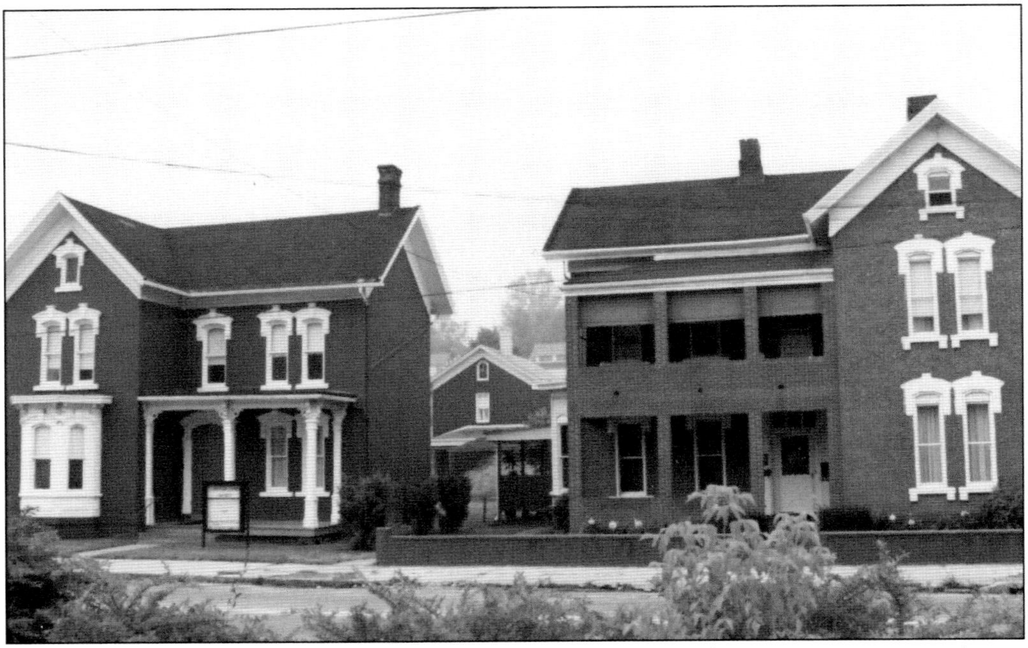

These two houses belonged to brothers John and James Blythe. John was a prominent architect who designed these two homes, along with several other houses and churches in town. His style can be seen in the Italianate beauty and elongated windows of each home. Another feature was the beautiful interior staircase. Both brothers took part in the building phase of John's designs.

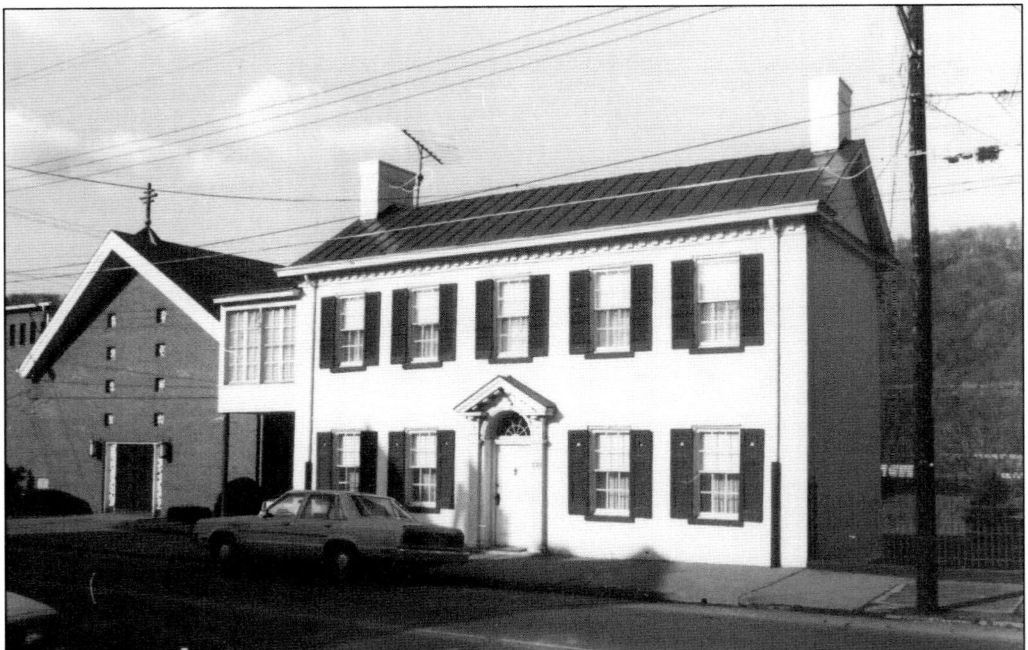

The Greek Revival–style Keenan House was built some time before the Civil War in the section of Monongahela originally called Georgetown. Georgetown was laid out by Adam Wickerham on part of his farm, which is now between Fifth and Sixth Streets. It is one of the last remnants of Wickerham's town planning efforts along West Main Street.

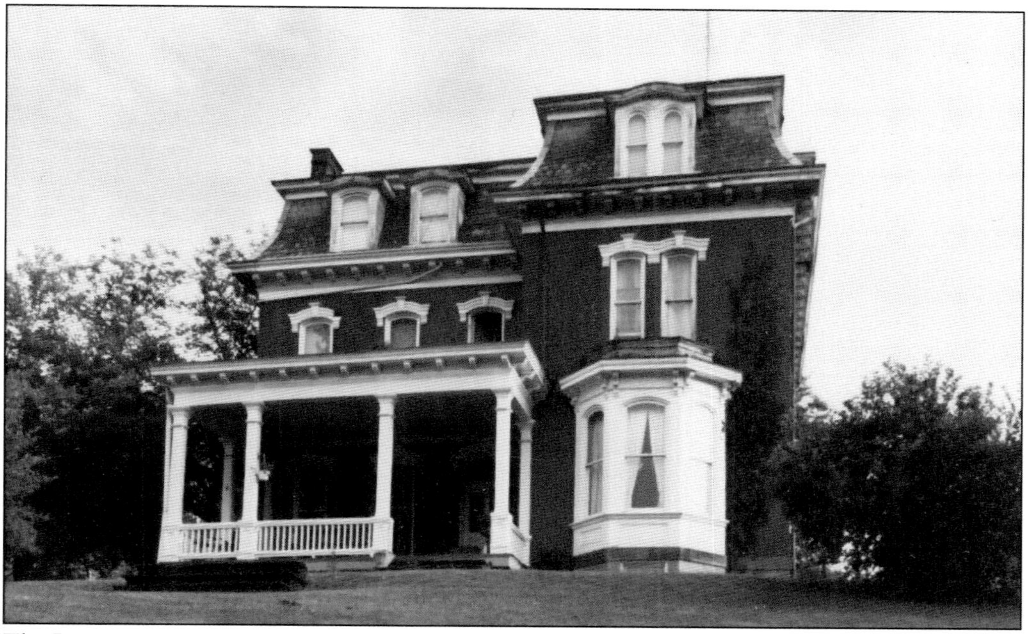

The Bowman House was the residence of Michael and Christina Bowman and family. Mr. Bowman was a merchant tailor by trade. This home occupied a city block and sat between Coal Street (now Marne Avenue), Howard Street, Meade Street, and Cherry Alley. The home was built in 1872 and was designed by John Blythe. The house was the first in town to be piped for gas lighting and the first to have a bathroom. The mansard roof gave the house a distinct look.

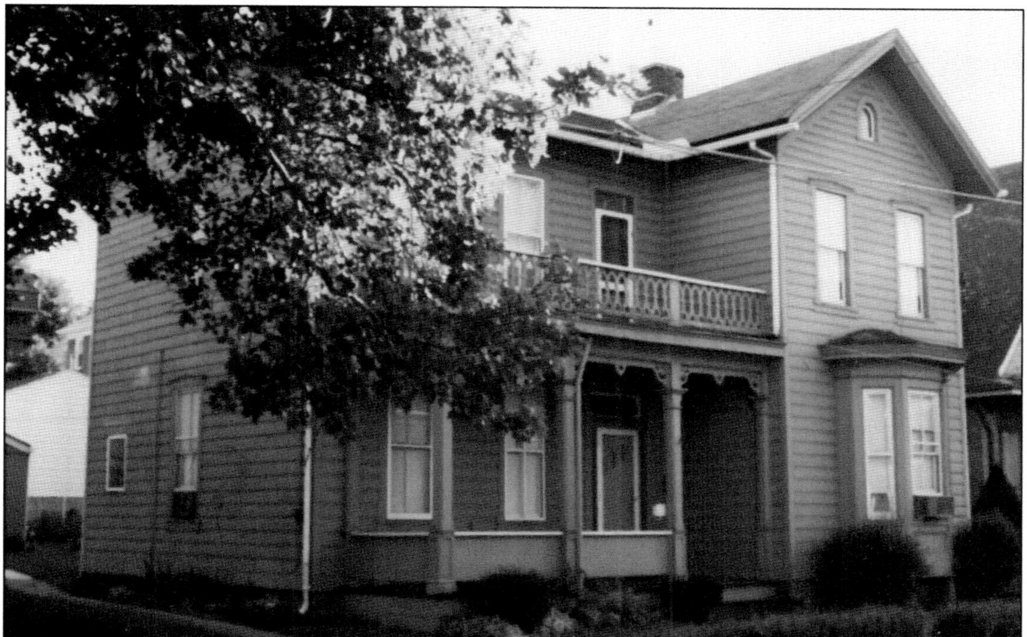

This house on Chess Street was the home of Dr. W.P. Taylor, the dentist in town who served on many of the committees, directed plays, and had several collections. The collection of 42 scrapbooks that was donated to the Monongahela Area Historical Society is one of his greatest contributions. From them came much information and many of the pictures used in this book.

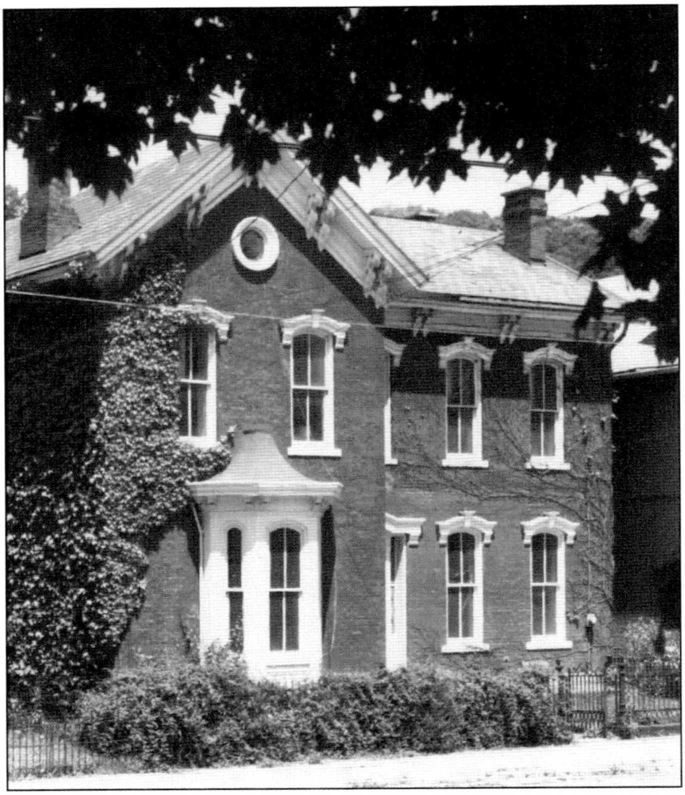

This home was built in 1872 for Capt. David Longwell. It was designed by architect John Blythe. Captain Longwell's first home was too close to the railroad tracks near the river, so he commissioned this house to be built. Its distinctive architectural design won it a place on the National Register of Historic Places on August 2, 1993.

This home on Main Street, in the Fifth Street block, was built in 1884 by William Wickerham. Adam Wickerham was the founder of Georgetown, later part of Williamsport. The home was originally red brick. Over the years, other prominent families, such as the Lytles and Herrons, resided here.

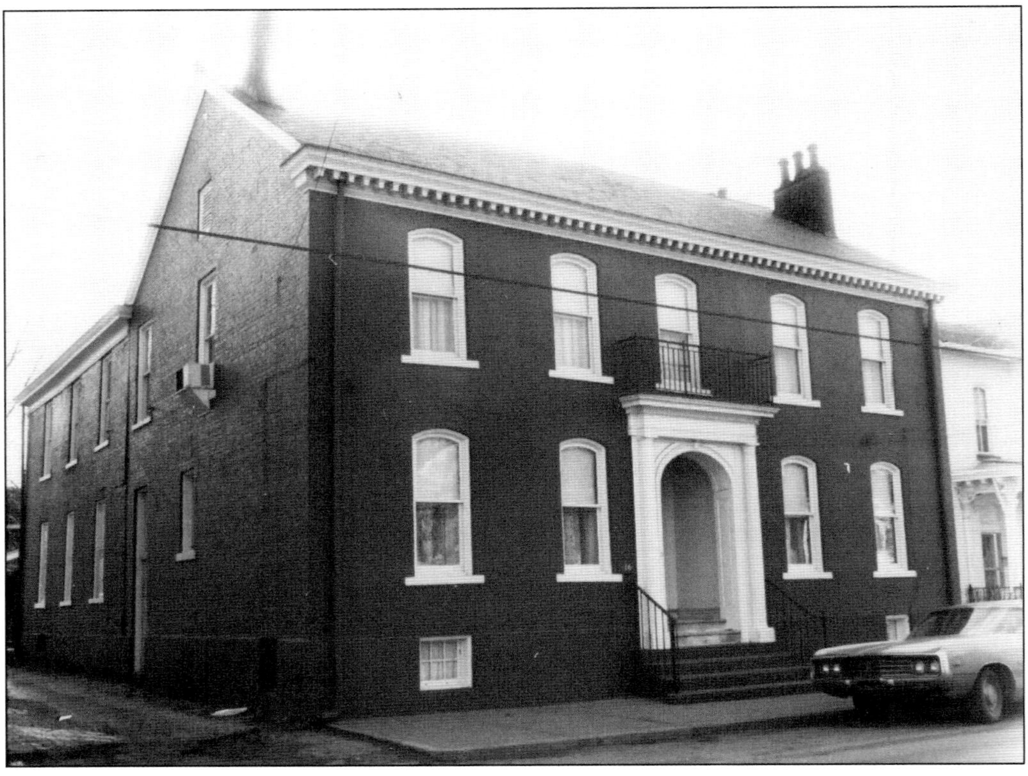

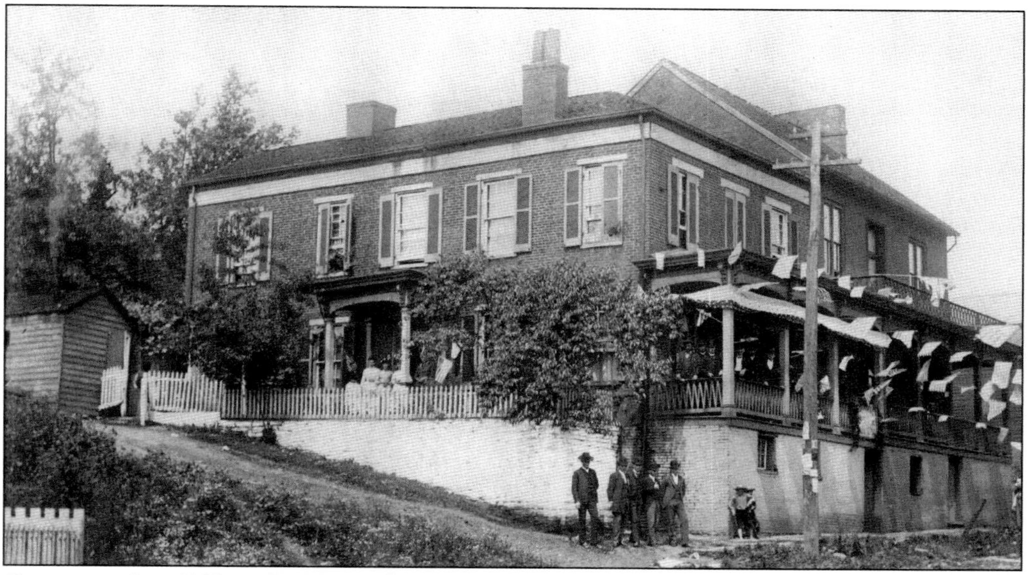

Constructed in 1802 on lot No. 1, the Irwin House, shown here, was the oldest brick house in Parkison's original plan of lots. It was built by William Irwin and later called the Kerr House. It was at the intersection of First and Main Streets. The hill alongside it is Bonacci's Hill. The present-day St. Anthony's Roman Catholic Church sits atop the hill.

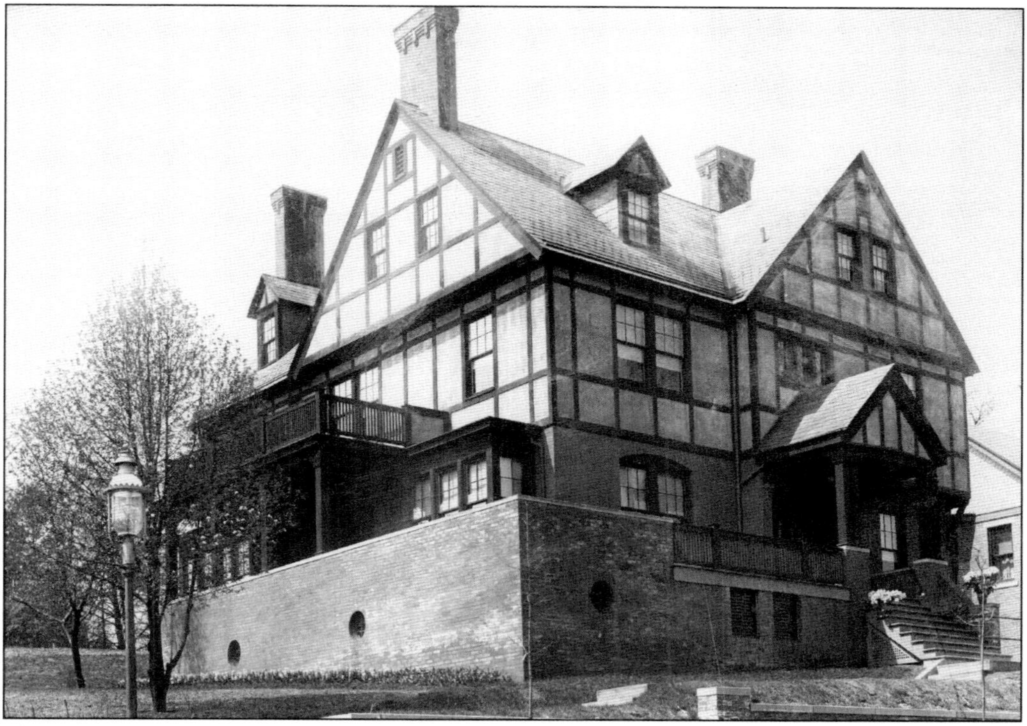

The Alexander House is a stately mansion that still stands on Meade Street. Built in 1828, it is the former home of the prominent Alexander banking family, who started one of the earliest banks in town. Joseph Alexander established the bank on the corner of Third and Main Streets in 1870. The bank closed its doors in 1931, during the Great Depression, never to open again. The PNC Bank building stands there now.

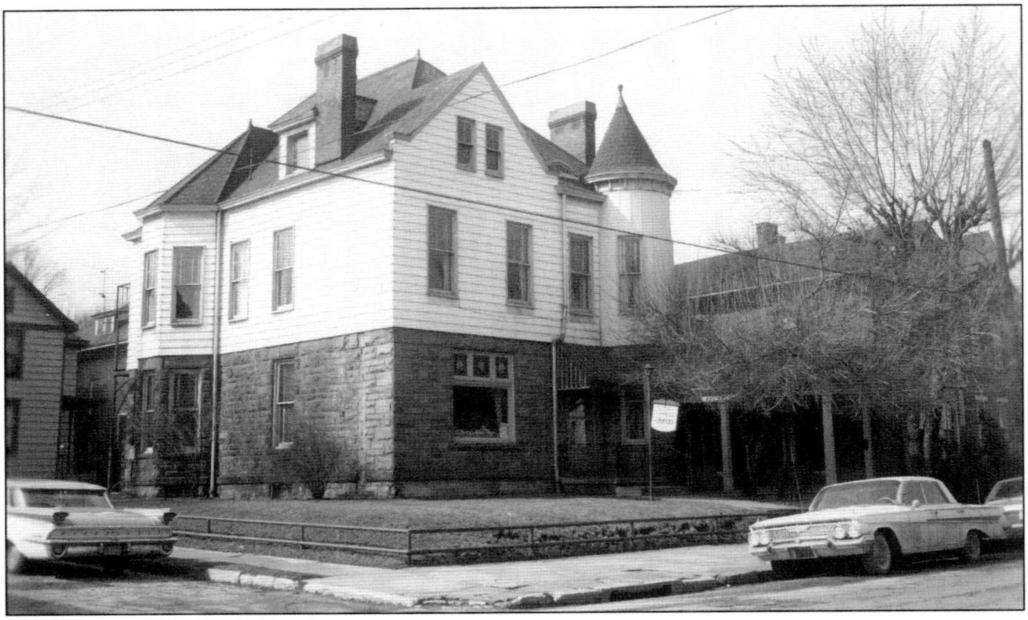

The original library, shown as it looks today, currently serves as an office for a local physician. It stands on the corner of Ninth and Main Streets, and many of the town's residents can still recall the many nooks and crannies of the reading rooms, where memories were made and imaginations flourished. The original turret and windows still remain today.

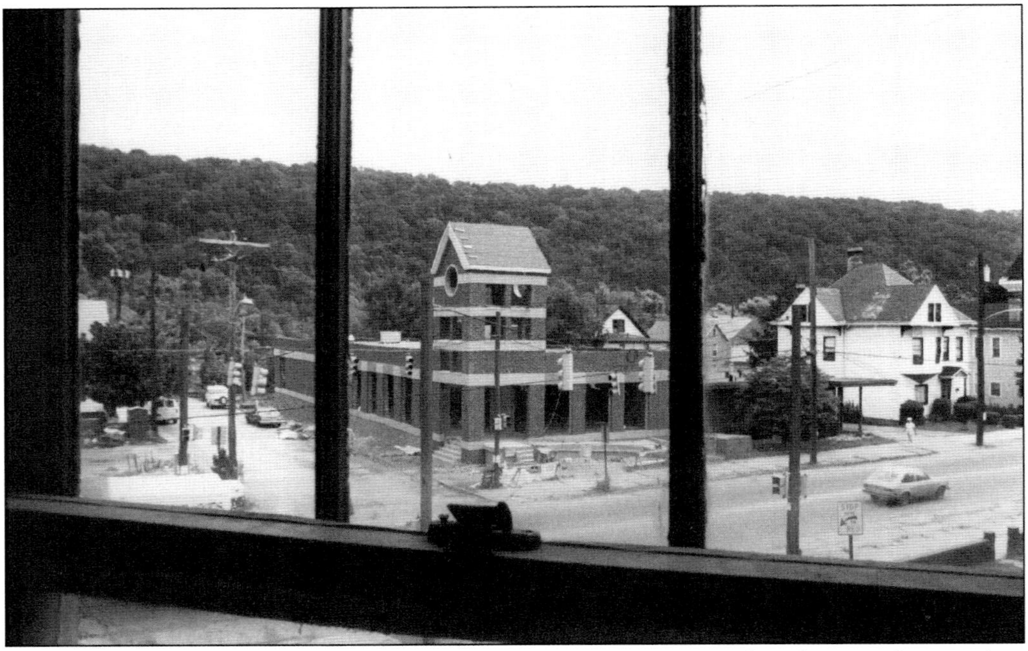

What a unique scene, contrasting the old and looking at the new. This photograph was taken looking out of the second-floor window of Byers Memorial Library, the old library, to Monongahela Area Library, the new library, which is across the street. Many still recall moving day, when volunteers formed a human chain across Main Street and handed the books bucket-brigade-style to transport them from the old library to the new. The books went directly from one bookshelf to another, with librarians directing the process. (Courtesy Scott Beveridge, *Observer-Reporter*.)

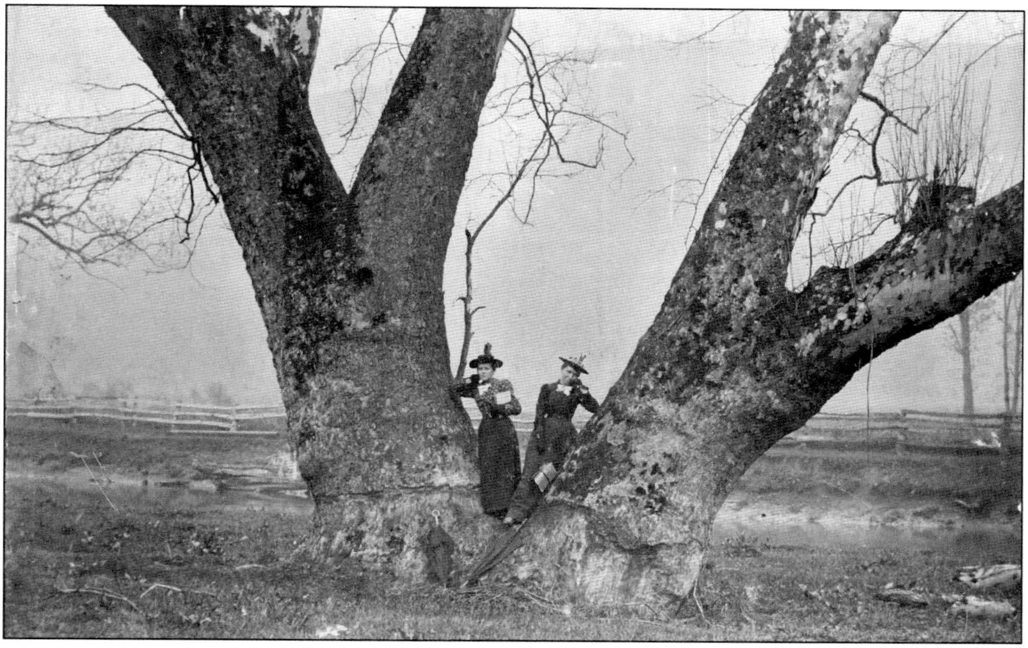

This old sycamore tree stood alongside the road on Park Avenue, across from the driving park. The tree's massive hollowed-out trunk was 36 feet tall and 7 feet in circumference. The story is told that John Howden and his wife were traveling to Bentleyville to set up a homestead. Along the journey, the couple sought shelter in the tree, using a few blankets and leaves for protection not only for themselves but for their new baby boy, who was born in the tree.

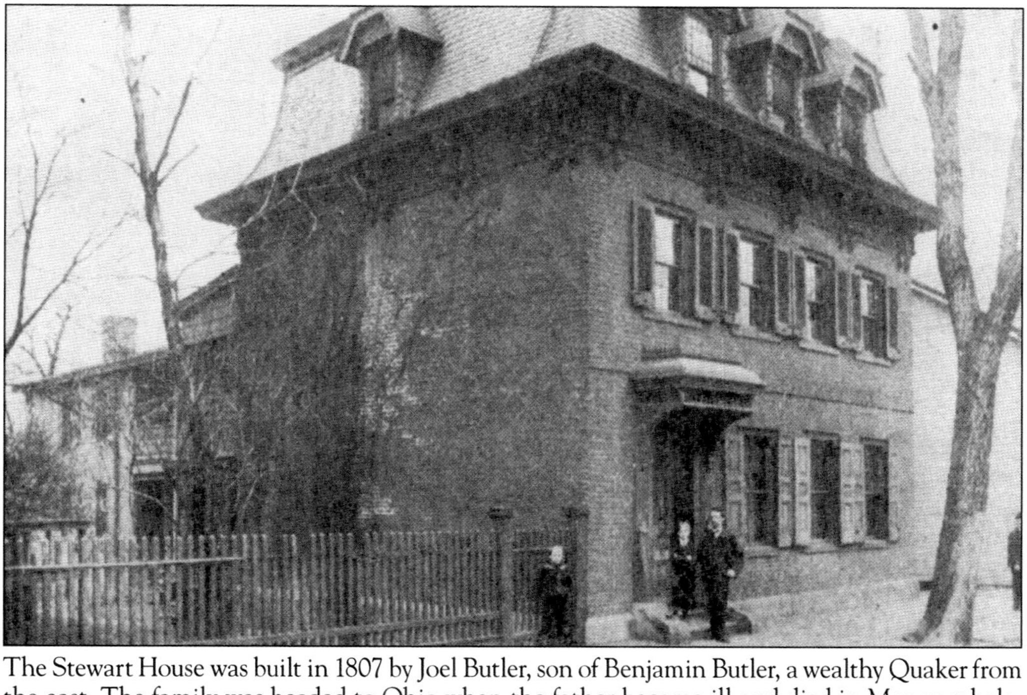

The Stewart House was built in 1807 by Joel Butler, son of Benjamin Butler, a wealthy Quaker from the east. The family was headed to Ohio when the father became ill and died in Monongahela. When the bridge was built in 1907, this house was saved and moved to its present location on Lawrence Street. It is a Washington County Landmark.

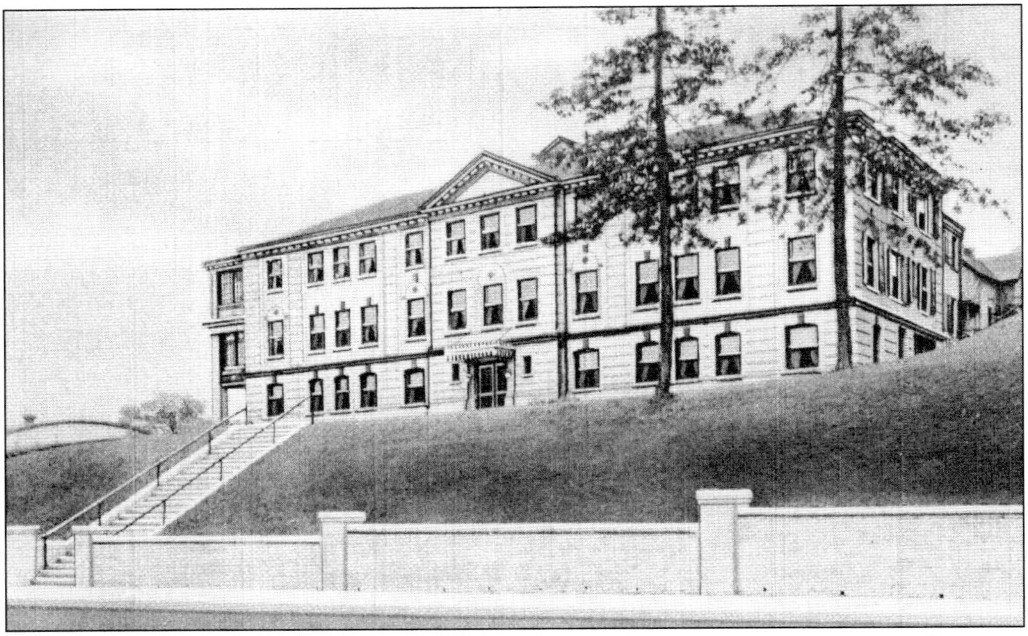

Built in 1902, the Monongahela Memorial Hospital, a wooden structure, was constructed to serve as a full-service community hospital. Area residents received cradle-to-grave care from obstetrics to surgery and geriatric care. In 1911, the Commonwealth of Pennsylvania gave $35,000 for construction of a new facility. A 95-bed hospital opened in 1914 and later served as a training facility for nurses. An addition comprised of critical care units and a pediatric unit was added in 1974. A state-of-the-art facility (Monongahela Valley Hospital) opened in October 1978, replacing the aging facility. (Courtesy the Joann Crow family.)

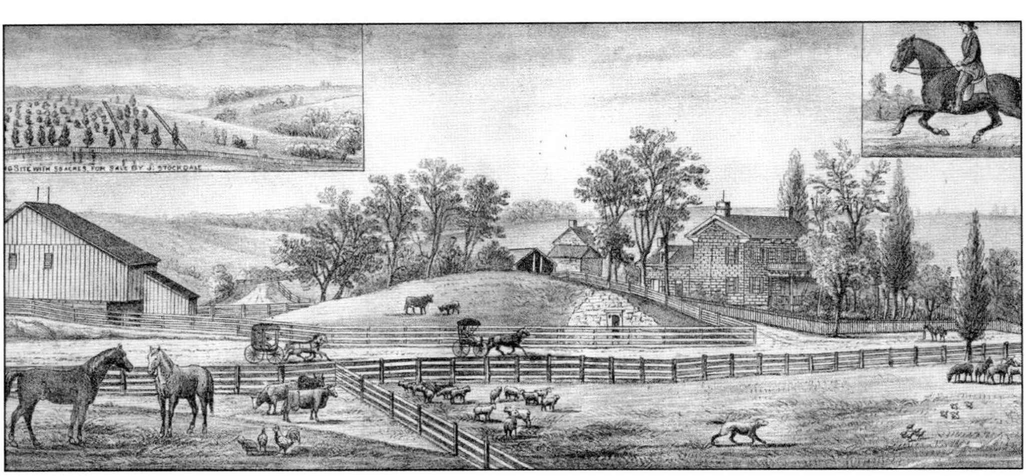

This intricate drawing illustrates the Stockdale Home of James Stockdale, located on the Washington Pike in Carroll Township two miles from Monongahela. In 1803, James Stockdale and Danny Heaton found bituminous coal. The sketch portrays the wealth and status of Stockdale. The area on Park Avenue, across the bridge on Pigeon Creek, was named Stockdaletown after him. (Courtesy scrapbook of Potente Zanardelli.)

Four

ENTREPRENEURS

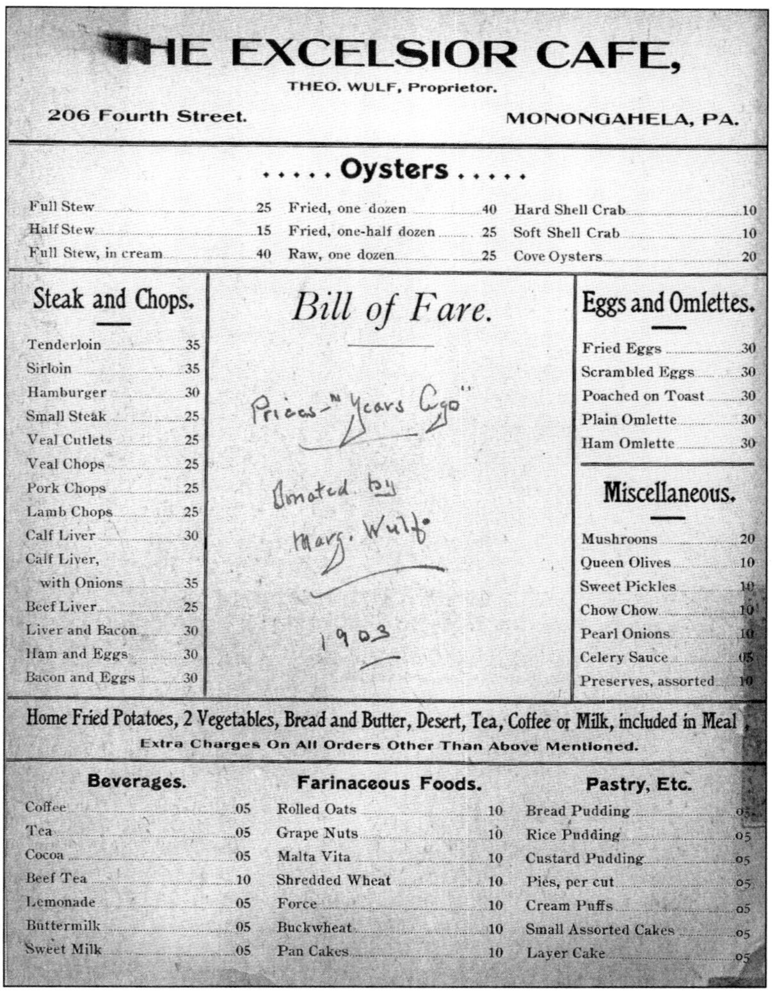

THE EXCELSIOR CAFE,

THEO. WULF, Proprietor.

206 Fourth Street. MONONGAHELA, PA.

..... Oysters .....

Full Stew	25	Fried, one dozen	40	Hard Shell Crab	10
Half Stew	15	Fried, one-half dozen	25	Soft Shell Crab	10
Full Stew, in cream	40	Raw, one dozen	25	Cove Oysters	20

Steak and Chops.

Tenderloin	35
Sirloin	35
Hamburger	30
Small Steak	25
Veal Cutlets	25
Veal Chops	25
Pork Chops	25
Lamb Chops	25
Calf Liver	30
Calf Liver, with Onions	35
Beef Liver	25
Liver and Bacon	30
Ham and Eggs	30
Bacon and Eggs	30

Bill of Fare.

Prices "Years Ago"

Donated by Marg. Wulf.

1903

Eggs and Omlettes.

Fried Eggs	30
Scrambled Eggs	30
Poached on Toast	30
Plain Omlette	30
Ham Omlette	30

Miscellaneous.

Mushrooms	20
Queen Olives	10
Sweet Pickles	10
Chow Chow	10
Pearl Onions	10
Celery Sauce	05
Preserves, assorted	10

Home Fried Potatoes, 2 Vegetables, Bread and Butter, Desert, Tea, Coffee or Milk, included in Meal.

Extra Charges On All Orders Other Than Above Mentioned.

Beverages.		Farinaceous Foods.		Pastry, Etc.	
Coffee	05	Rolled Oats	10	Bread Pudding	05
Tea	05	Grape Nuts	10	Rice Pudding	05
Cocoa	05	Malta Vita	10	Custard Pudding	05
Beef Tea	10	Shredded Wheat	10	Pies, per cut	05
Lemonade	05	Force	10	Cream Puffs	05
Buttermilk	05	Buckwheat	10	Small Assorted Cakes	05
Sweet Milk	05	Pan Cakes	10	Layer Cake	05

This menu is from the Excelsior Café, which was located at 206 Fourth Street in the late 1800s and was operated by Theodore Wulf. Who knew that it was possible to walk "uptown" and order a dozen softshell crabs or raw oysters? For 25¢, diners could have had veal chops served with home-fried potatoes, two vegetables, bread and butter, dessert, and a beverage. There is a whole offering of healthy "farinaceous" items and 5¢ desserts. Those were the days!

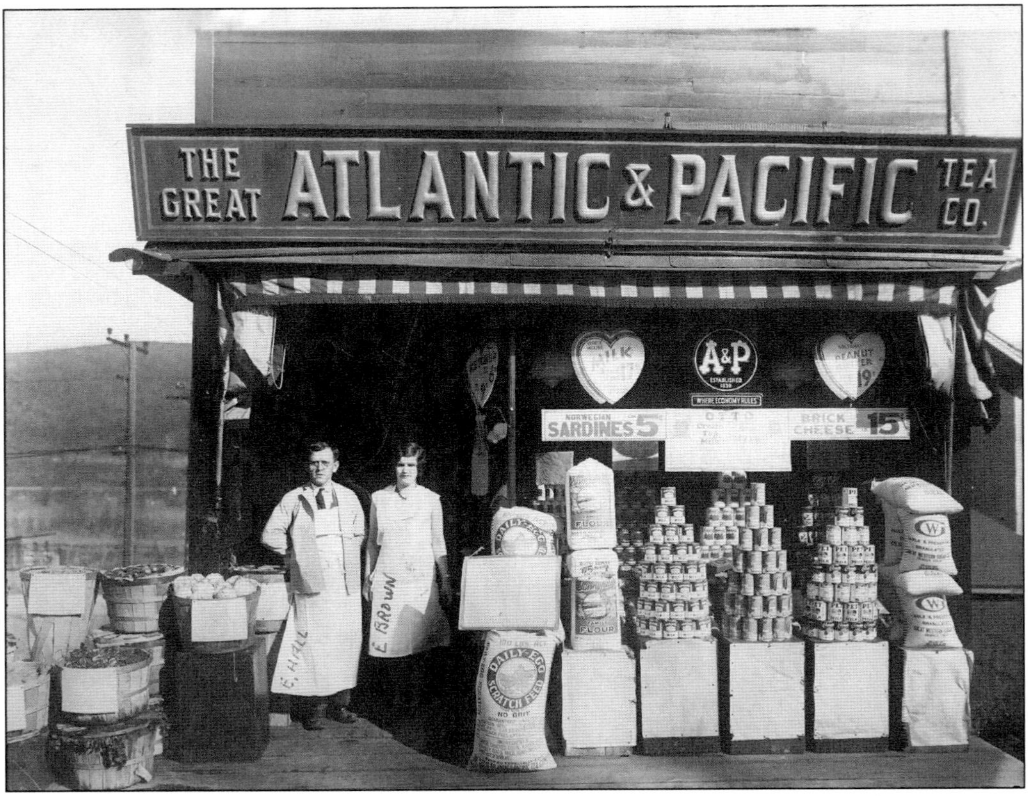

The A&P Tea Company supermarket was established in 1859, and its slogan was, "Where Economy Rules." Here, E. Hall (left) and E. Brown are standing in front. Some popular items were Otto milk (cream top), brick cheese (15¢ a pound), sardines (5¢ a can), ketchup (6¢ or 9¢ a bottle, depending on the size), and Daily Egg Scratch Feed.

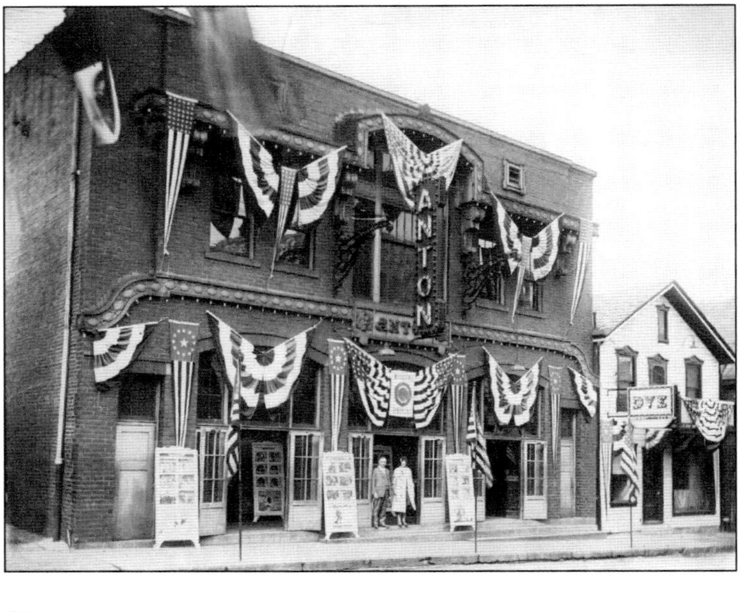

The Anton Theatre was established in 1911 and was one of three theaters in town during that time. The other two were the Ideal Theatre (1906) and the Bentley (1914). People came from all over Washington County, via train or horse and wagon, to enjoy the entertainment offerings. Like elsewhere, vaudeville-type acts became regular showings in local venues, including the Anton.

The Ashcraft Hauling Company, which began in Monongahela in the early 1900s, was founded by Harry J. Ashcraft, who did feats of magic in moving very large items. This photograph shows the Ashcrafts moving a huge water tank out of a field near Monongahela. Because the railroads did not want unfair competition from Ashcraft, he continually made photographic documentation of his work to show he was hauling in areas where there were no railroad tracks. (Courtesy George Ashcraft.)

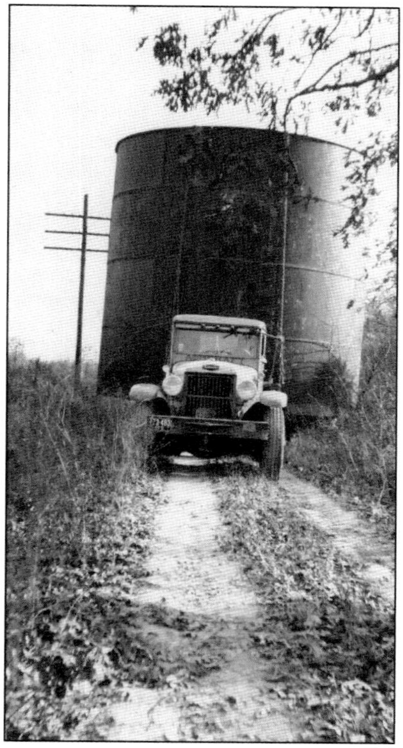

Harry J. Ashcraft was born in 1889 in a log cabin in Ohio and came to Monongahela in 1908 to begin his hauling business, first using teams of horses and wagons and later using trucks. This picture shows several trucks linked together to move a Dinky steam engine in 1928–1931 for Vang Construction, which was building the dam in Cumberland, Maryland. Ashcraft, Inc., is functional today in Monongahela under the direction of Harry's son George Ashcraft. (Courtesy George Ashcraft.)

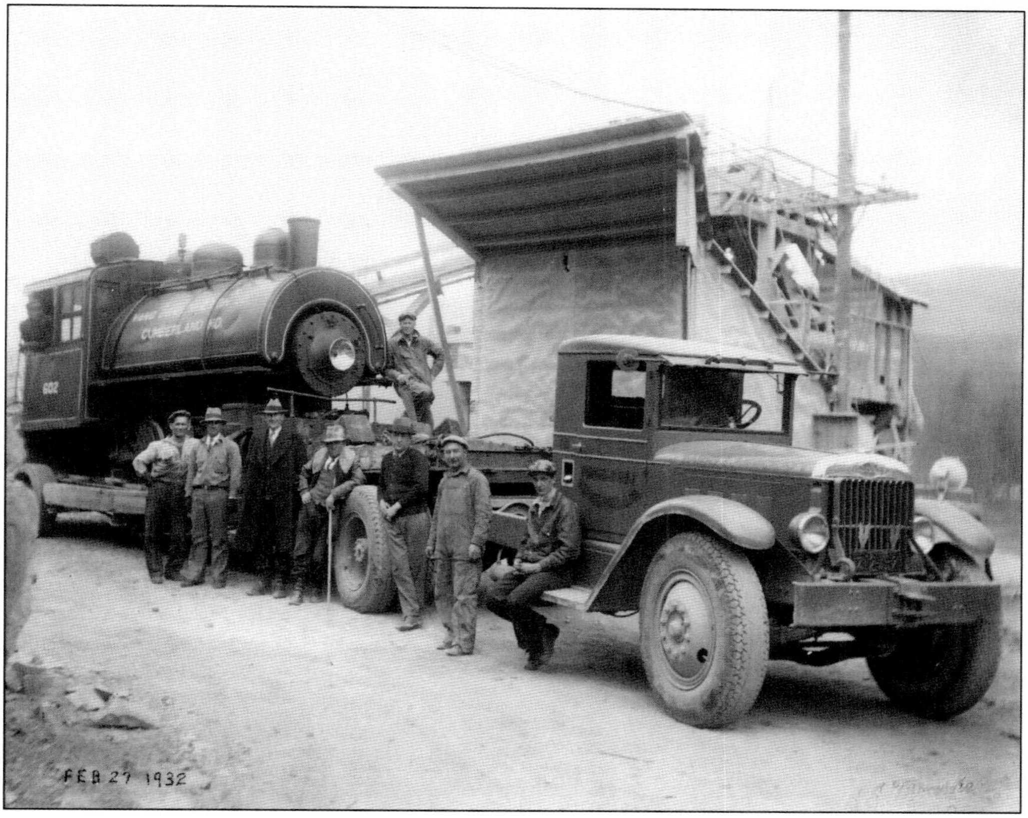

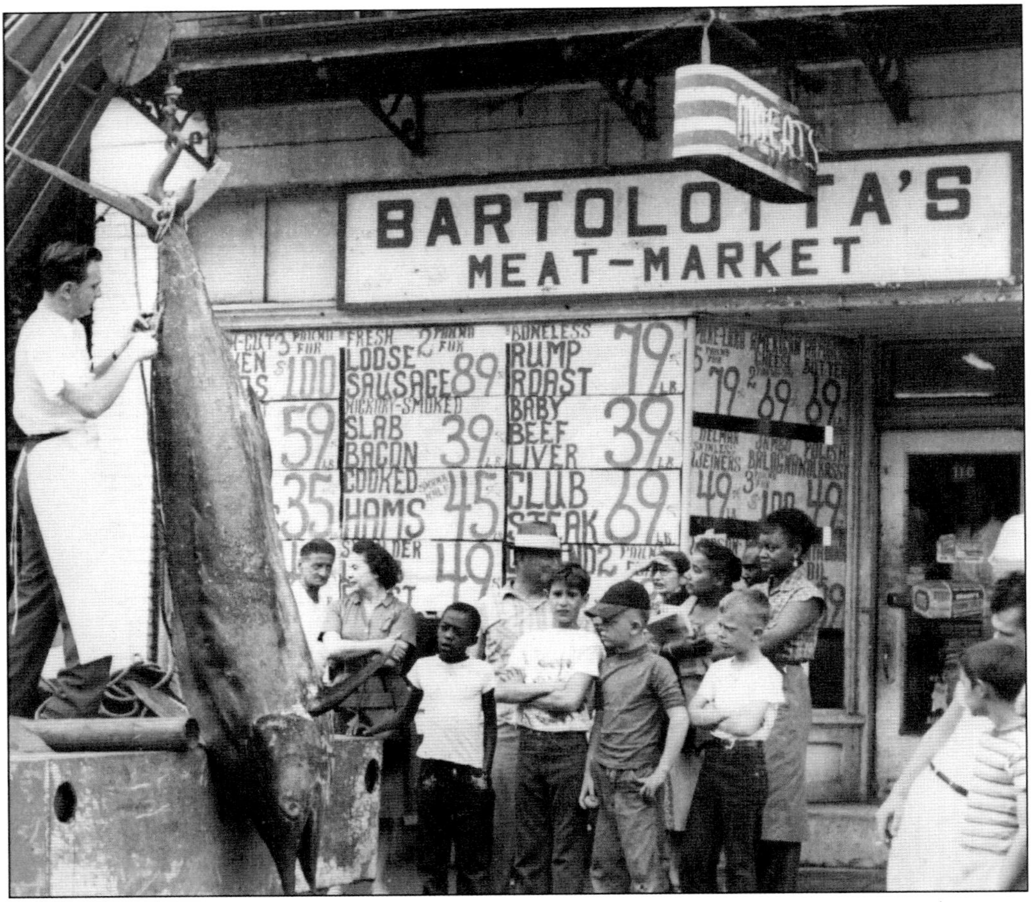

Bartolotta's original meat market was located at 110 Main Street near Park Avenue. Shown in this photograph is Leo Bartolotta with a great catch (not from the Monongahela). The children and adults certainly enjoyed catching a glimpse of such a large fish. Leo, Aldo, and the Bartolotta family have a long history of being successful grocers in the region and are known for their fine products and generous support of the community. (Courtesy Aldo Bartolotta.)

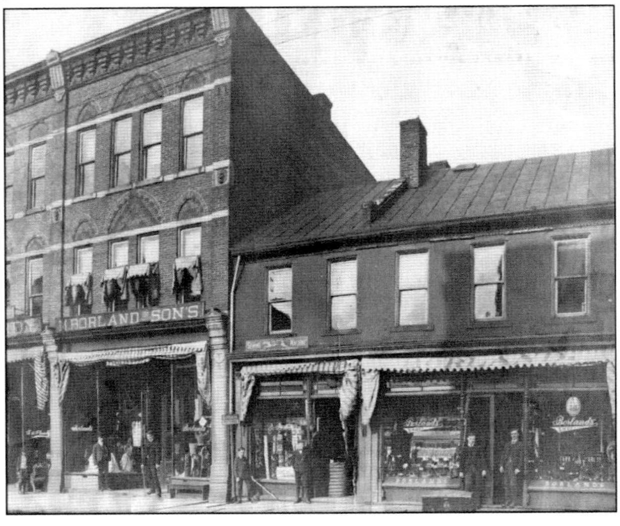

The Borland family consisted of five brothers, the sons of Mark Borland. The Borland brothers had several businesses known as Borland and Sons that took up most of the Fourth Street block in the 1800s. Their establishments included a dry goods store, wallpaper store, and shoe store. In its day, their monopoly surely would have given Wal-Mart a run for its money.

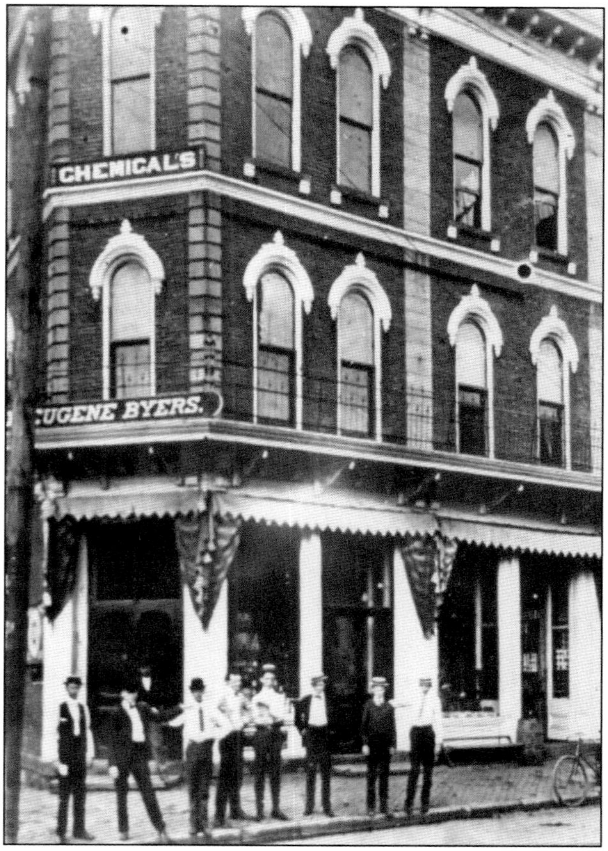

Shown in 1901 is the Byers Drug and Grocery Store. Located at Fourth and Main Streets, the Byers Drug Store was a long-standing institution in Monongahela, fondly remembered for its soda fountain. Adjacent to the drugstore was a dry goods store, also owned by the Byers family. The gentlemen standing in front for this photograph are, from left to right, Mr. Goodwin, Joe Herron, Jake Ambrose, Clyde Hooker, Bob Byers, Frank Dinsmore, Dr. E.L. Yohe, Don Herron, and Ben Haines.

Clem Pizzutelli's grocery store is shown in 1915. The store was located on Second Street and sold many of the staples needed by the community. In the photograph are, from left to right, Dora Zanardelli, Mary Zanardelli, unidentified, Clem Pizzutelli, Mary Remen, William Turri, and Tom Morelli. (Courtesy scrapbook of Potente Zanardelli.)

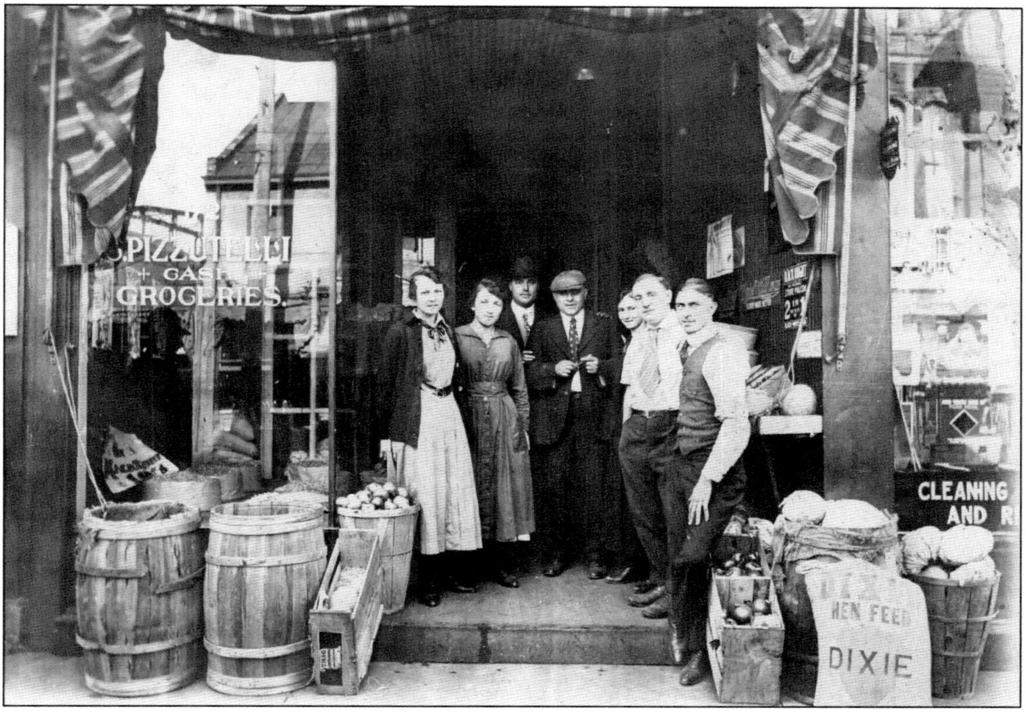

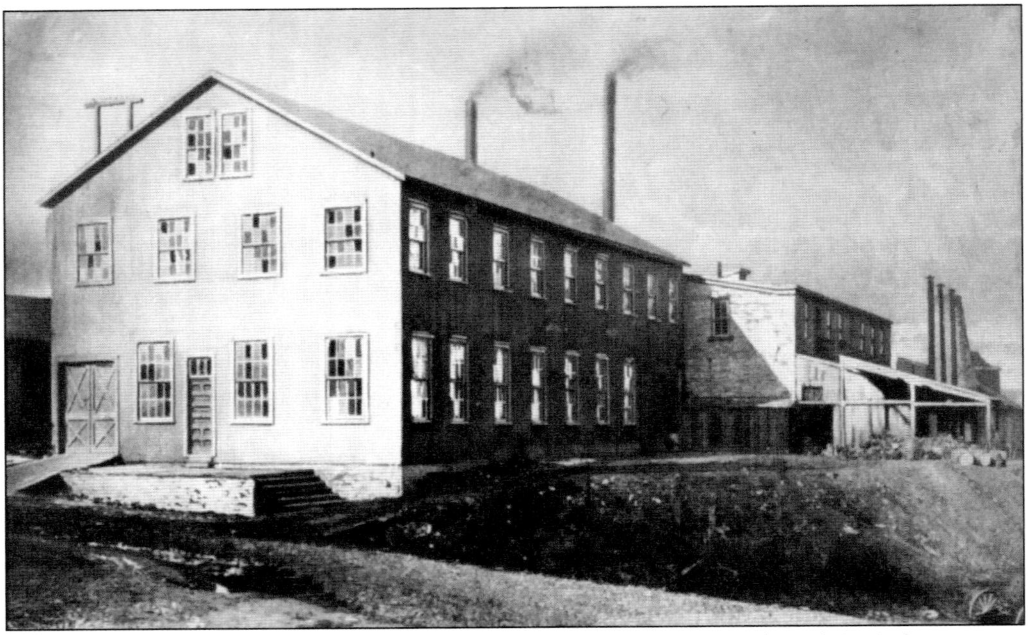

The Carborundum Company, started by Carborundum inventor Edward G. Acheson, was organized on September 21, 1891. He incorporated it for $150,000 and had 50 men employed at the company by 1894. The plant was near the river behind a local lumberyard. The city council refused Acheson's request to expand the company on the riverbank, and by the fall of 1896, the company was moved to Niagara Falls, later becoming Union Carbide.

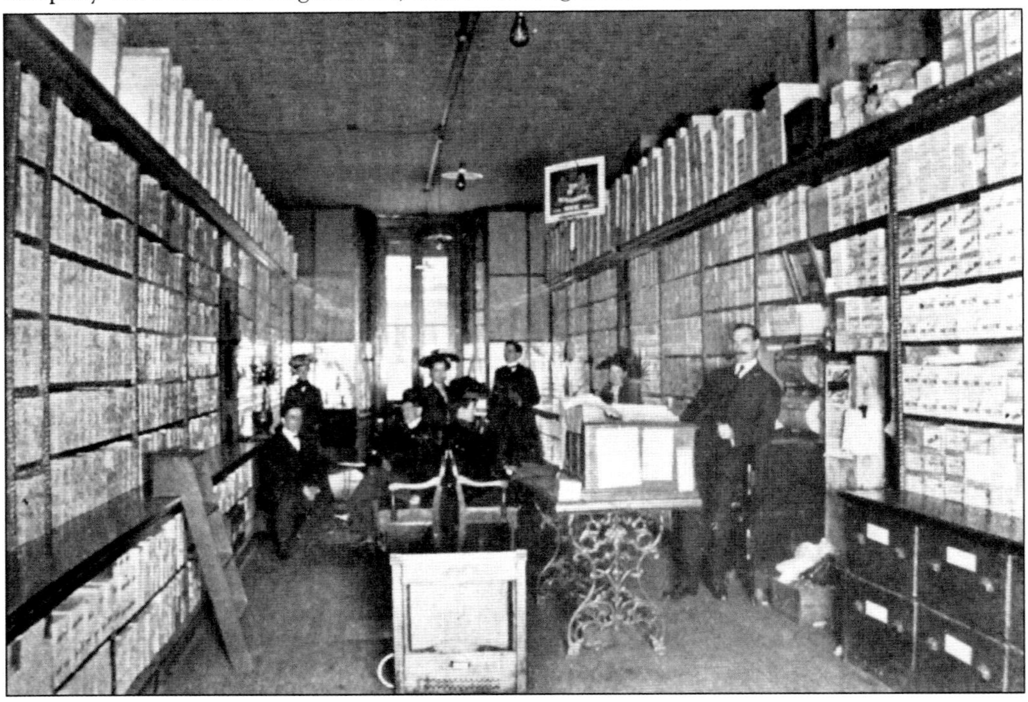

The Howard Borland Shoe Store, on the Fourth Street block, is shown in the 1800s. The stacks of shoes ran to the ceiling. The shoppers seemed pleased with such a selection. This photograph proves once again that, at one time, a person could purchase everything he needed right here in town.

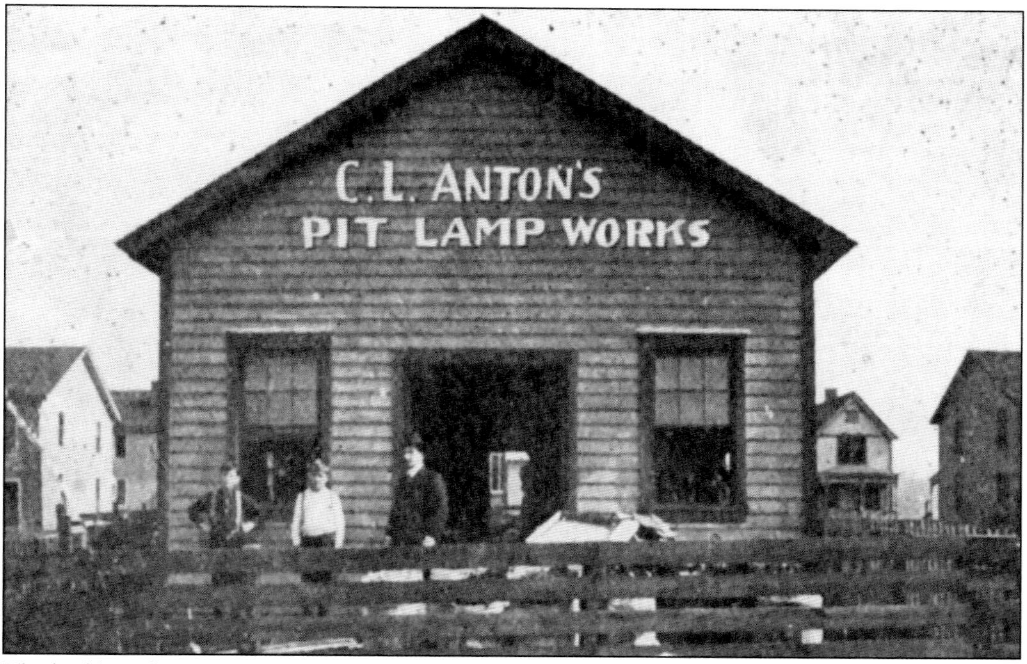

The building shown was C.L. Anton's Pit Lamp Works, which manufactured the Anton Lamps used by miners worldwide. They were manufactured by George Anton and Brothers in Monongahela, the premier wick lamp makers in the United States. The Star Lamp, first sold in 1898, was the best-selling mine lamp of its time, owing to its quality construction, attractive logo, and superior light.

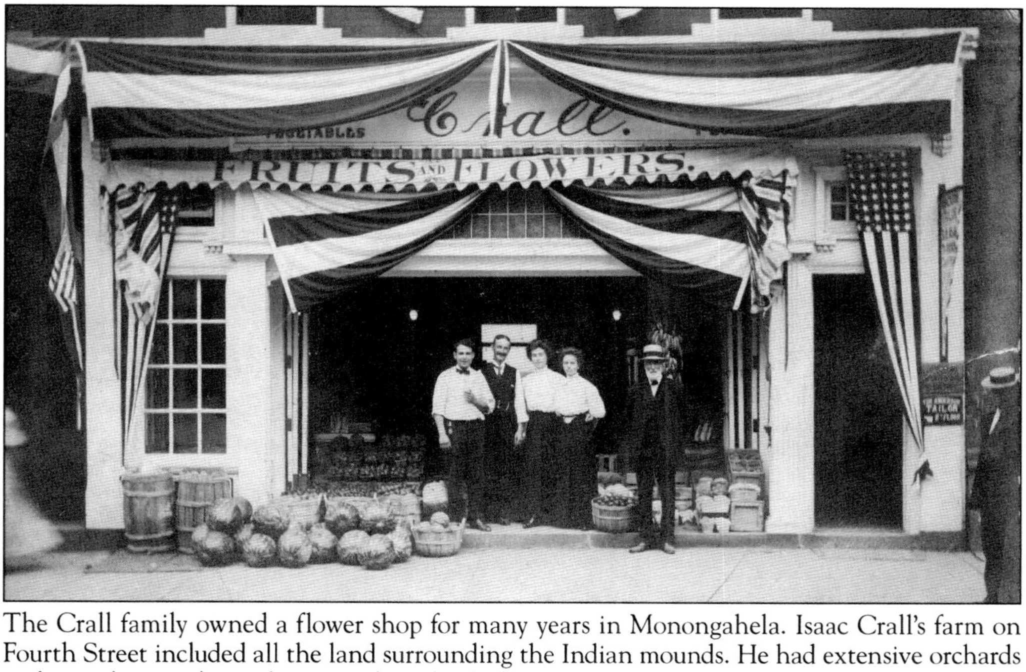

The Crall family owned a flower shop for many years in Monongahela. Isaac Crall's farm on Fourth Street included all the land surrounding the Indian mounds. He had extensive orchards and greenhouses there, thus providing the fruits and vegetables he sold in town. Shown in the photograph are, from left to right, Pete Rocco, H.M. Griffith, Flora Thompson, Nora Summerville, and Bill Wilson.

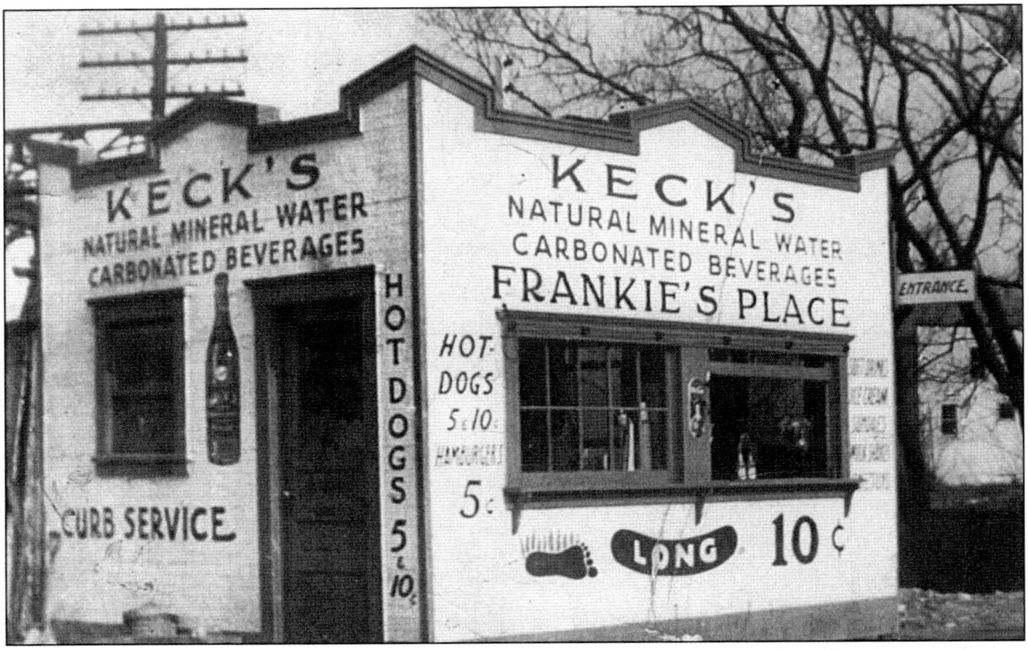

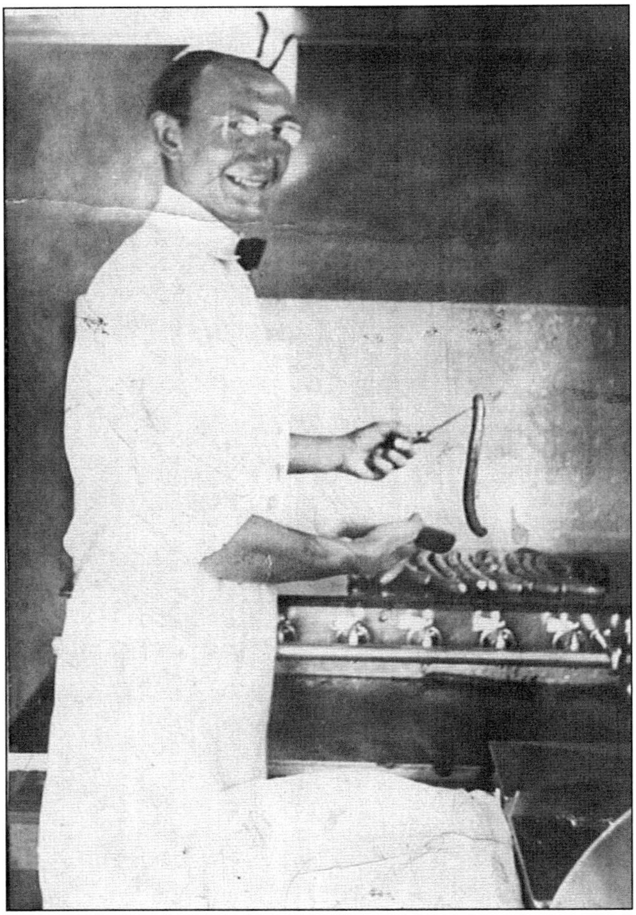

Frankie's Place hotdog stand was a popular spot to eat in Monongahela. It was started by Frankie Ketcher, a true entrepreneur at an early age. He quit high school in his senior year, opened the eatery in 1939, and ran it until it closed in 1960. When Frankie served in the Army during World War II, his wife kept the stand going until his return.

Shown is Frankie Ketcher and his famous foot-long hotdog, sold at Frankie's Place from 1939 to 1960. He is credited with being the first to serve a foot-long hotdog, even though he never patented his creation. The stand also had curb service, and according to his daughter Janice, the thing that made the hotdogs taste so good was that he always steamed his buns.

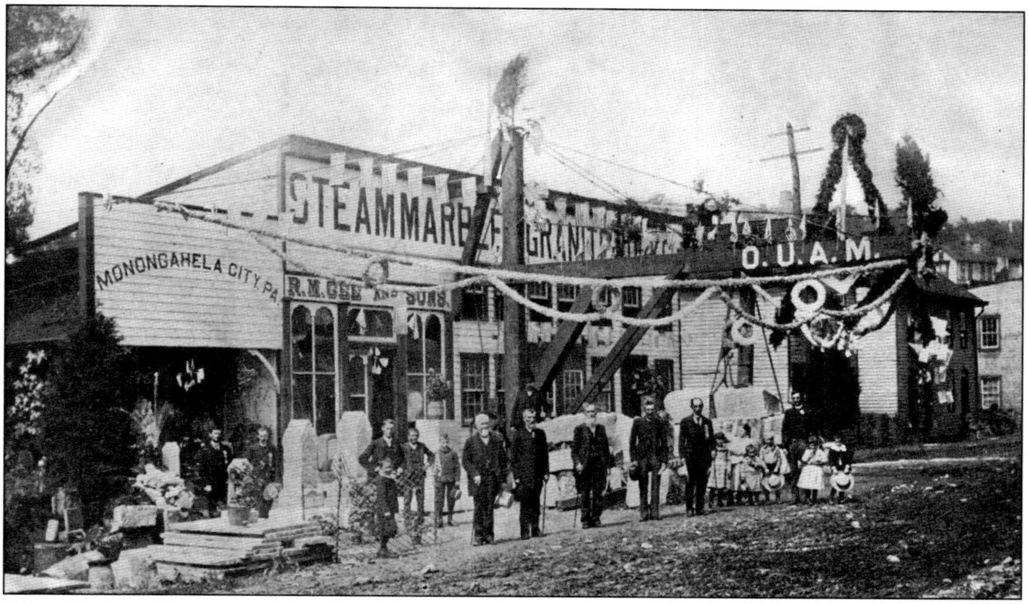

The old Gee Granite and Marble Works was built by R.M. Gee in 1852. It stood on East Main Street near the railroad crossing. This picture was taken on July 4, 1889. In front of the shop was a stand set up by the Order of United American Mechanics (OUAM), whose agenda was aimed at subverting immigrant prosperity in America.

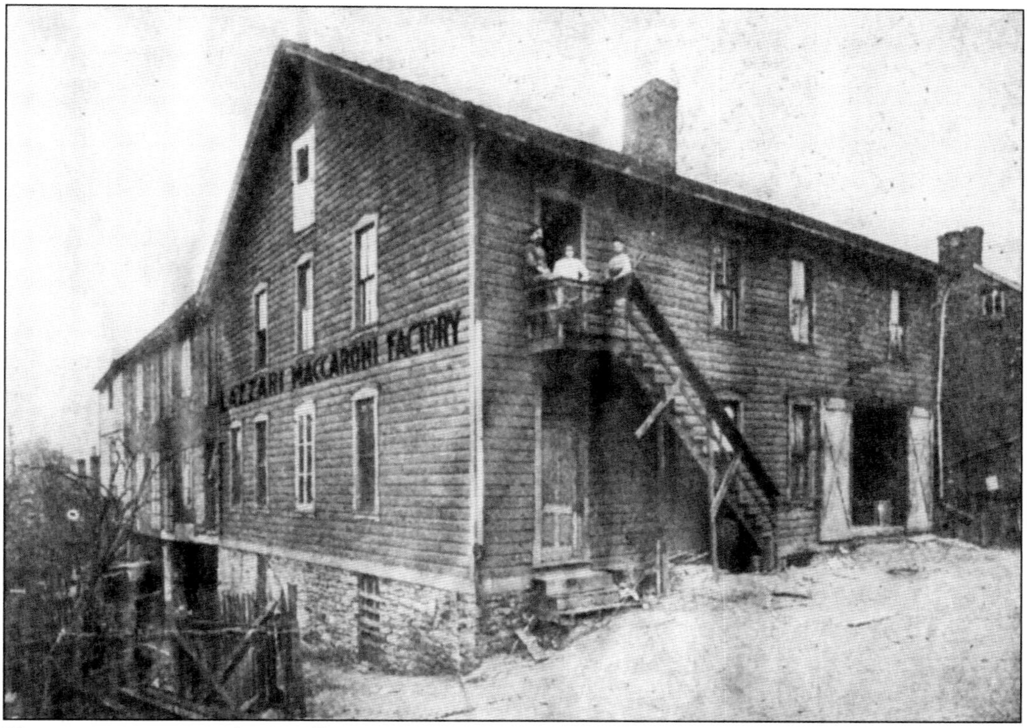

How many towns can boast of having a macaroni factory as early as 1903? The photograph depicts the exterior of the Monongahela Macaroni Works, which was on Marne Avenue between Fourth and Fifth Streets. It was originally built as a carriage factory in the 1880s. As printed on the side, it was owned by the Lazzari family.

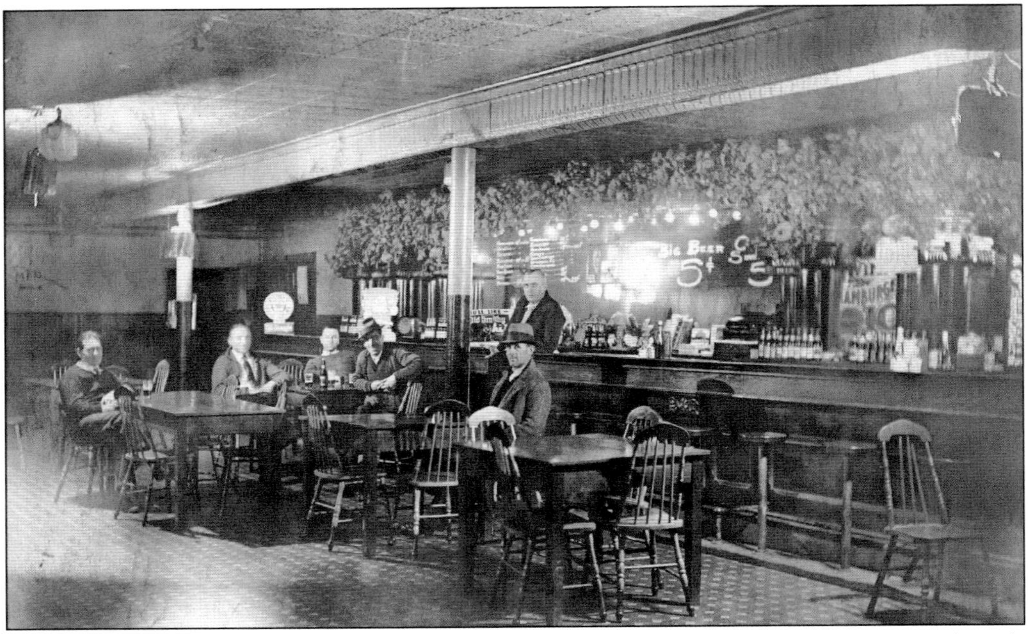

The Hotel Main barroom is shown in 1933. The hotel was known for its comforts and good meals and welcomed visitors throughout the years. An advertisement in the 1908 Homecoming Week book boasted that, in addition to its large dining room, it was the largest rathskeller (basement tavern) in the valley. Shown in the photograph are, from left to right, F. Dievart, A. Ferrello, F. Barber, F. Caruso, and J. Barnett (manager).

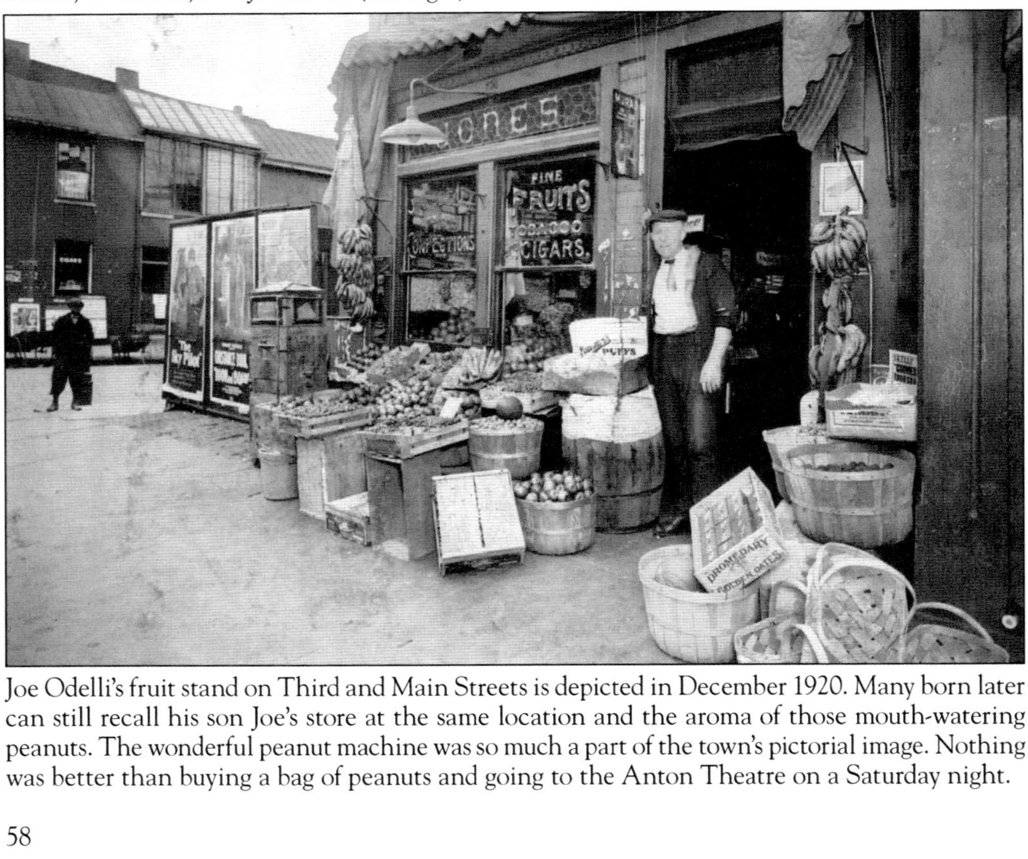

Joe Odelli's fruit stand on Third and Main Streets is depicted in December 1920. Many born later can still recall his son Joe's store at the same location and the aroma of those mouth-watering peanuts. The wonderful peanut machine was so much a part of the town's pictorial image. Nothing was better than buying a bag of peanuts and going to the Anton Theatre on a Saturday night.

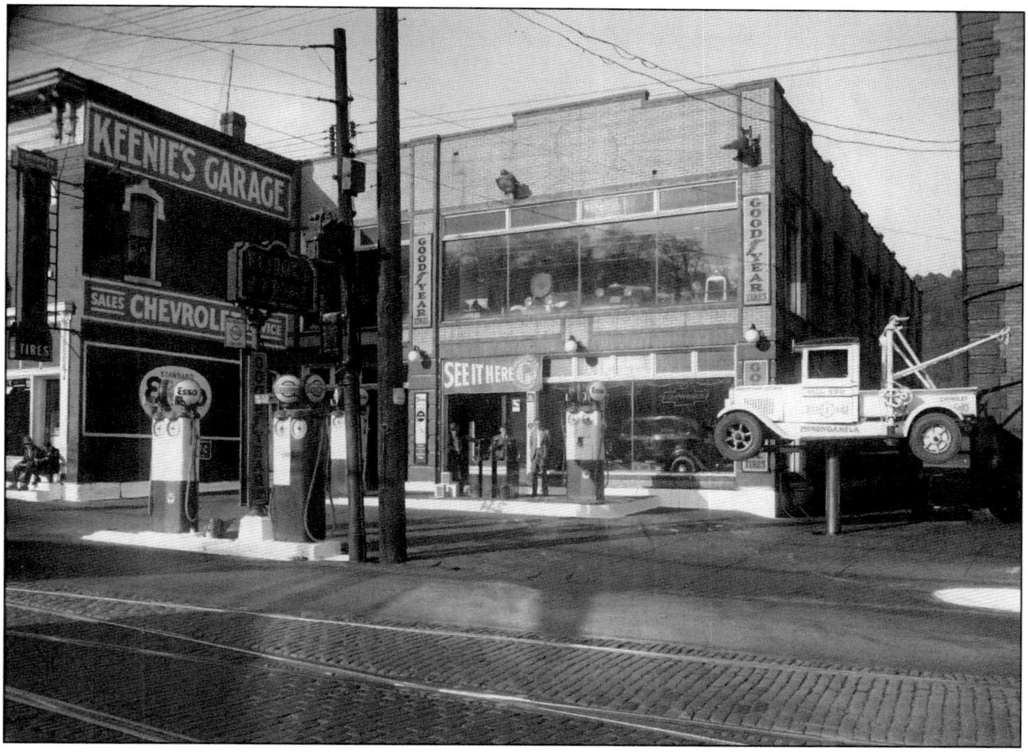

A familiar sight throughout the years had been the garage and car showroom found on Main Street across from Park Avenue. In 1928, it was known as Keenie's Garage. Shown are Alfred Turri (left) and A.K. "Keenie" Turri (right), who were brothers. Ray Pickering, an employee, is also pictured. Later, when the business changed hands, it was also known as Vickers Chevrolet and then Vaughn Chevrolet. (Courtesy scrapbook of Potente Zanardelli.)

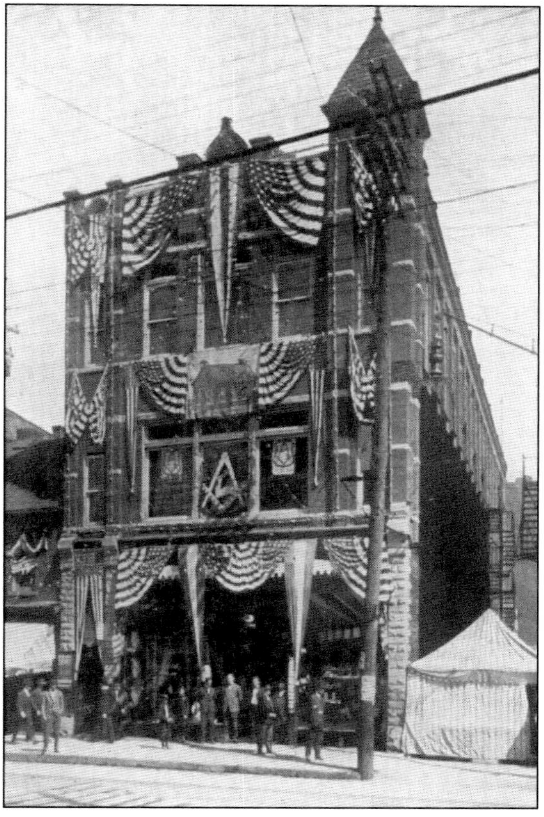

Landefeld's, known as the "Big Store," was established in 1878 by Henry Landefeld and grew until it stood at the head of the list as the largest exclusive clothing and furnishing store in the Monongahela Valley. It carried men's clothing, children's clothing, furnished goods, and trunks and offered merchant tailoring. The store was located at 235–237 Main Street.

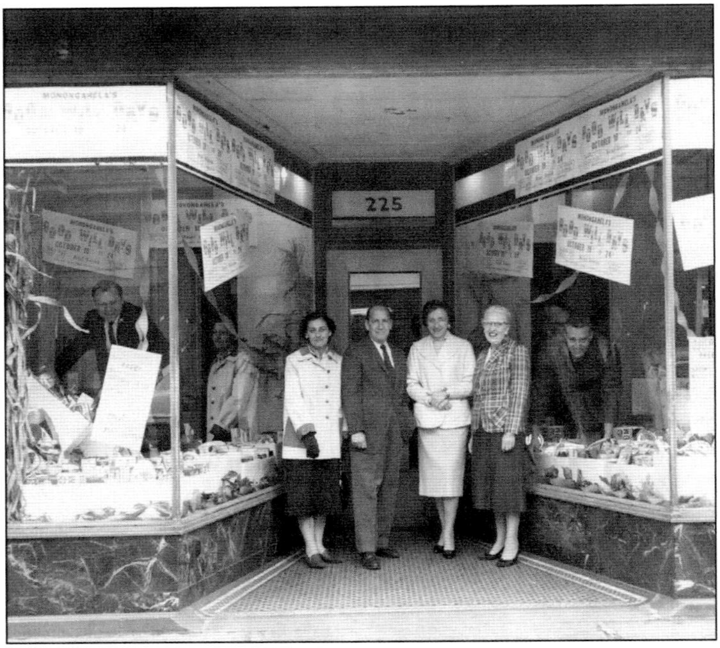

The Monongahela merchants in town have always come up with inventive ways to promote the great city. This photograph was taken on October 16, 1959, during Monongahela Goodwill Days, celebrated each year. The Goodwill Days celebration was sponsored by the chamber of commerce. Pictured are, from left to right, Patsy Pileggi (in the window on the left), Mrs. William Hill, Alfred Turri, Helen Yohe, Estelle Osterhaut, and Bill Granato (in the window on the right).

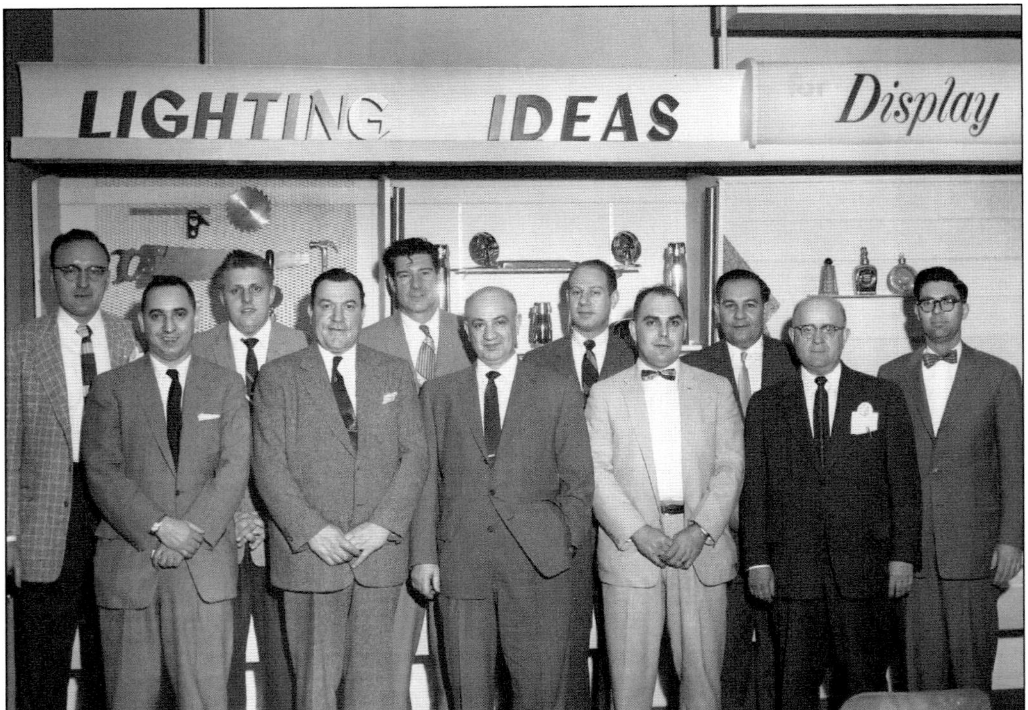

Pictured here are Monongahela-area chamber of commerce members in the 1950s. They are, from left to right, (first row) Bernard Marcus (of Dierken's), William B. Hill (mayor), Sam Fireman (of William's Store), Ed Matheny (representative, West Penn Power), and Paul Traversari (of Traversari's Photography); (second row) Dan Wible (of Wible's Appliances), Dick Kopsack (of Friend-Lee Bakery), Bill Urban (chief of police), Ted Krause (of Sun Wallpaper), John Bove (of Zimmer Printing), and Sam Hoffman (chamber director).

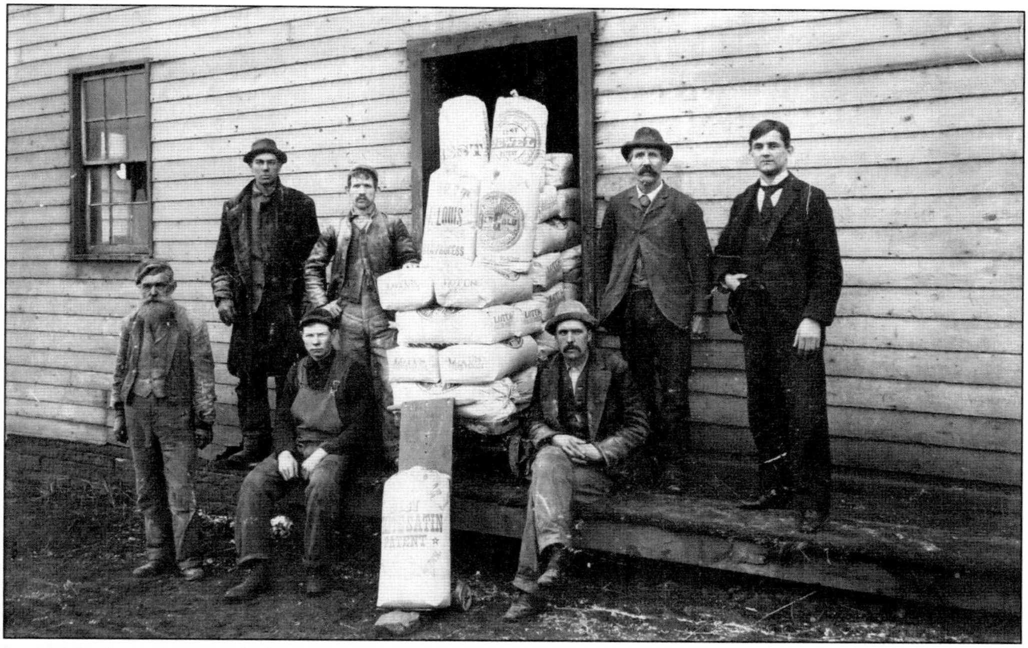

In 1895, the Monongahela Flourmill was a "flourishing" business in town. Hundreds of sacks of Lotus roller-process flour, with names such as People's Choice, Old Gold Fancy Flour, and Best Jewel, were sent out to different companies daily. The aroma of just-baked bread in many homes had its beginning at the flour mill.

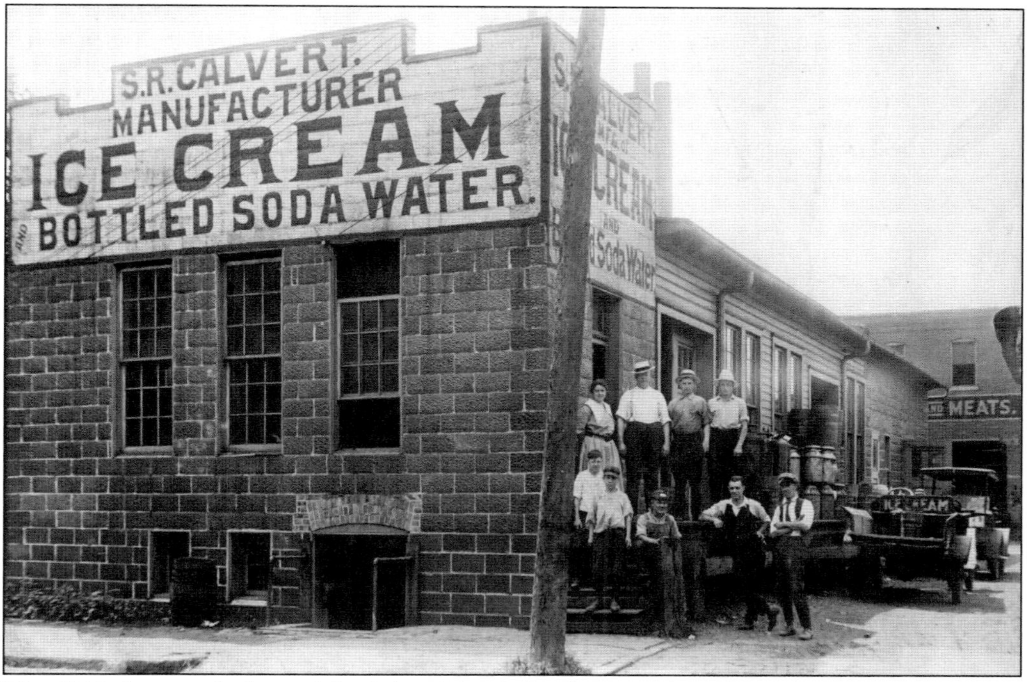

This 1916 photograph shows C.R. Calvert's bottled soda water plant, located on East Main Street. It remained a bottling plant, in later years becoming the Coca-Cola plant. In the background is Hank's Meat Market and Slaughterhouse. Pictured are, from left to right, (first row) Ray Casner, Bill Foster, and unidentified; (second row) Neil Calvert, S.R. Calvert, Jack Dodds, and unidentified.

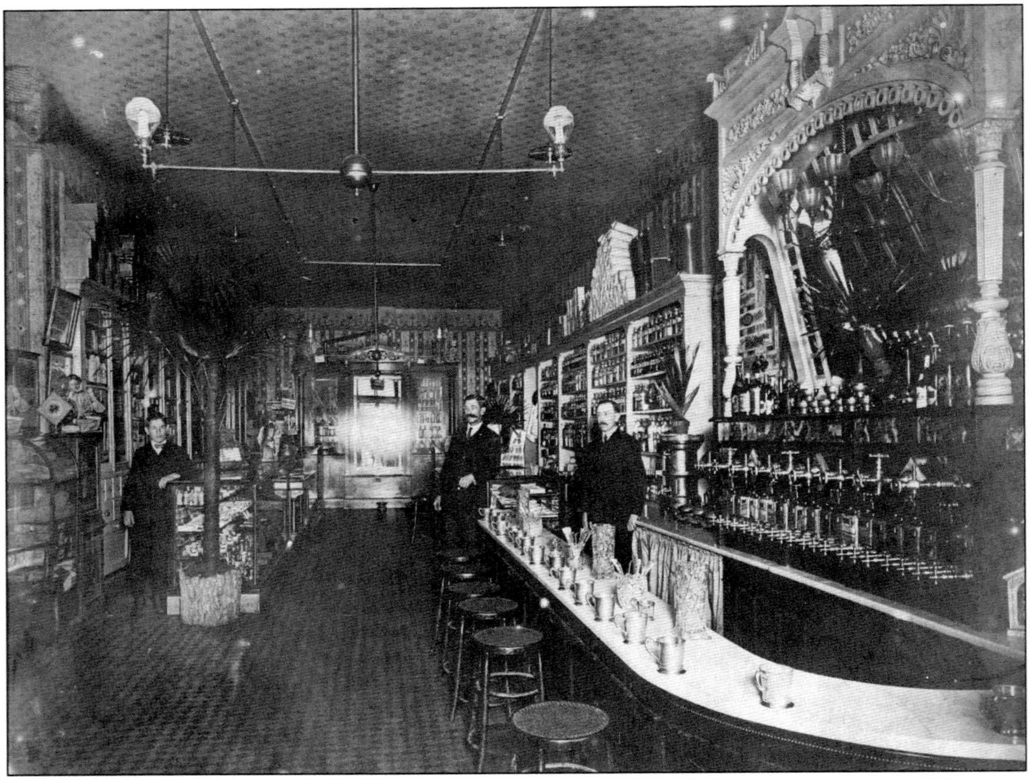

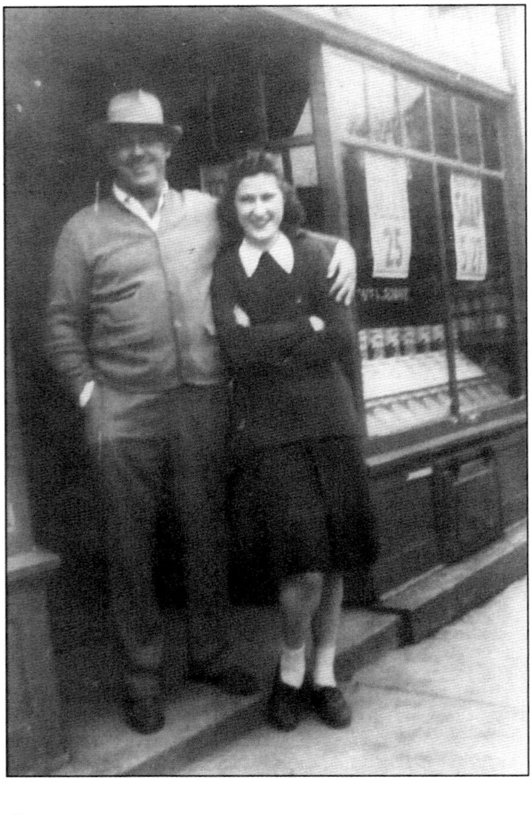

McCallister's Drugstore was owned by druggist W.C. McCallister, best friends with Edward G. Acheson, inventor of Carborundum. The two men gave the chemical its name. The drugstore was a favorite stop both to and from the electric plant. McCallister was a financial investor in Acheson's endeavor. His drugstore was open early and late, and McCallister saved leftover sandwiches from his lunch trade to share with Acheson when he joined him in the laboratory around midnight.

Bill Richert, popular owner of the Clover Farm grocery store, located on Park Avenue across from Cuff Alley, is shown with Liz Coulter Podrosky. Clover Farm was a favorite stop for students on their way home from school and provided some locals with their first job. Many neighbors remember the cowboy who would sit on the sidewalk and regale people with his guitar and songs. (Courtesy Gladys Frye Sholtis.)

Five

FOUNDATIONS

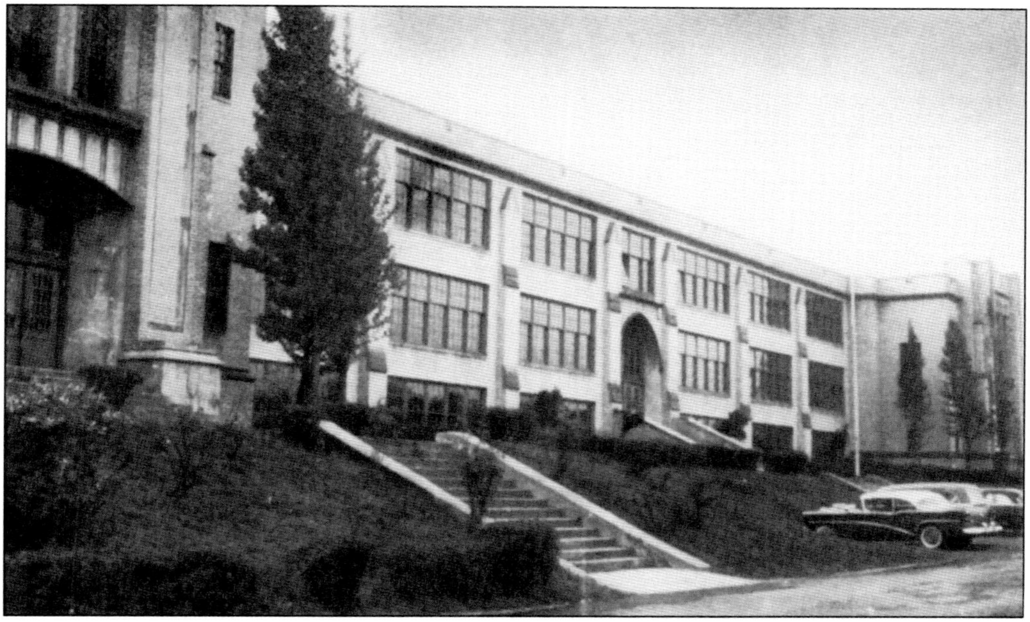

Monongahela High School was erected in 1924. "High above Mononga's waters, stands our dear old school, Hail to thee our Alma Mater, Hail, Oh Hail to thee, Red and White, Red and White, flying high above, colors that we love, Hail to Thee our Alma Mater, Hail oh hail to thee." This was one of a series of alma maters written for Monongahela High School. This one was sung through the 1950s.

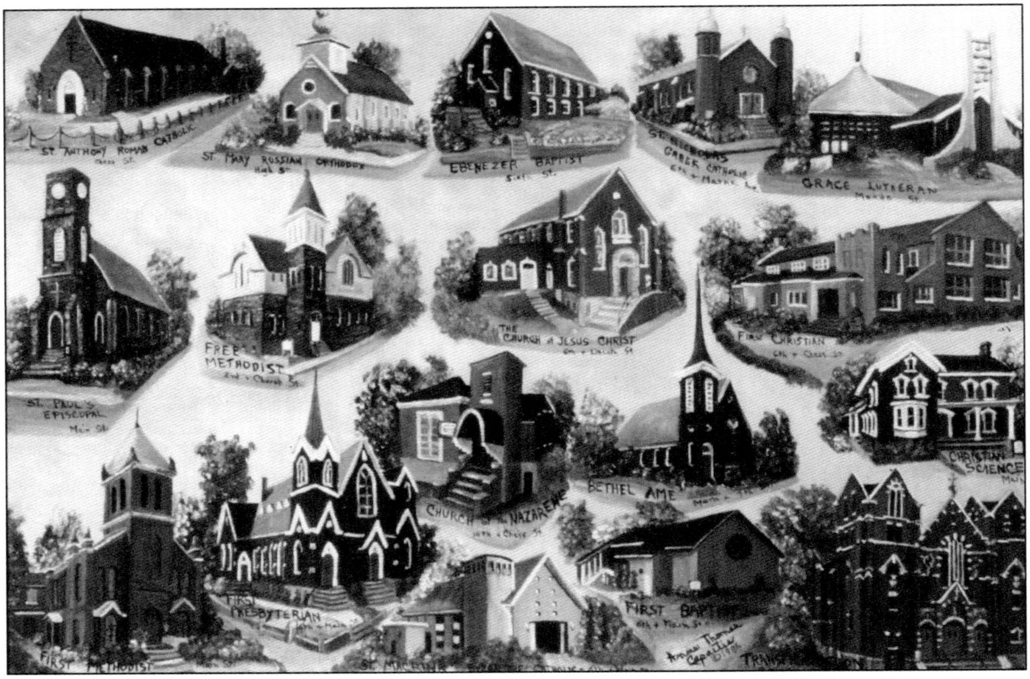

This painting was done by local Monongahela artist Anne Cepaitis in 1986. Monongahela is known as the "City of Churches," and this painting proves it. The churches shown are St. Anthony's, the Nativity of the Virgin Mary, Ebenezer Baptist, St. Nicholas Greek Catholic, Grace Lutheran, St. Paul's Episcopal, Free Methodist, the Church of Jesus Christ, First Christian Church, First United Methodist, First Presbyterian, Church of the Nazarene, Bethel AME, Christian Science, St. Macrina, First Baptist, and Transfiguration. (Courtesy Anne Thomas Cepaitis.)

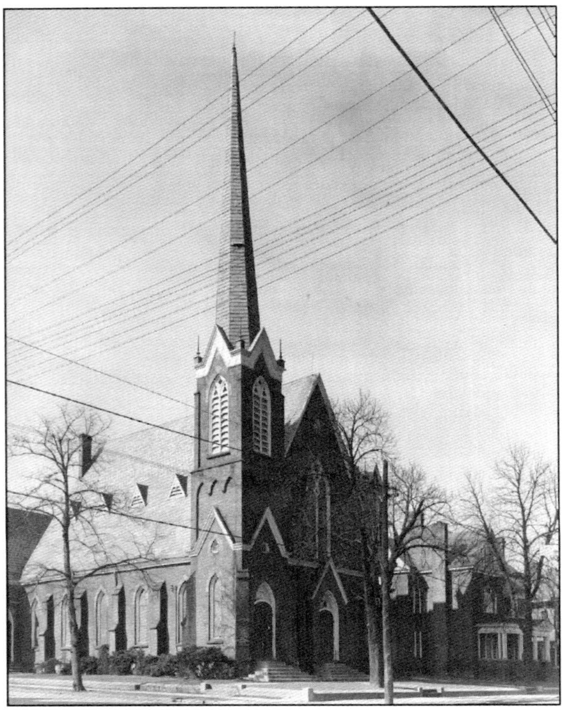

The lot for building a new church for the Presbyterians was purchased on October 28, 1869, for $440. In 1871, Foster, Blythe, and Company was awarded the contract for the design and construction of this elegant church. It was bordered by Main, Chess, and Sixth Streets and West Alley. John Blythe kept the off-center entry for a simple and sound reason: no man comes to God on a straight path.

The First Baptist Church was organized in the public school hall on February 9, 1860. On February 24, it met in the Presbyterian house of worship and was organized as a Baptist church. The first church edifice was dedicated in January 1871. The present-day church sits on Main and Sixth Streets.

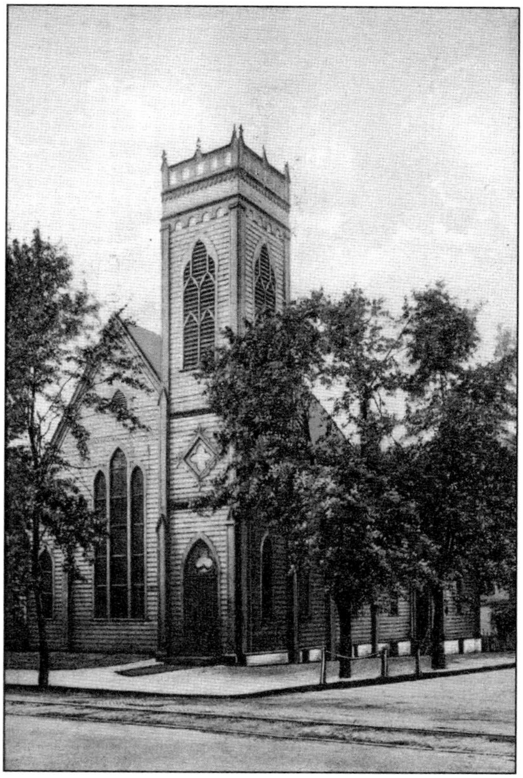

The Nativity of the Virgin Mary, an Orthodox church, was organized on September 30, 1914. The first service was celebrated in the McGregor Building on Main Street when immigrants from Russia, Czechoslovakia, and the Austro-Hungarian Empire wanted a church to worship in their own faith. The existing location is called "The Miracle on High Street." It is a jewel, with impressive murals, icons, gold leafing, liturgical vessels, and a stunning crystal chandelier. (Courtesy Rev. Deacon David Rostcheck.)

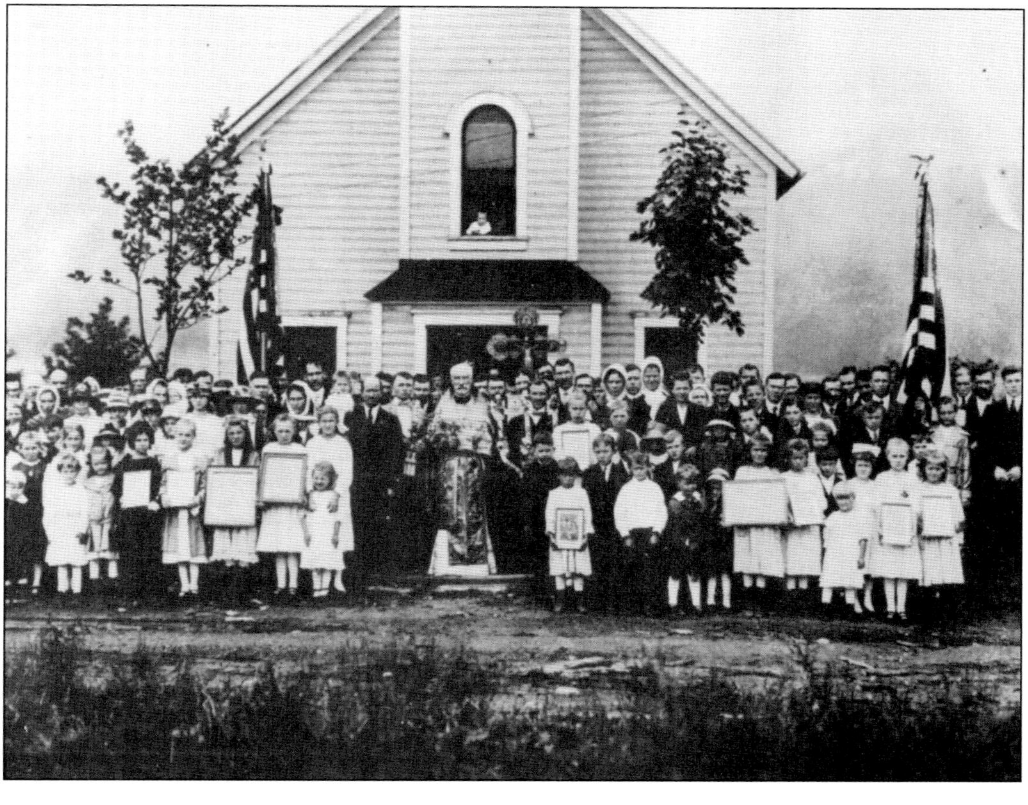

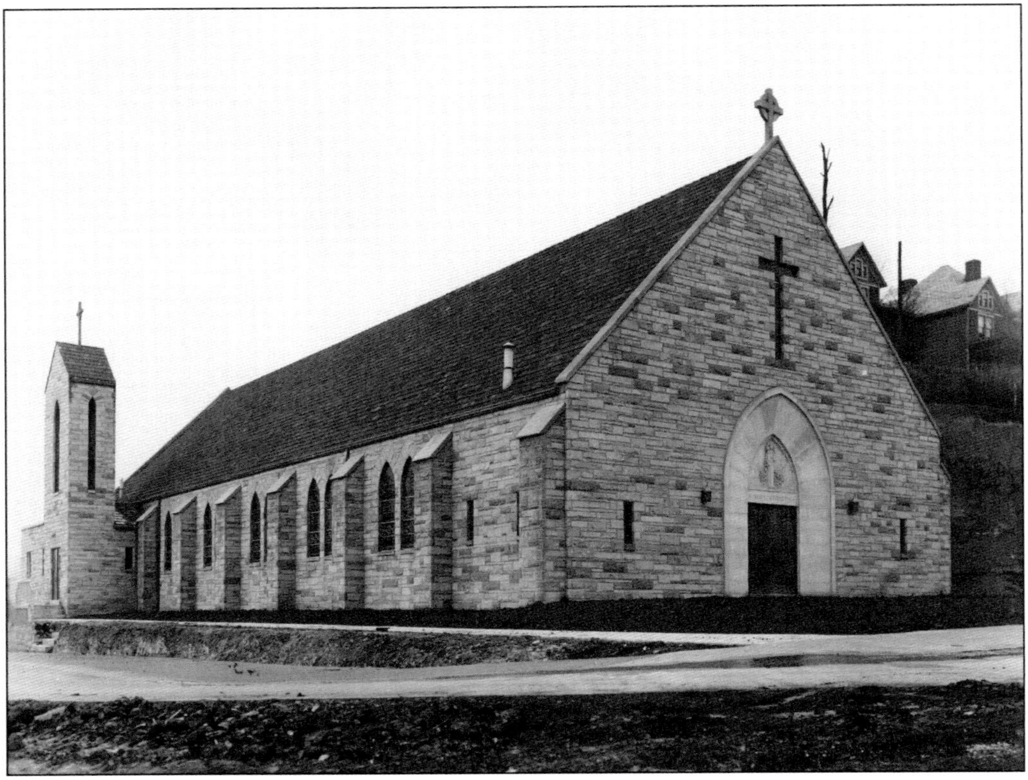

The original St. Anthony's Church on Park Avenue was dedicated on December 17, 1905. The present-day church, under the direction of Fr. Joseph L. Abbate, was dedicated on May 14, 1950, on the site that was Whiskey Point. The cornerstone for the new school adjacent to the church was blessed in July and dedicated in October 1957. Church history says the name Anthony was chosen in part to honor the Anton family for donating the land on Park Avenue where the original church was built.

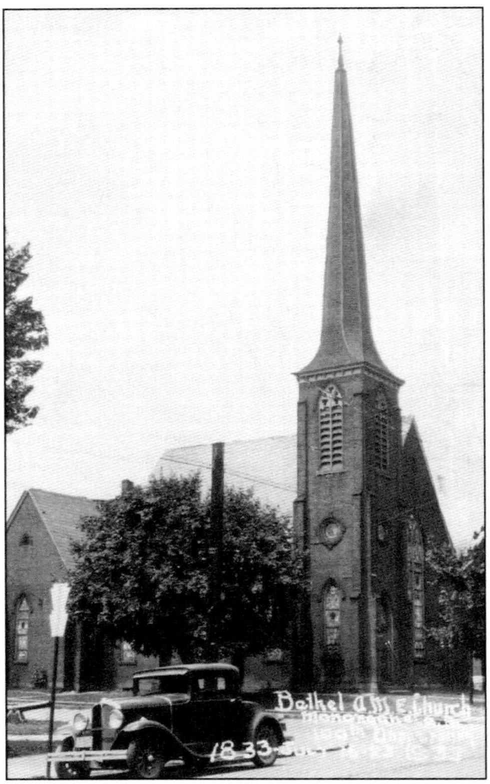

The Bethel African Methodist Episcopal Church of Monongahela City was built in 1871 and added to the National Register of Historic Places in 2002 with the assistance of Monongahela native Terry A. Necciai, RA. The church was designed by prominent Monongahela architect John Blythe. It is an outstanding example of Gothic Revival design. The original steeple was destroyed by lightning in 1987 but was accurately reconstructed afterward based on an 1876 atlas drawing. This congregation has served as an educational, religious, and social focal point for African Americans for generations.

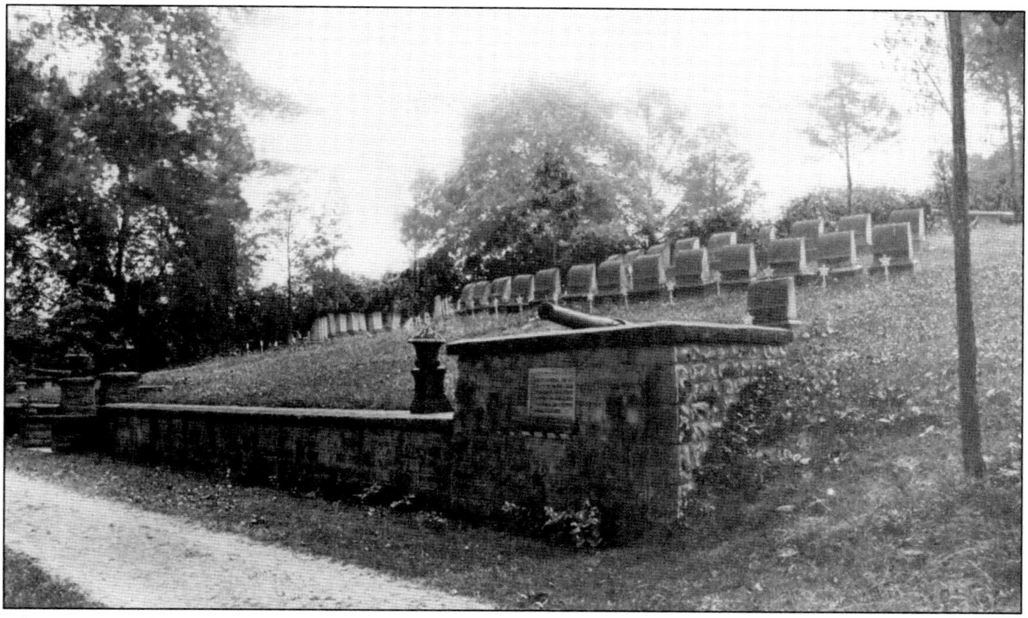

The picture shows the Civil War section of the Monongahela Cemetery. All able men of the Monongahela Valley were enlisted in the war effort. Sadly, many returned to their home ground in wooden coffins. The small city cemetery soon reached capacity. A parcel of land was purchased to provide a final resting place for the Civil War heroes.

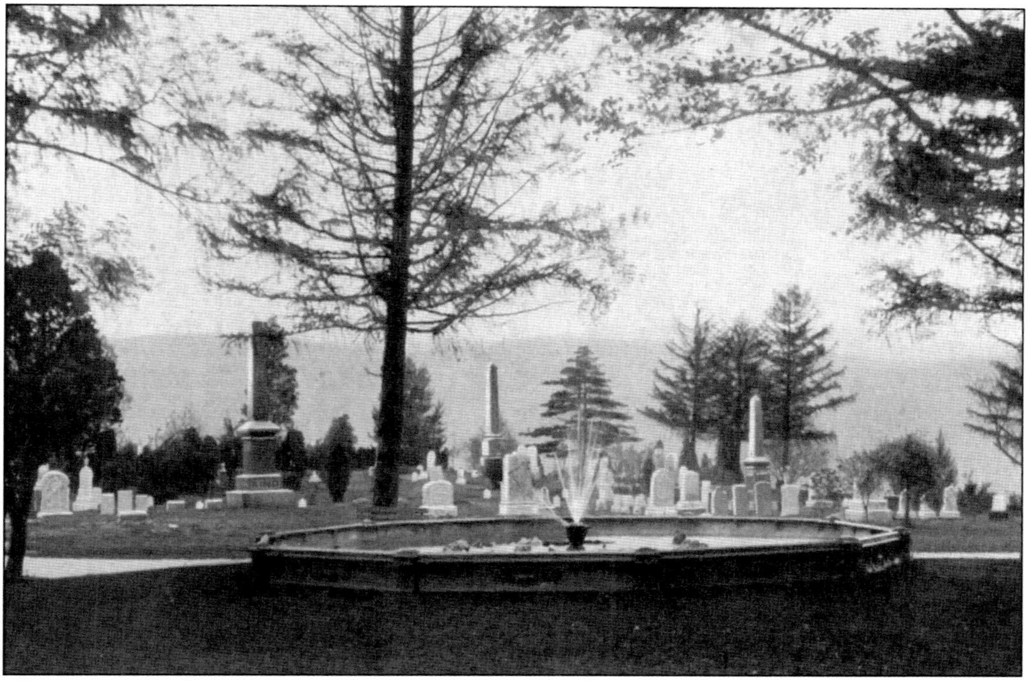

The Monongahela Cemetery fountain, complete with goldfish pond, was a favorite place to visit before it was removed to build the present office and parking area. Hare & Hare, 19th-century landscape architects of national repute, designed the cemetery grounds. Their work and effort laid the foundation for what is today one of the most picturesque and well-maintained cemeteries to be found.

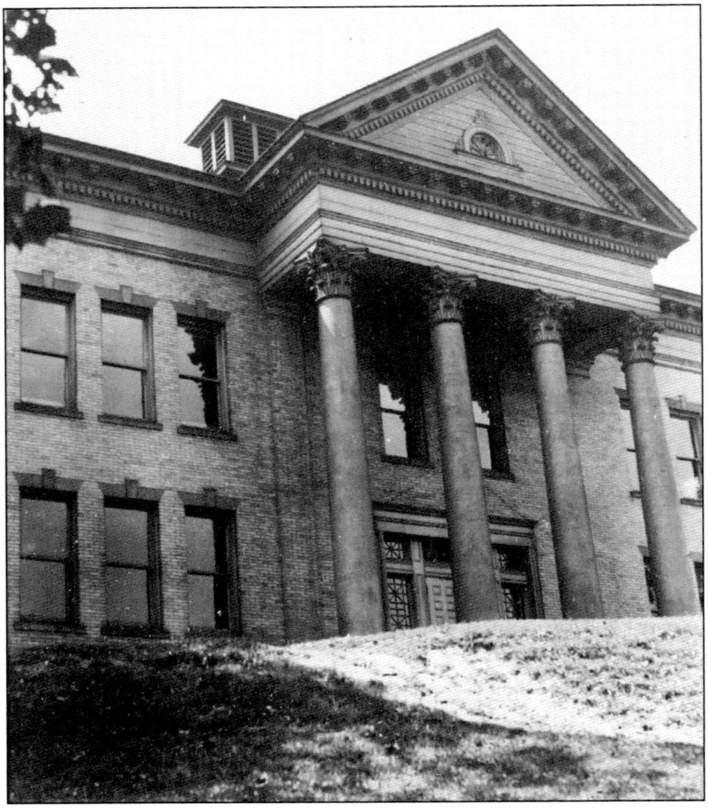

Williams School was the first of the city elementary schools built. It was built in the First Ward. Students remember this alma mater: "There's a school upon a hillside/ with its pillars stately tall/ and its sturdy keystone arches, holding firm the outer walls./ And the bell within the tower,/ calling children day by day/ to the school that's known as Williams,/ where they learn and work and play./ Hail to thee O Williams School,/ Praise to thee we sing,/ Hail to thee O Williams School,/ Let our voices ring."

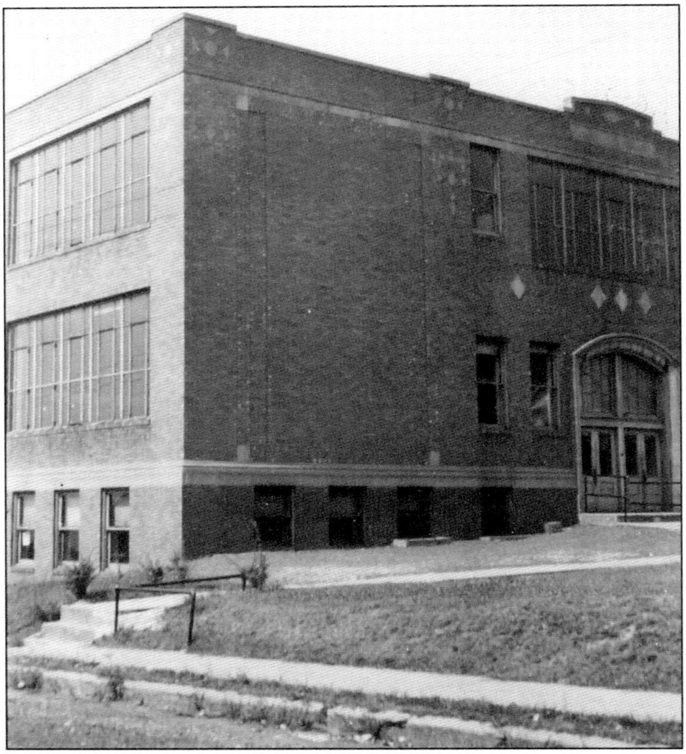

Waverly School is another elementary school remembered in song: "In the town- Monongahela,/ high above the winding river,/ where the Indians roamed and hunted,/ where the settlers built their homes,/ stands a noble place of learning,/ stands the school we love so well,/ and to it our thoughts are turning,/ as we sing our song of praise./ Hail to thee, dear Waverly./ Hear our song, our song of praise./ Hail to thee, dear Waverly,/ May you live, always."

Lincoln School was the second elementary school built. Its proud school song is, "In a green and pleasant valley,/ where Monongahela flows,/ there stands a school that's named for honest Abe./ It's a place we'll all remember,/ where we spent our early years,/ a firm foundation for our future laid./ Lincoln School, O Lincoln School,/ the pride of all who work together here,/ Lincoln School, O Lincoln School,/ No other school can e'er with you compare."

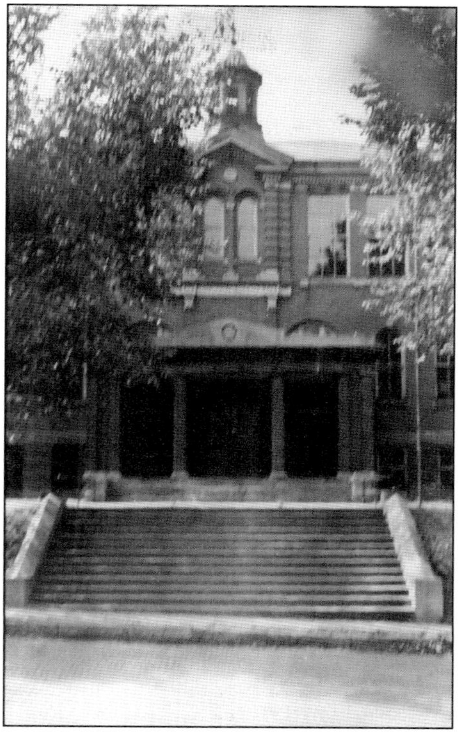

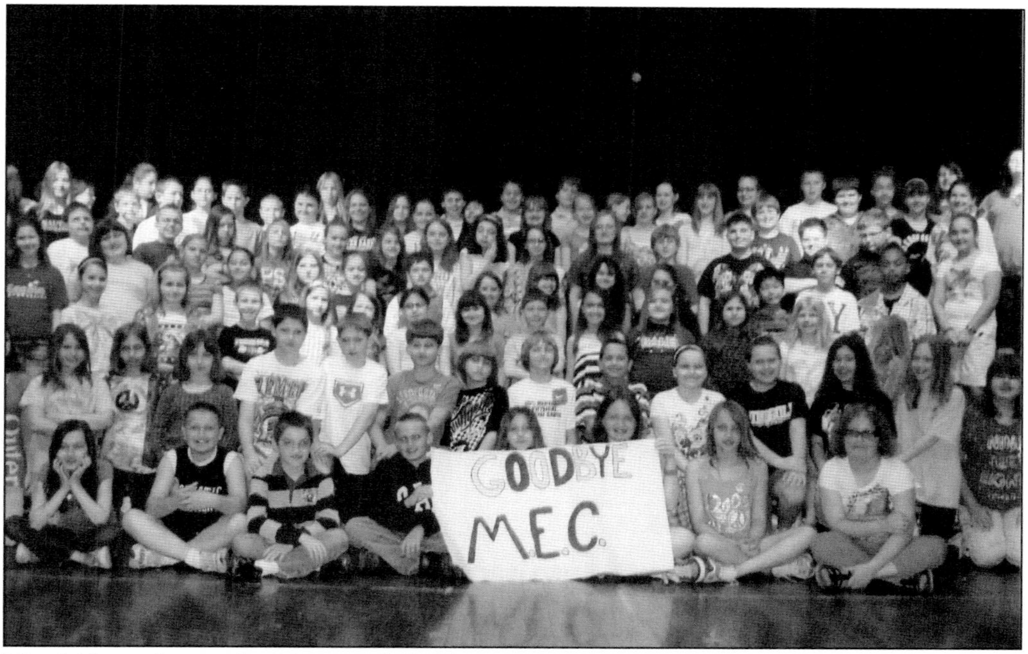

The fifth graders at the Monongahela Elementary Center (MEC) are shown holding a sign saying "Goodbye MEC" as they presented the final performance in the auditorium to close the school year in 2011. As a farewell to the building, the students presented a superb production that celebrated the various musical and historical eras experienced by students in the building. MEC opened in 1979 when a grade school building was established in the former Monongahela High School. (Courtesy Shannan Winkleblech.)

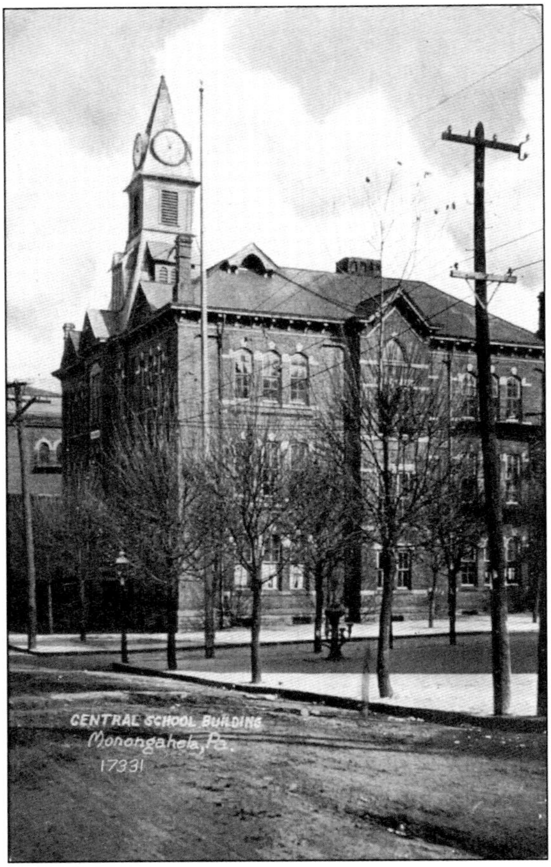

Central School was constructed in 1881; it burned and was rebuilt in 1883. The wooden structure was three stories tall, housing seventh- and eighth-grade classes. The clock atop the building was a town landmark and served as a guide for river boats. The bell that was placed in the school had been cast in 1865, even before the school was built. The bell was saved when the building was razed in 1961. After that, the bell was moved to Chess Park. In 2010, the bell was moved to the plaza in front of First Niagara Bank at the corner of Fourth and Main Streets, the original location of the school.

Pictured here are the members of Sadie Freeby's Sunday school class in the Methodist Episcopal church for the 1867–1868 year. Members are, from left to right, (first row) Mary Downer, Sarah Wormsford, Mary Gibbs, Amanda Filson, and Sadie Freeby (teacher); (second row) Emma Clark, Miss Cott, unidentified, Becky Hayley, and unidentified.

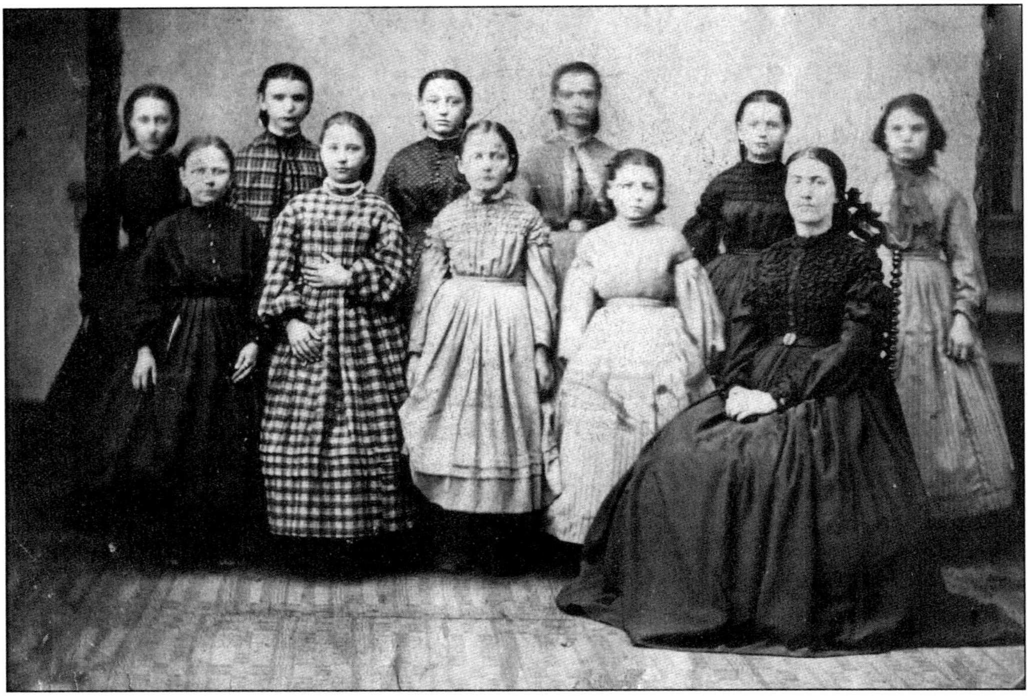

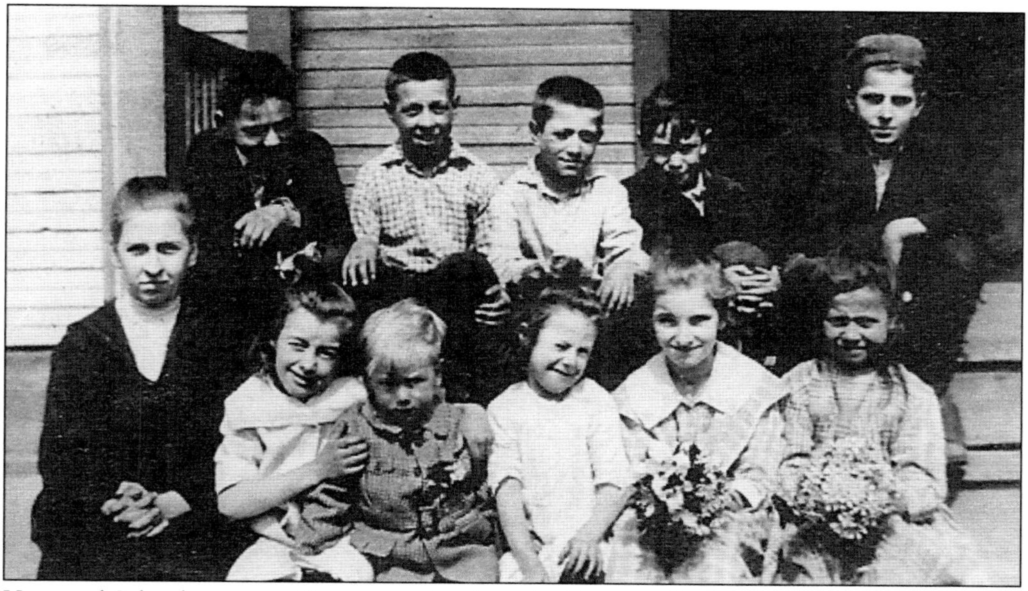

Haywood School was a small country school on the Haywood family farm property, located on Crackerjack Road on the outskirts of the city. Pictured here are, from left to right, (first row) Gladys Yohe (teacher), Elsie Williams, Grace Eugene, Catherine Haywood, Annie Liptak, and Annie Robb; (second row) Joseph Green, Patsy and Joseph Robb, Benjamin Haywood, and David Liptak.

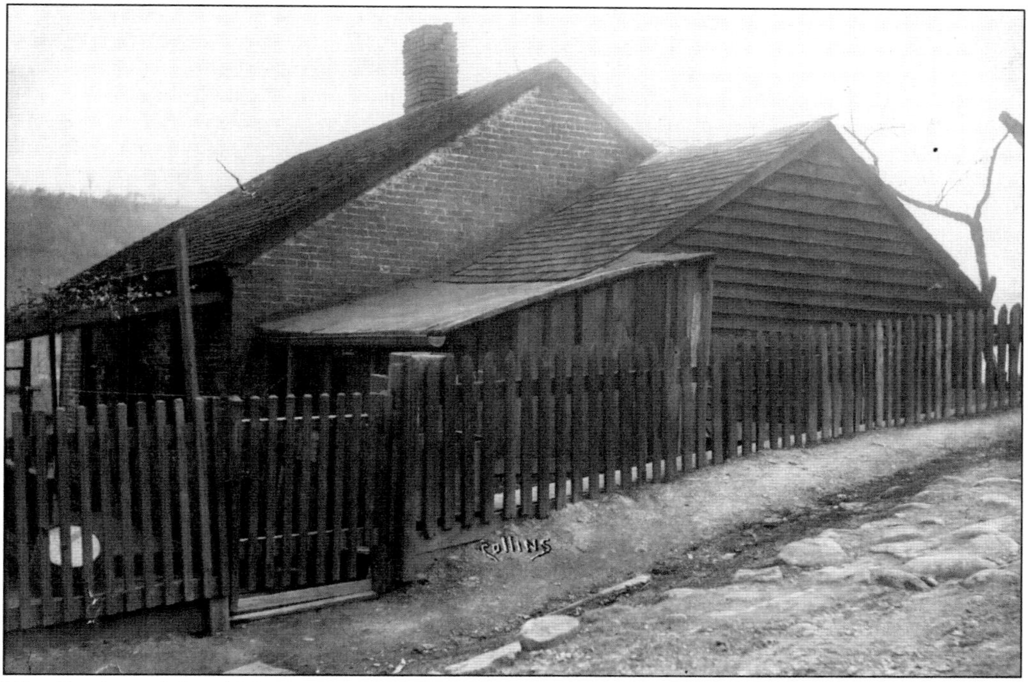

The Catsburg School House stood on Cemetery Street in Catsburg (Black Diamond). The brick portion in the picture was where the Catsburg boys and girls received their education. The boys usually attended only through the fifth reader. It was a well-known fact that the directors would not employ a teacher unless he could handle a rod, and the teachers generally used a rod—not that the boys needed it, just as a force of habit, of course.

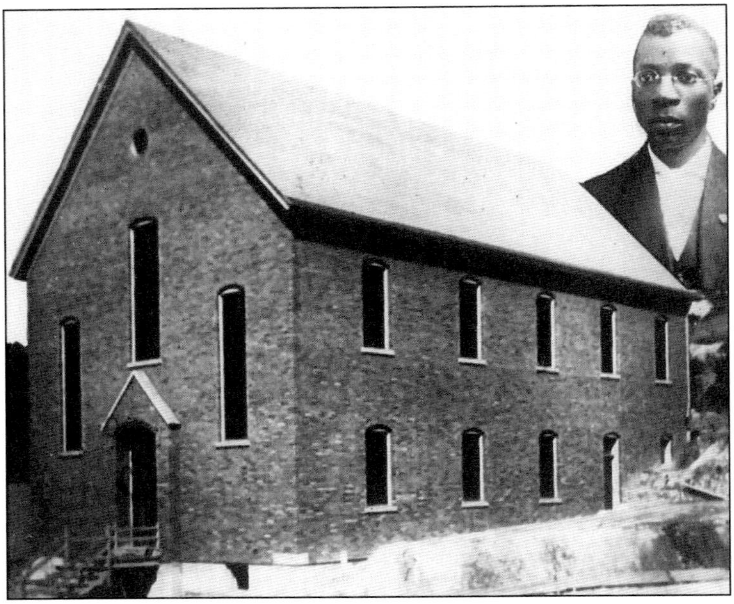

The Ebenezer Baptist Church was built in 1911 and is located on Sixth Street. While Bethel AME members date back to pre–Civil War days, the congregation of Ebenezer Baptist Church was made up more of new families who came to the area later to work in the coalmines and other industries. This African American church is still active today. This picture shows Pastor Sylvester Ernest Callaway. (Courtesy James D. Lee.)

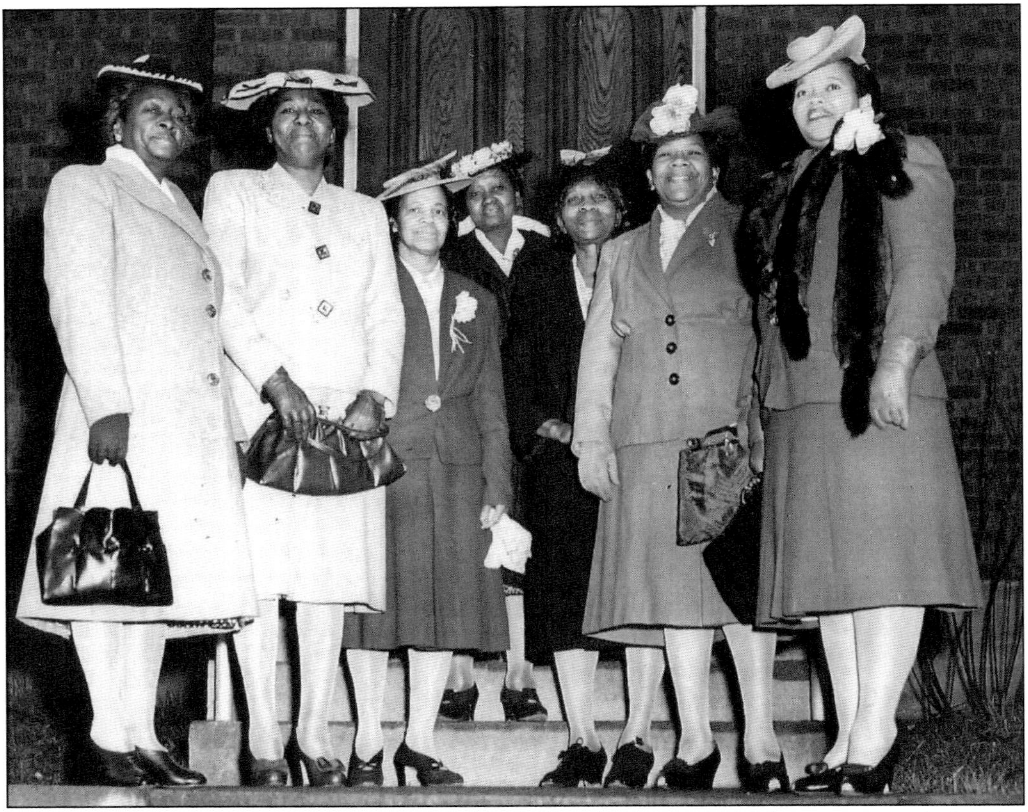

The women of the Ebenezer Baptist Church redefine the meaning of dressing in one's Sunday best. Much care was taken in designing each outfit: well-heeled shoes and matching handbags, suits or coats, festive hats, gloves, hose, handkerchiefs, some corsages, fur pieces, and big beautiful smiles. Because of evidence of a flash, it appears these women were either attending an evening service or stayed all day after a daytime function. (Courtesy James D. Lee.)

The Methodist Episcopal church began in 1864, and the stately church still stands today on Main Street. The Sunday school room was opened for worship in 1867, and the audience room was completed in 1873. The entire church cost $45,000. The elegant manse that graces Chess Street was added during the pastorate of Rev. John Conner, who served from 1892 to 1897. In 1903, a new pipe organ was installed, the gift of Andrew Carnegie.

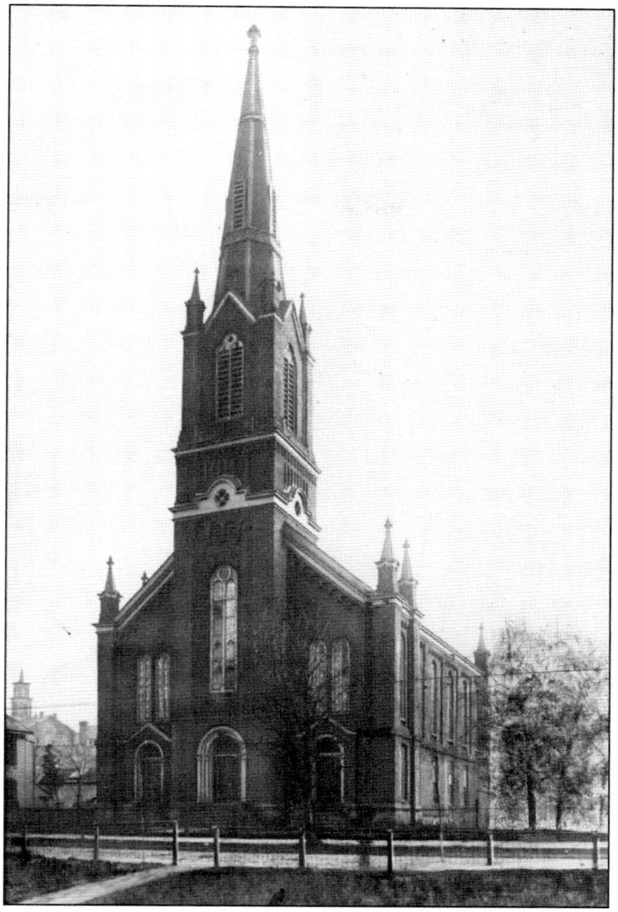

What a proud day it was for the Methodist Episcopal church when the congregation dedicated its new set of 11 bells in November 1925. Each bell weighs between 525 and 3,000 pounds, is made of 80 percent copper and 20 percent tin, and was manufactured by the McShane Bell Foundry of Glen Burnie, Maryland. No other southwestern Pennsylvania church has such a set of bells still in operation in 2011. They were donated by lumber mill owner Charles E. Stephens at a cost of $10,000.

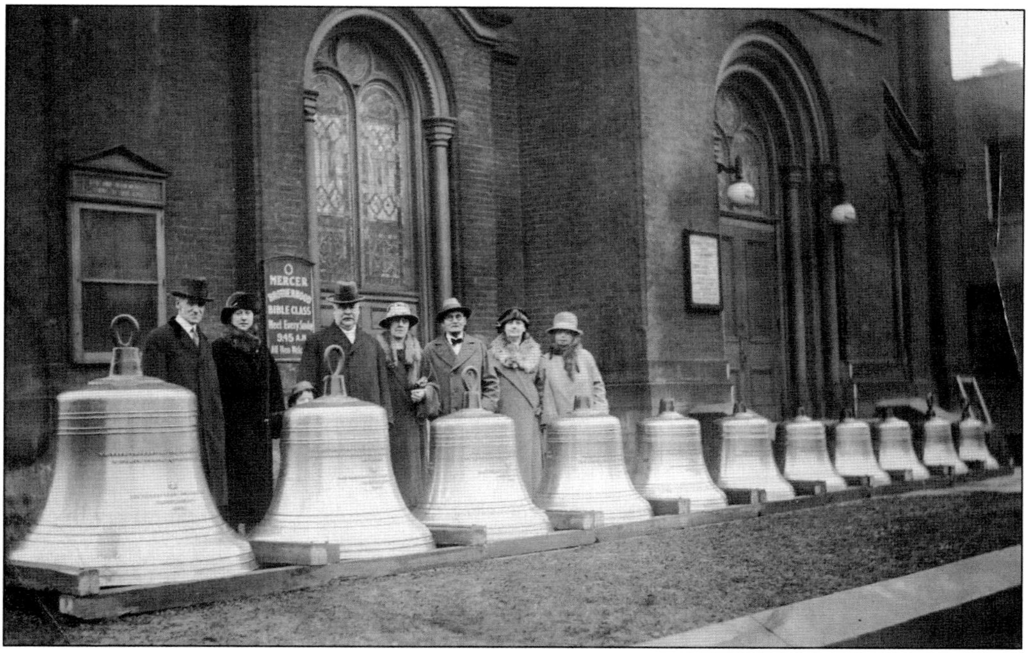

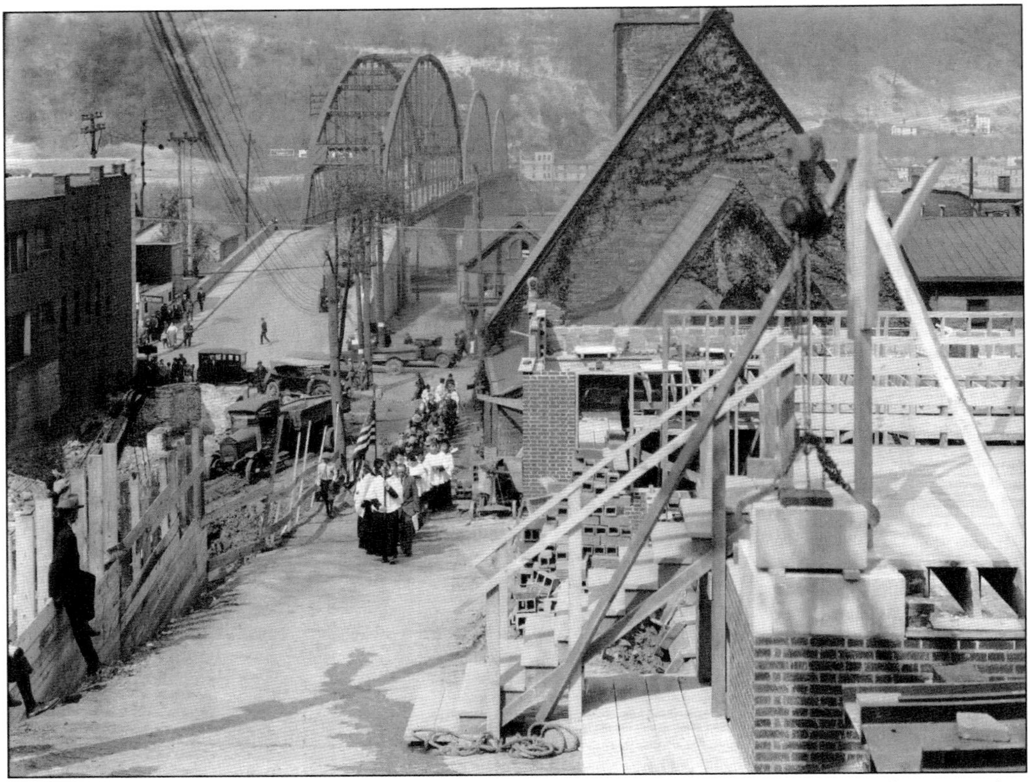

St. Paul's Episcopal Church dates back to the 1800s and is one of the oldest in the city. This photograph shows the processional at the Parish House ceremony. The cornerstone was being laid in 1925. The church is Gothic in design and built of native grey stone 18 inches thick. Inside the entrance of the church stands the font, believed to be the first font west of the Alleghenies.

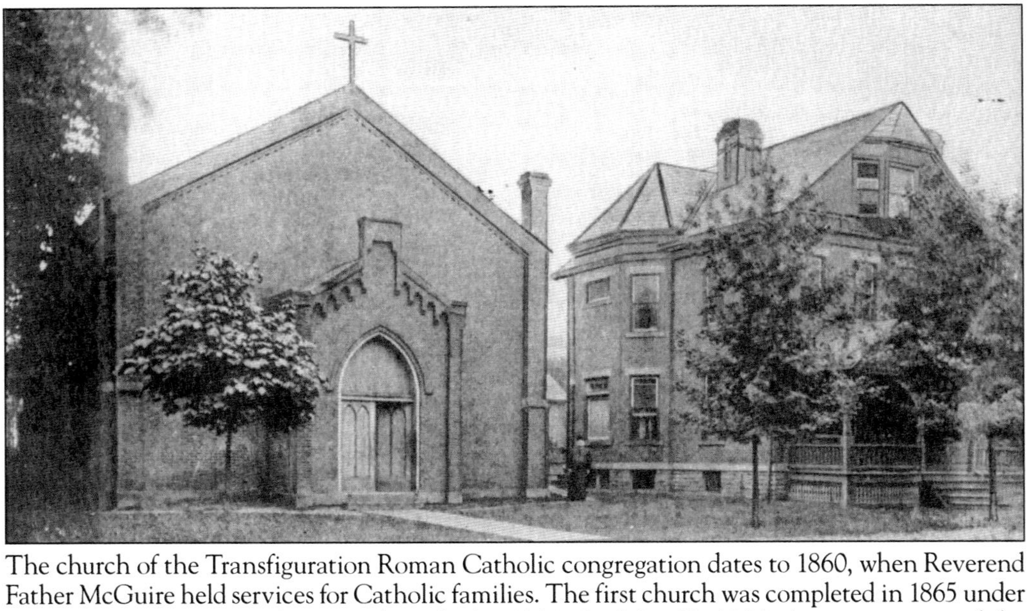

The church of the Transfiguration Roman Catholic congregation dates to 1860, when Reverend Father McGuire held services for Catholic families. The first church was completed in 1865 under Rev. Dennis Kearney and was used until May 1904. On May 30, 1906, the cornerstone of the present church was laid. It was completed at a cost of $75,000.

Six

Gatherings

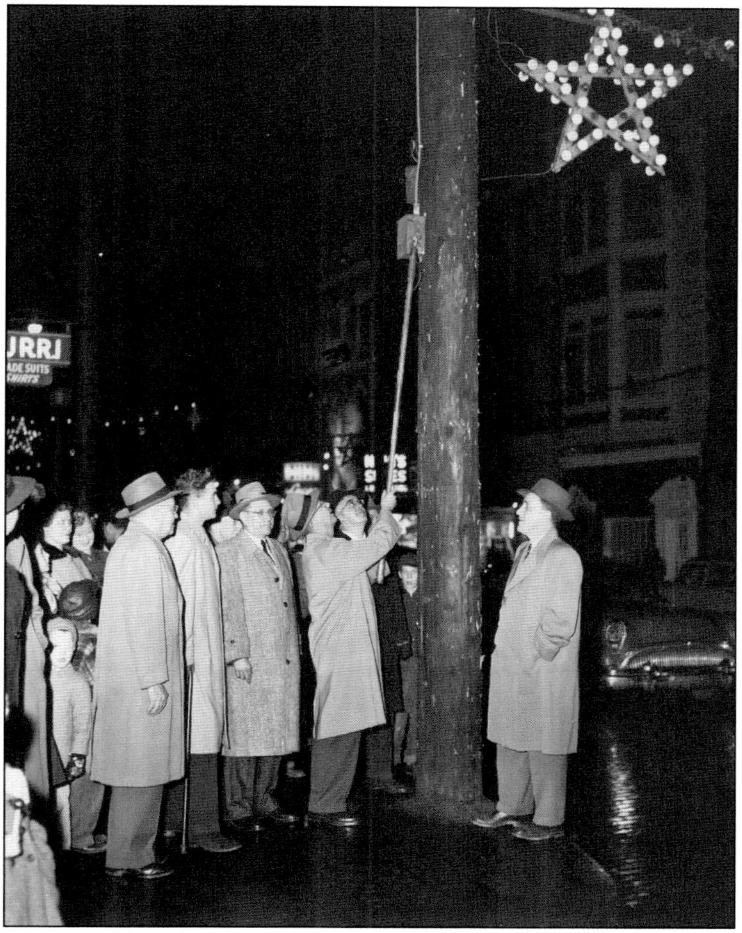

One of the most exciting events downtown during the Christmas season was the lighting of the Christmas stars that started at First Street and continued throughout the town. The town was illuminated on Thanksgiving night each year and continued through New Year's Eve. The red and green stars were made by Vincenzo Malena in his blacksmith shop on Railroad Street, and one is on display at the Monongahela Area Historical Society's museum.

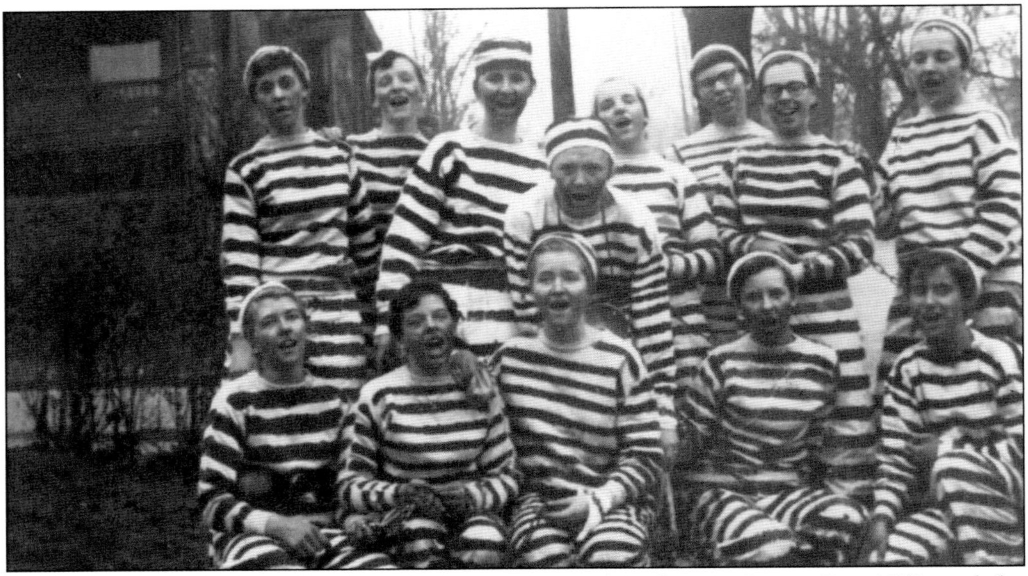

The Chain Gang (the Ravens) is a group 13 lifelong friends. It is Senior Day 1950, and the custom was to dress in costumes. The girls were chained together as they all followed one girl's schedule. From left to right are (first row) Irene Warne, Georgie Peters, Joan Daniels, Mona Rae Williams, and Betsy Oehrle; (second row) Shirley Balliard, Barbara Underwood, Grace Houston, Donna Weber, Marilyn Mitchell, Peggy Rutz, JoAnne Benford, and Sally Seaman. (Courtesy Mona Rae Williams.)

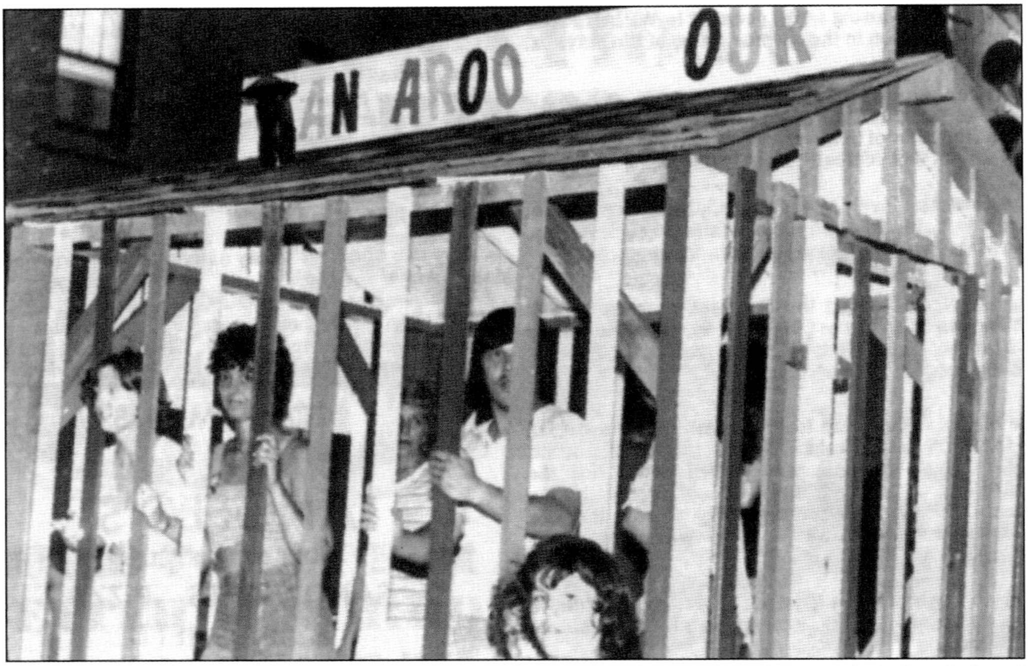

Monongahela celebrated its bicentennial from June 27 to July 4, 1969. Monongahela bustled and thousands attended, many wearing pioneer attire. Men were required to purchase and carry a permit if they chose to be clean-shaven, and women did the same if they chose not to wear pioneer attire. Offenders were sent to Kangaroo Court. Sample punishments ranged from being required to handle a garter snake to playing a song on a musical instrument or be doused with water.

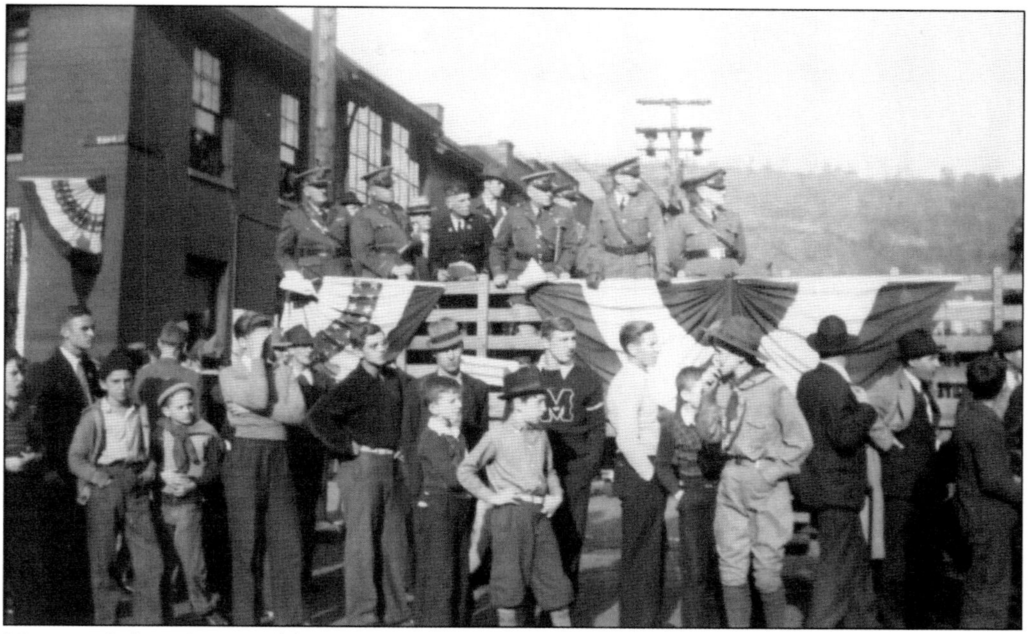

Monongahela is shown celebrating Armistice Day with one of its many parades. The picture was taken in front of the judges' stand erected at Main and Third Streets. Armistice Day, also known as Remembrance Day, is on November 11 and commemorates the armistice signed between the Allies of World War I and Germany, at Compiegne, France, for the cessation of hostilities on the Western Front.

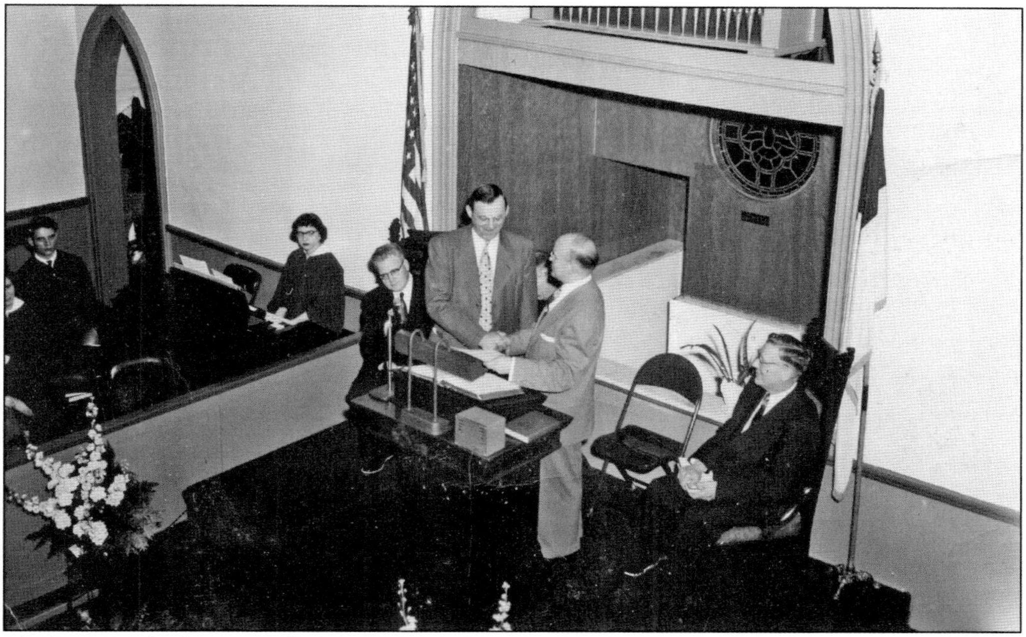

The Reverend Glenn Hazel of the First Baptist Church at Sixth and Main Streets is presenting a certificate of appreciation to Lawrence V. Frye during a Sunday service. Frye, owner of Lawrence V. Frye Lumber at Sixth and Railroad Streets, and his nephews Harold and Wilbur Frye donated services to build six windows for the church addition in the 1950s. Onlookers as the presentation is made are two members of the congregation and the church organist.

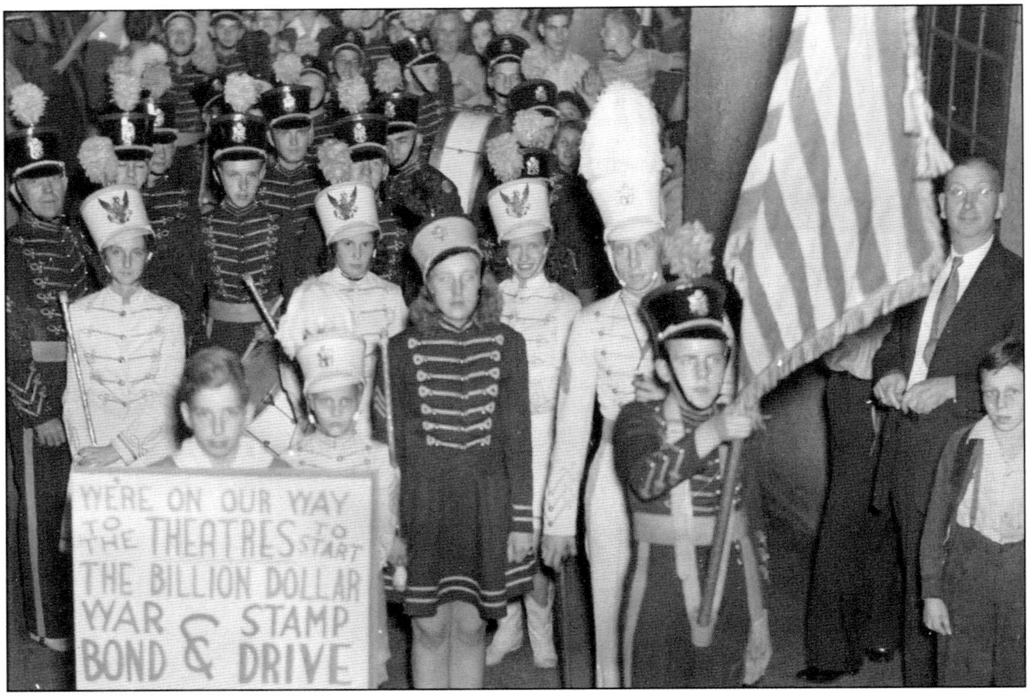

The gathering took place at the opening of the Monthly Billion Dollar War Bond and Stamp Drive, held at the Bentley Theatre on Main Street. The high school band was playing and leading the way, carrying the American flag. War bonds were debt securities issued by a government for the purpose of financing military operations during times of war.

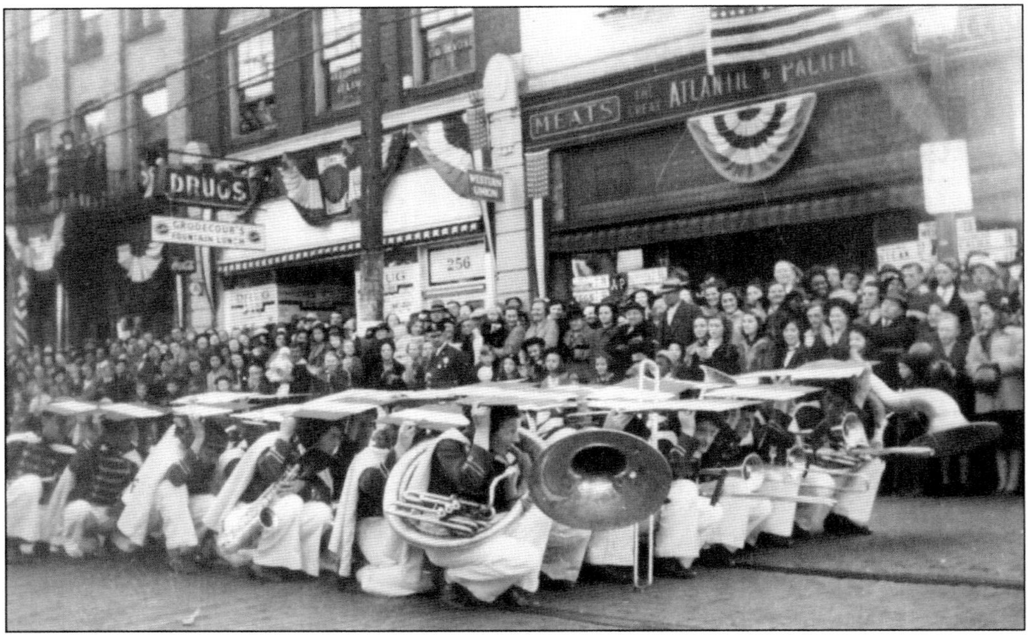

The Monongahela High School Band was at the top of its game as it performed for the judges during one of the city's many parades. The band members are kneeling, and in a synchronized motion, they are holding over their heads what becomes a single American flag. The onlookers in the crowd are surely impressed, as the judges must have been, as the band displayed its American pride.

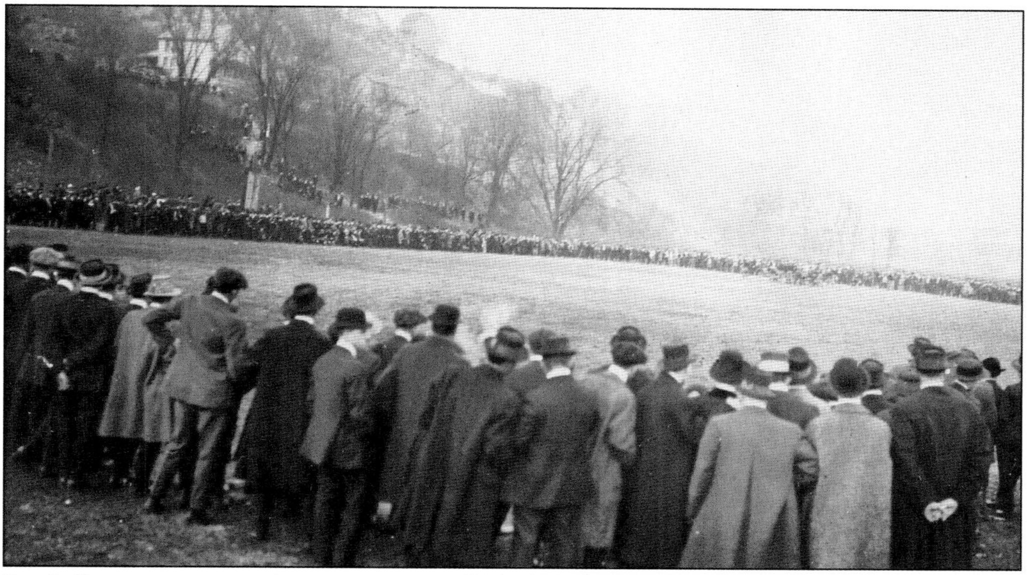

Football was an emerging American sport in 1914, when this photograph was taken on Thanksgiving Day at Bryant's Field in Monongahela. The National Football League would be formed six years later, in 1920. Not only were men in suits and hats lined up three deep surrounding the entire field, but many were lined up on the hillside as well. This football game was between Charleroi and Monongahela, and Monongahela won, 14-0. Any guesses where the women were on this Thanksgiving Day?

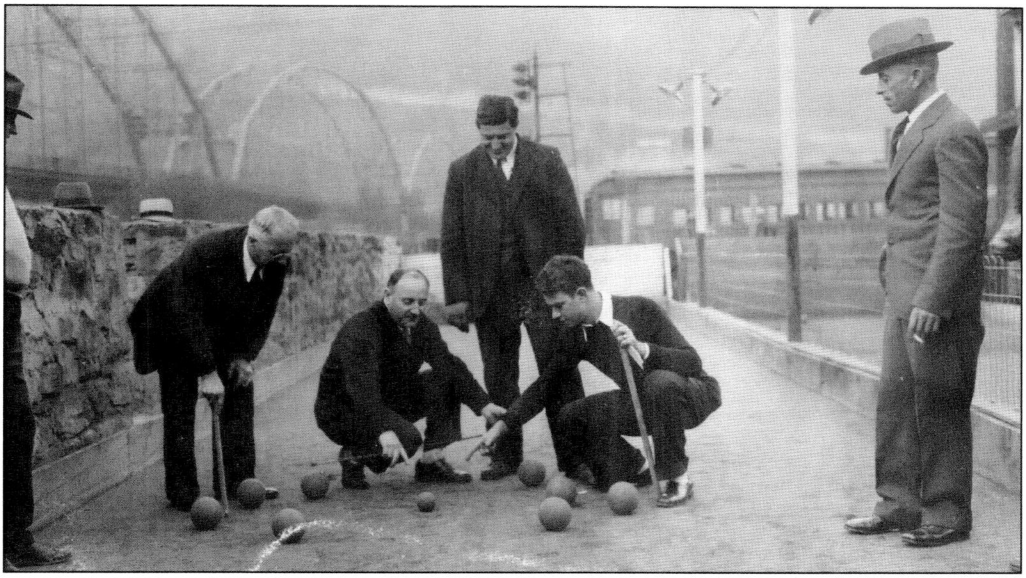

The bocce diamond, located behind the Italian Citizens Club between First and Second Streets, was a familiar and favorite spot of many of the Italian gentlemen in town. The sound of the balls hitting together, along with groans and cheers, could be heard nearly every night. The players are Mr. Paoleschi, William Turri, Mr. Cattaneo, and P. Inserra. The game was being played in 1931. (Courtesy scrapbook of Potente Zanardelli.)

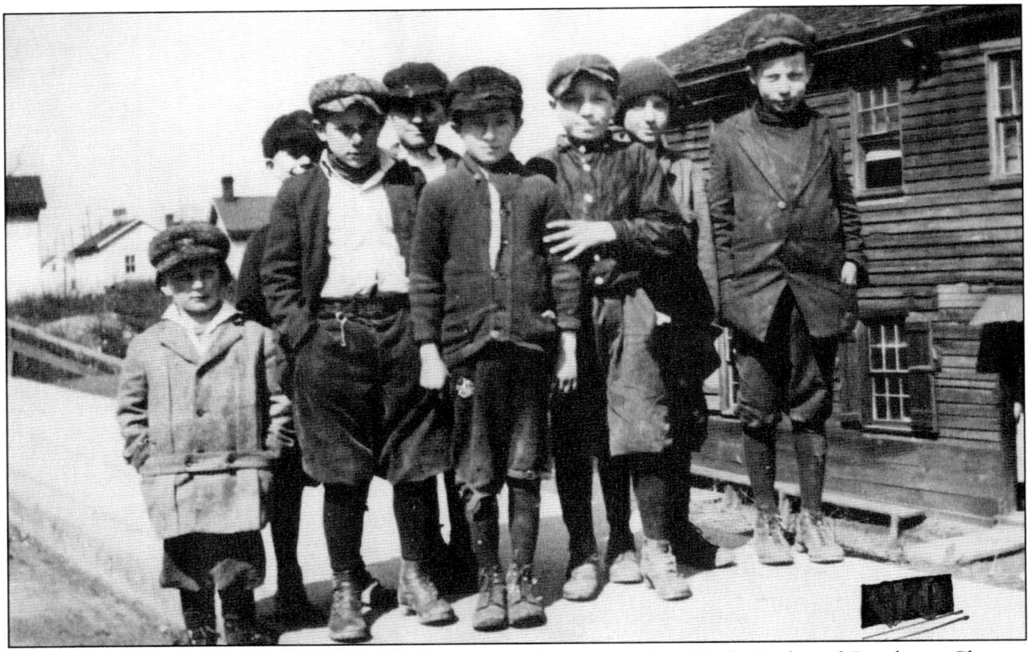

Catsburg had its own version of the Little Rascals, known as the Black Eagles of Catsburg. Shown here in 1917 are, from left to right, B. Kozon, J. Salesky, V. Pezzoni, J. Pezzoni, Thomas Lazzari, P. Zanardelli, E. Sposetti, and James Lazzari. Some said that Catsburg was named for Biddie Caldwell and her kittens. Others swore it was because she and her daughter argued all the time—sounding like cats. (Courtesy scrapbook of Potente Zanardelli.)

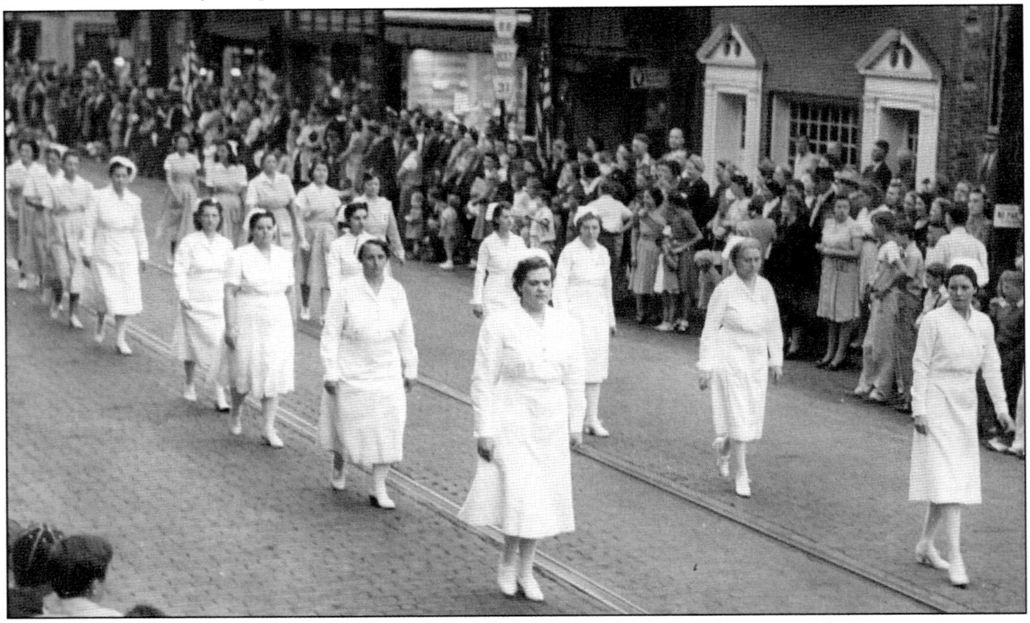

Monongahela parades always included a variety of service organizations of the city. Pictured here are the nurses from Monongahela Memorial Hospital on June 15, 1942, marching in their starched white uniforms and caps, showing their support for and dedication to the community. The Monongahela Memorial Hospital was always an integral part of the town, and the commitment continues today through the excellent care provided by the Monongahela Valley Hospital.

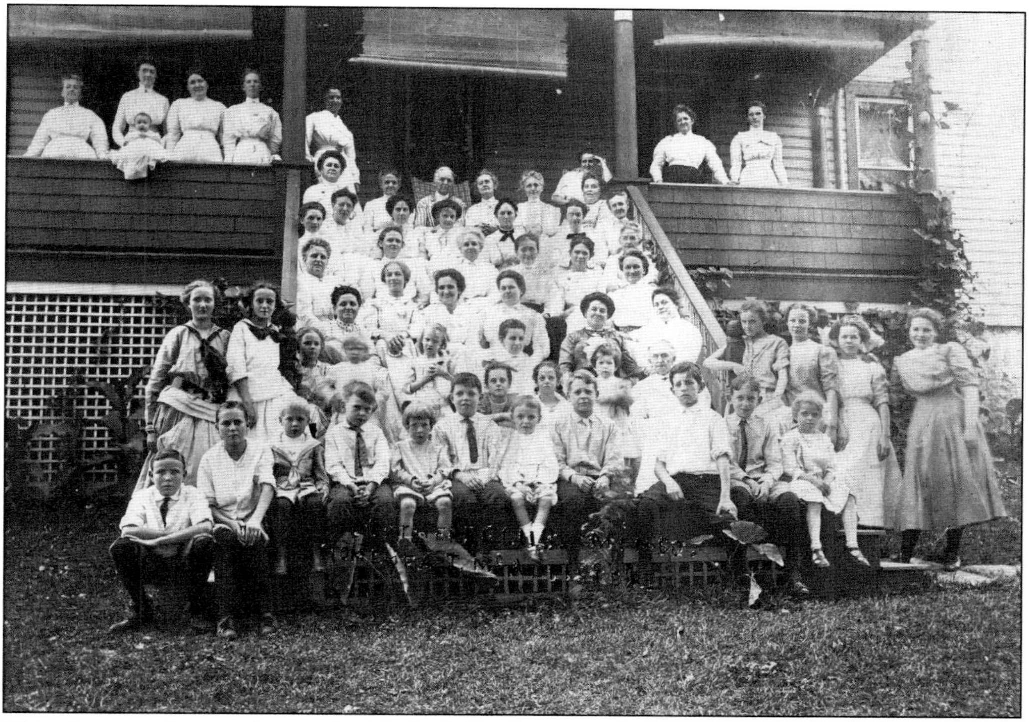

This photograph was taken at the Mother's Day Picnic at the McAlister farm near Mingo Creek. The Monongahela Mother's Club was organized in 1902. Its daughter organization, founded as a junior section in 1938, is the present Monongahela Women's Club, which assumed senior club status in 1945. The club is still active today and does many good works for the city.

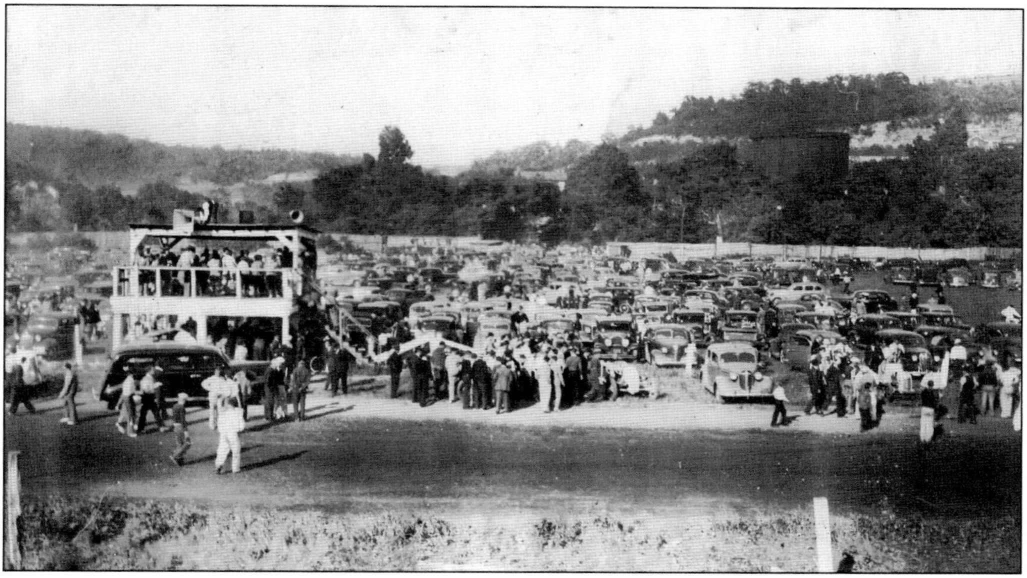

Opening day for automobile racing at the Old Driving Park on Park Avenue was always an exciting time. This race took place on July 4, 1938. In the late 1800s and early 1900s, the track was used for horse racing and was run by a group of men who formed the Monongahela Valley Agricultural Association. Later in the 1900s, a Pittsburgh interest group reconditioned the track for automobile racing. The sport continued until the late 1930s.

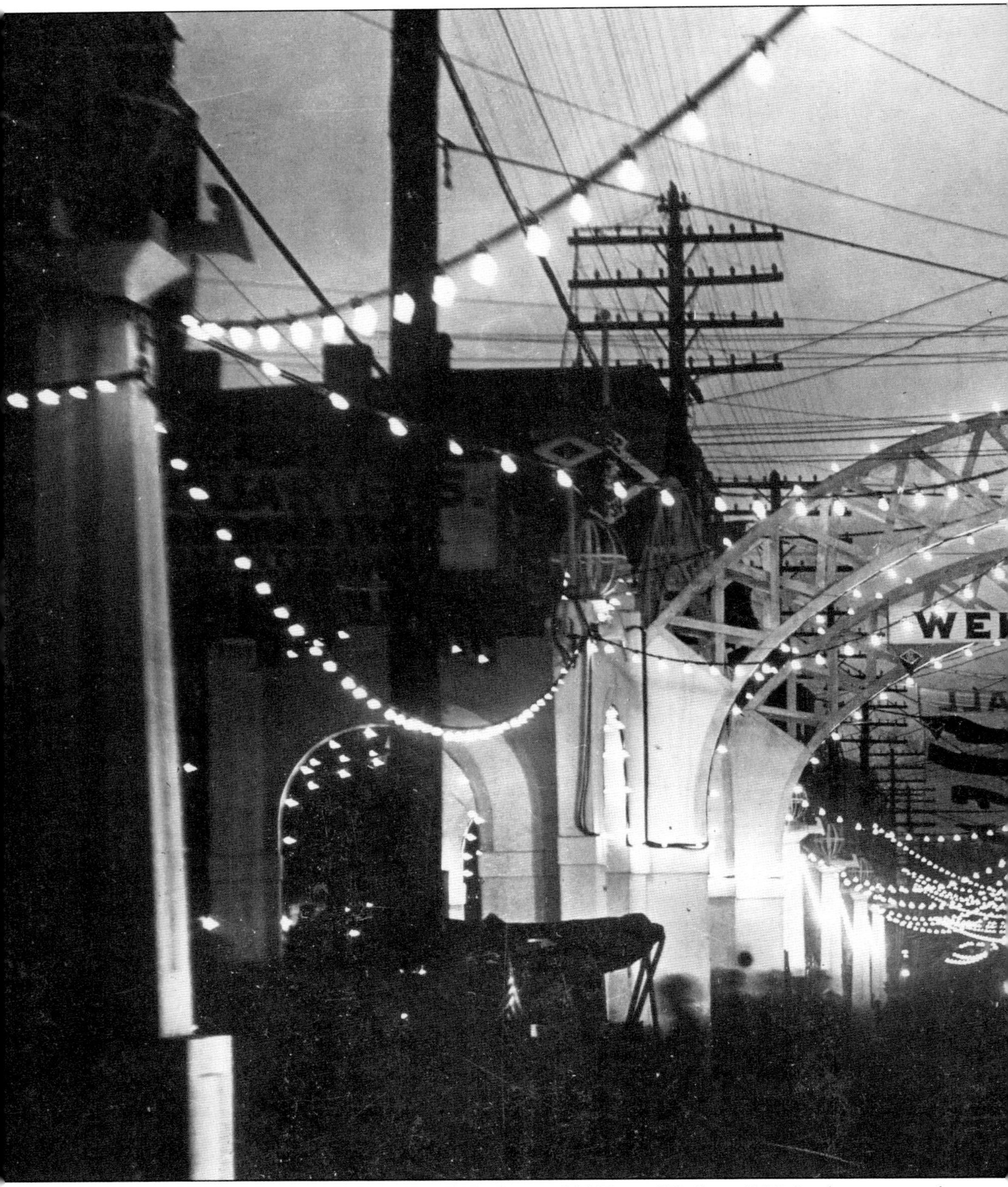

Monongahela City certainly shone brightly during Old Home Week in 1908. In this spectacular photograph, thousands of electric lights illuminate Main Street. Monongahela had a number of gifted photographers with the talent to produce high-quality timed exposures such as this. And Edward Acheson must again be credited with changing the face of Monongahela City, the city he adopted for a time. Acheson was having little luck elsewhere getting his inventions off the ground. He came to Monongahela City upon acquiring an electrical company located along the

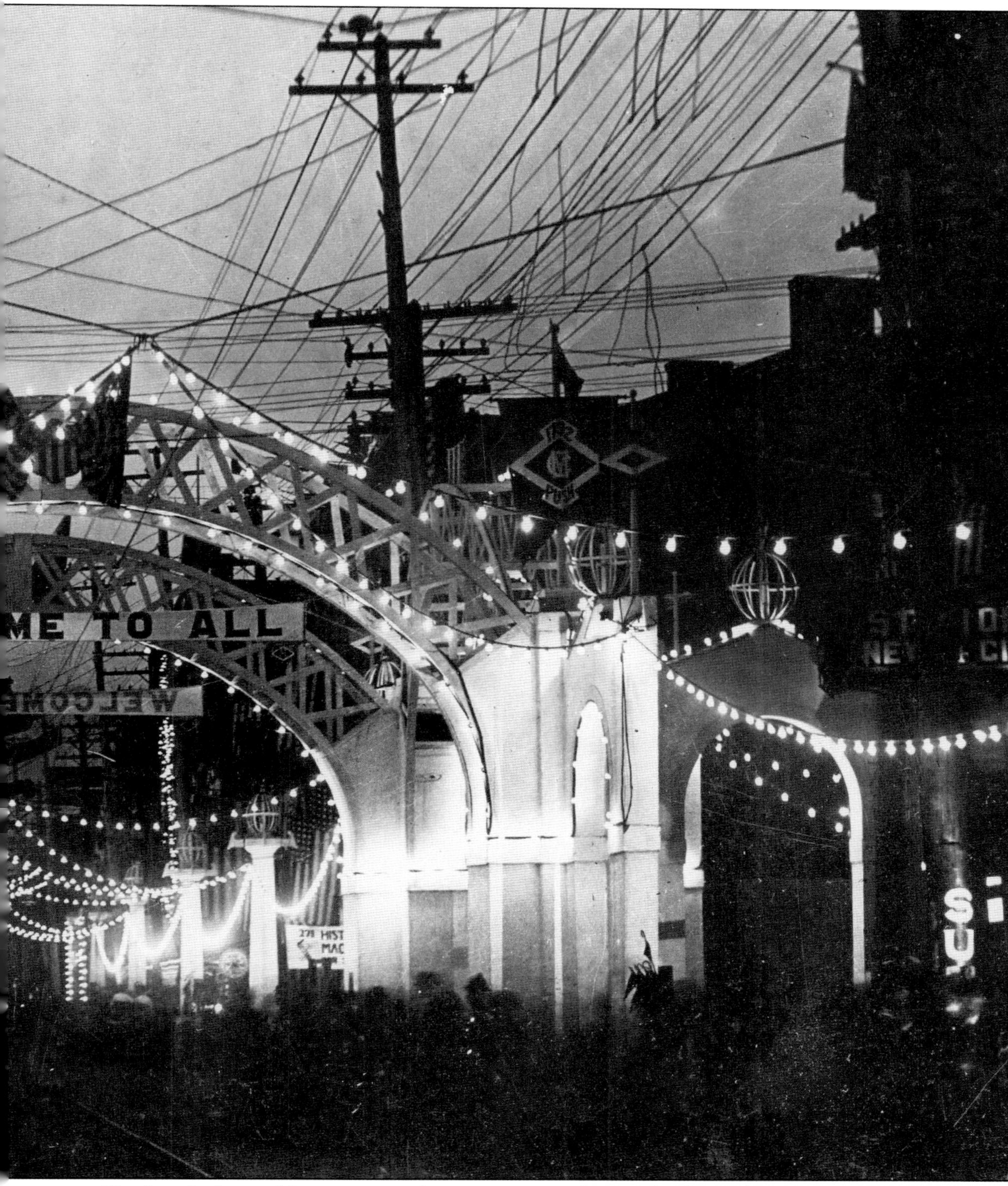

river. He thought he could use it to conduct experiments during the day and generate revenues by illuminating the town at night. However, because Monongahela City already had gas lights, there was little interest in generating lighting with electricity. Town history documents that Acheson became politically active to change the thinking. He worked to change anti-electric-light Republicans into pro-electric-light Democrats—and was then able to get back to the business of inventing.

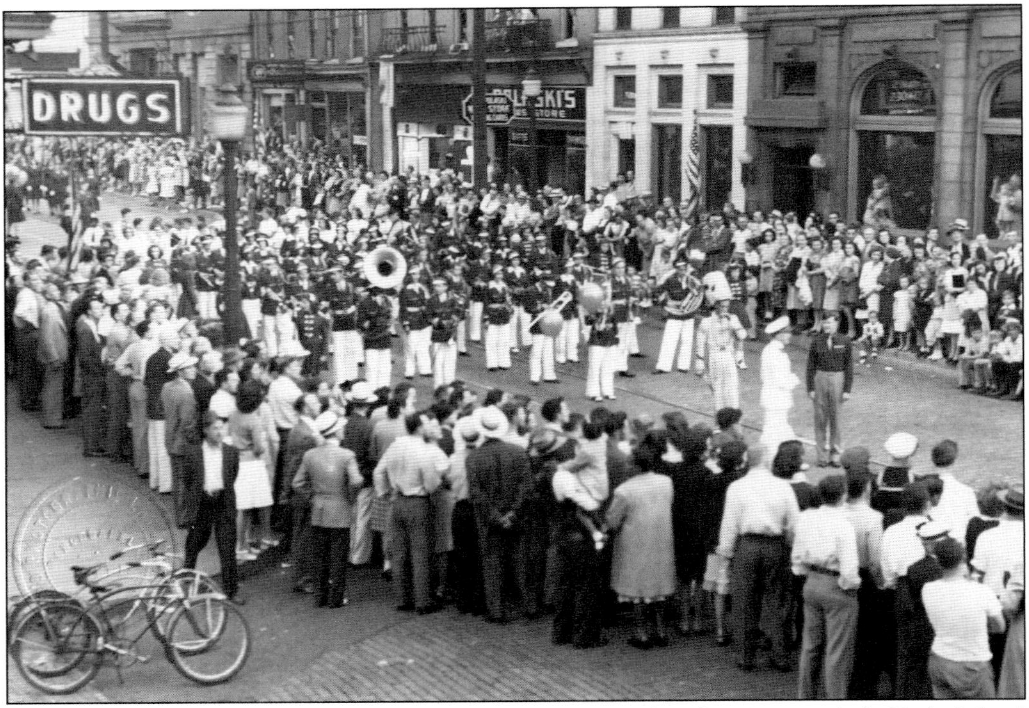

Main Street was the place to be for this World War II parade. The Monongahela High School Band had center stage, with the Women's Defense Corps following. The scene is set between Third and Fourth Streets, with Polaski's New Store in plain view. The Alexander Bank is on the left side of the photograph, with a Bell of Pennsylvania office on the second floor, and the First National Bank is on the right. Members of the military are in the crowd, which is four and five people deep. The kids left their bikes to get a spot in the front, and the men and women are dressed in their Sunday best, with several men wearing fedoras.

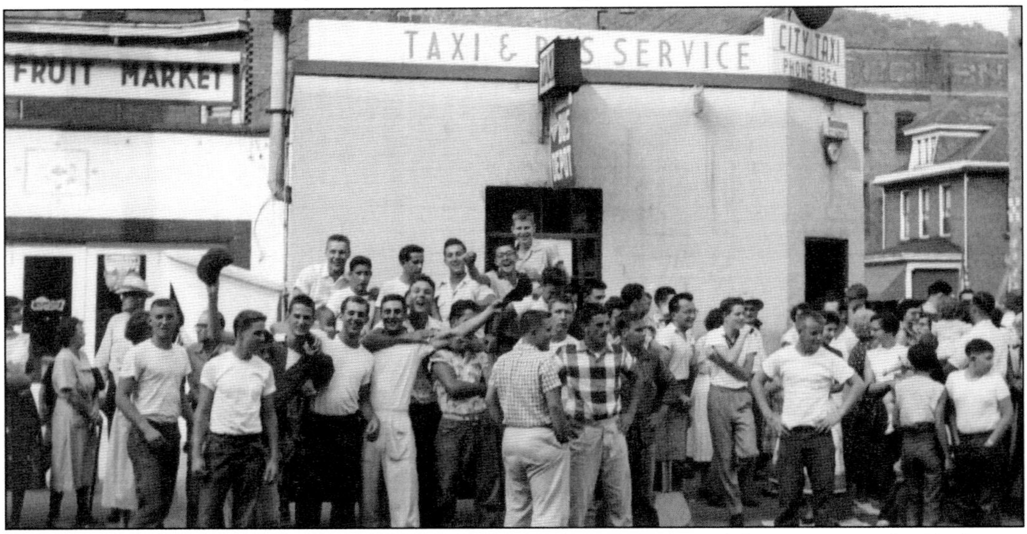

The 1954 Pony World Series Championship gave sports fans one of their greatest thrills during Monongahela's first 200 years. Fans lined up everywhere along Main Street to welcome their heroes with a parade. Little League baseball got its start in Monongahela in 1950, and four years later, under the management of Harry Sickles Sr., the team captured the Pony World Series crown.

A photograph of women eating watermelon might seem like an ordinary picture, but during the period it was taken, it really was not ordinary. Many photographs that were taken were formal, posed portraits, where smiles were a rarity. Film was expensive and photographs were luxury items. Here, a group of women appear to be enjoying themselves immensely as a candid shot captures them leaning over carefully to avoid getting watermelon juice on their outfits. Washing clothes was no small chore.

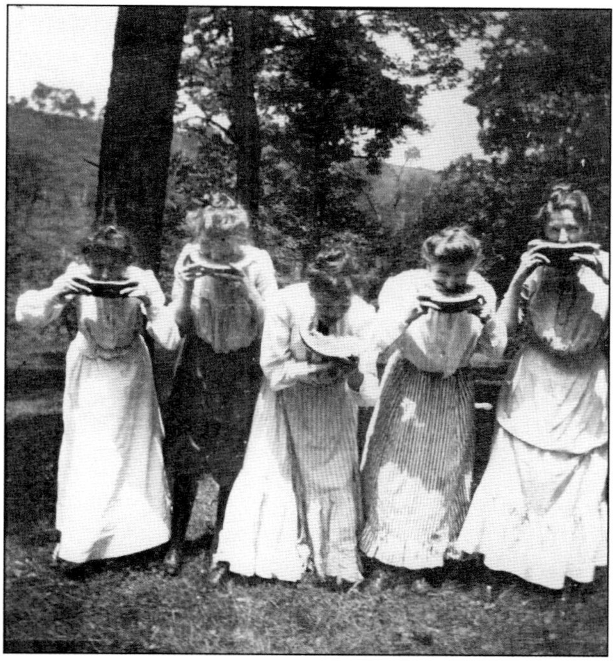

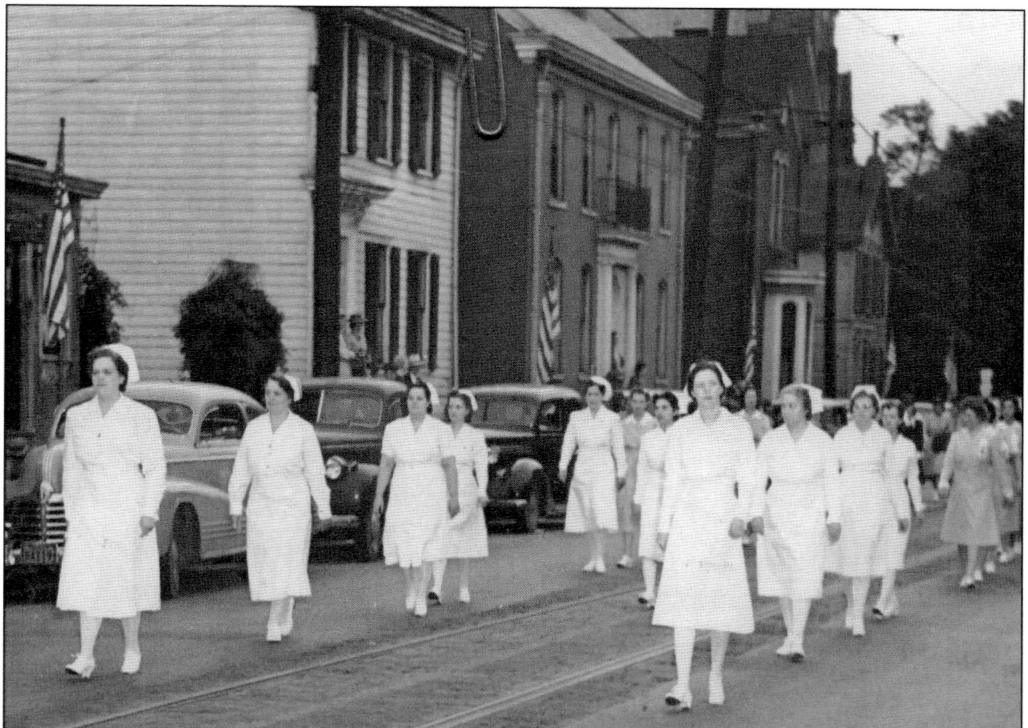

Much like the rest of the country, Monongahela continued to hold parades to celebrate during World War II. Nurses are proudly marching past townspeople who always came to demonstrate their support of the troops. Women were an important part in the war effort, taking over many of the men's jobs to keep the country going during that difficult time. Nurses were central in caring for the wounded and deserving of recognition.

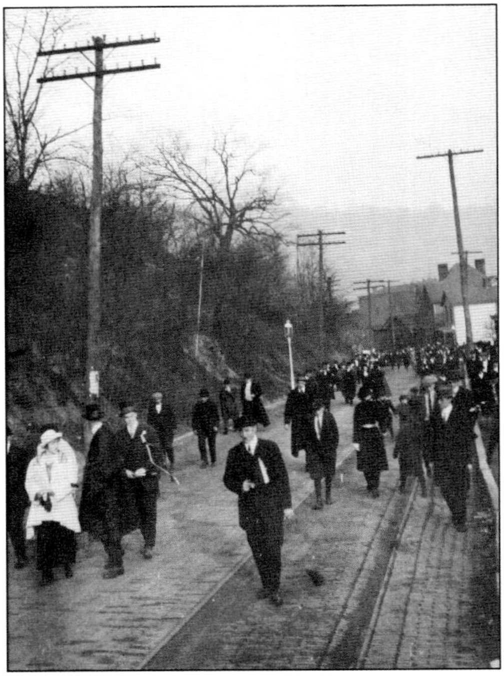

A crowd of people fills Park Avenue in the vicinity of St. Anthony's Church. The picture can only be dated by the clothing the people are wearing and the age of the streetcar tracks. The caption says they are "walking to the game." The photograph includes mostly men, but some women and children are present. Note the gas streetlamp near the center of the photograph.

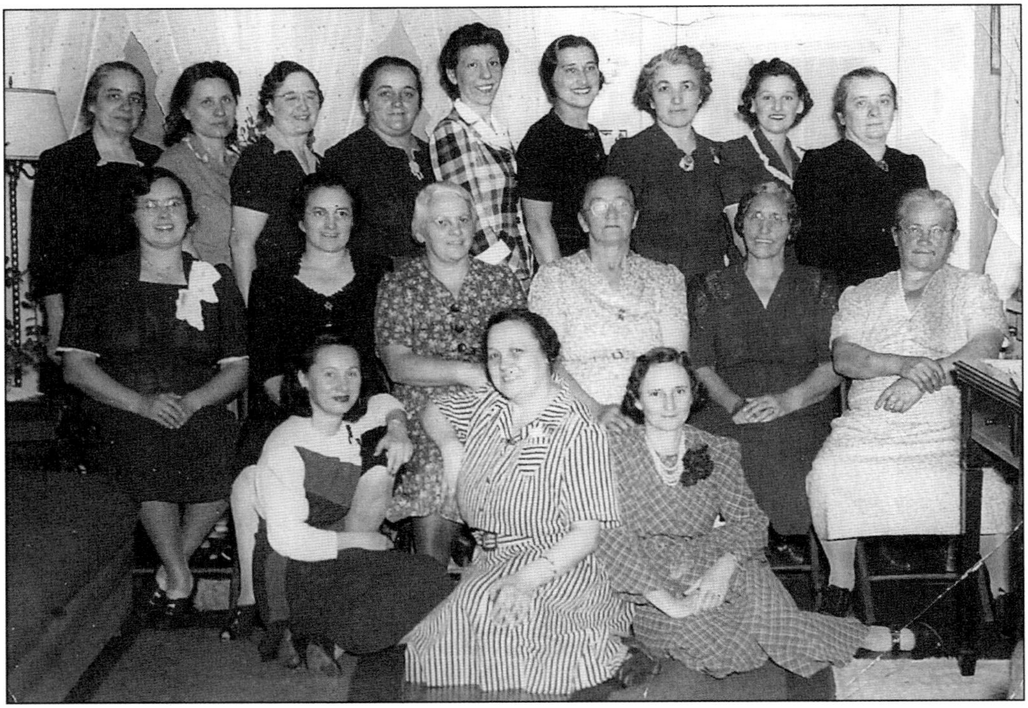

Shown here is a group of women who gathered as a send-off for Florence "Pia" Zanardelli, who was moving with her husband, August, to Tucson, Arizona, in 1943. The women pictured here are, from left to right, (first row) Vicki Paterlini, Dora Turri, and Mary Nagy; (second row) Vickie Giuliani, Florence Zanardelli, Elisa Giuliani, Minnie Lazzari, Annie Paterlini, and Maria Zanardelli; (third row) Maggie Veraldi, Mary Dolfi, Geneva Durieux, Josephine Zavarello, Lena Lazzari, Josephine Inserra, Mary Previtali, Lucy Miklos, and Mary Pollard. (Courtesy Betty Lou Gainer Tuite.)

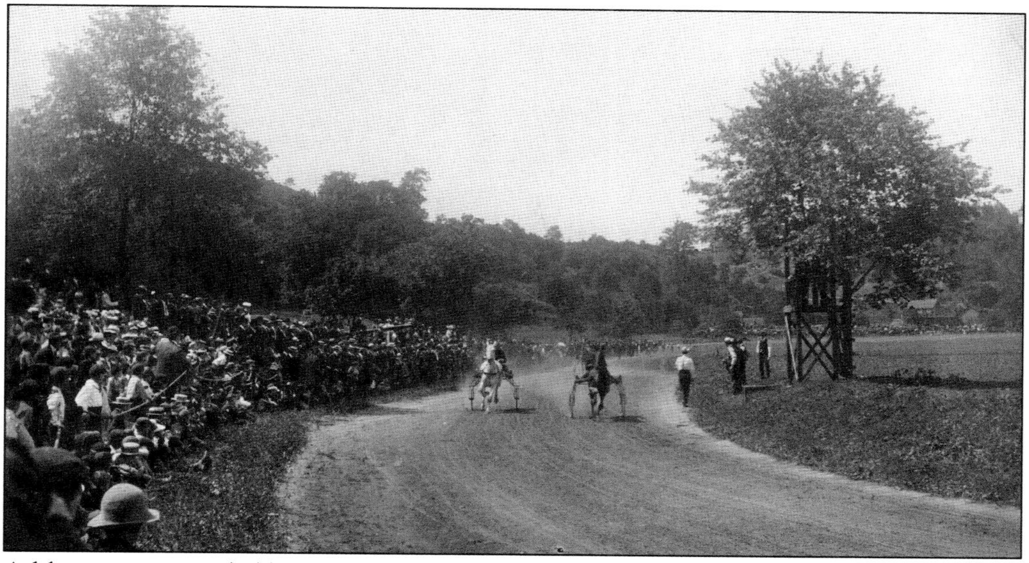

Athletic events were held at the racetrack on Park Avenue as early as 1861. Prominent horsemen of the time included Harvey VanVoorhis, with his famous little horse Hawkeye, and Frank Bentley, who owned a mare called Sweet Lips. Horses were brought to the track from as far away as Waynesburg and White Hall around the turn of the century.

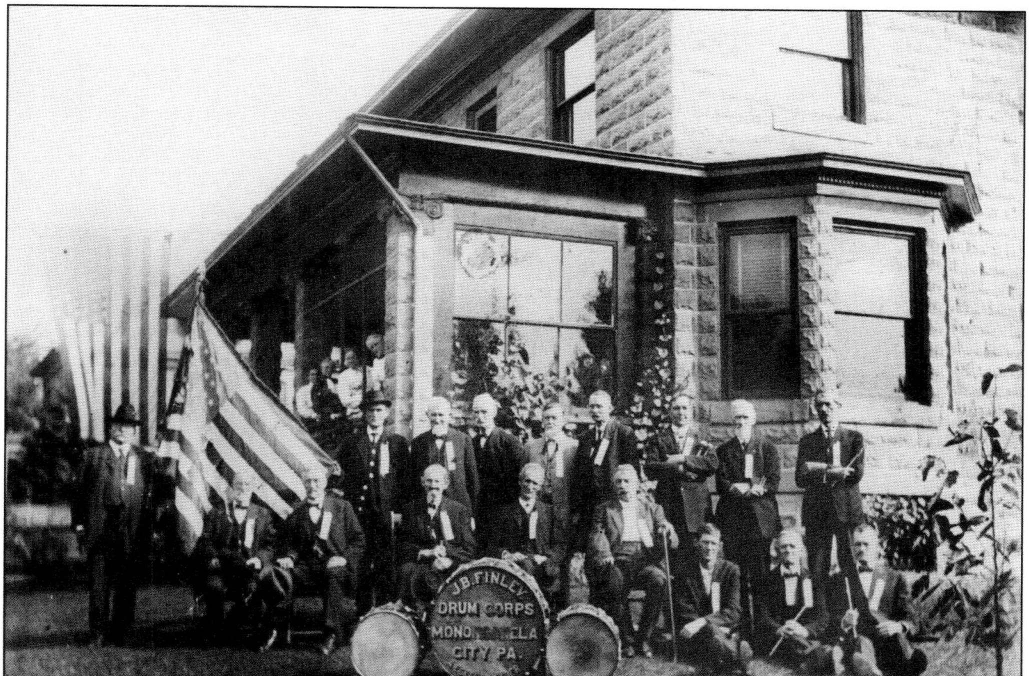

Pictured here is the J.B. Finley (Eckels) Drum Corps at the home of Isaac Yohe on Stanton Street. The group included the reunion of Company B, 79th Pennsylvania Volunteer Infantry. From left to right are (sitting) Alex O'Donovan, Luke Beagel, William Butler, William Woodward, George Gibson, Charlie Eckels, Amzi Eckels, and Joe Coatsworth; (standing) Joe Wolfe, William Miller, Sparks Cooper, unidentified, Isaac Yohe, unidentified, Fred Eckels, John Berringer, and Bub Eckels.

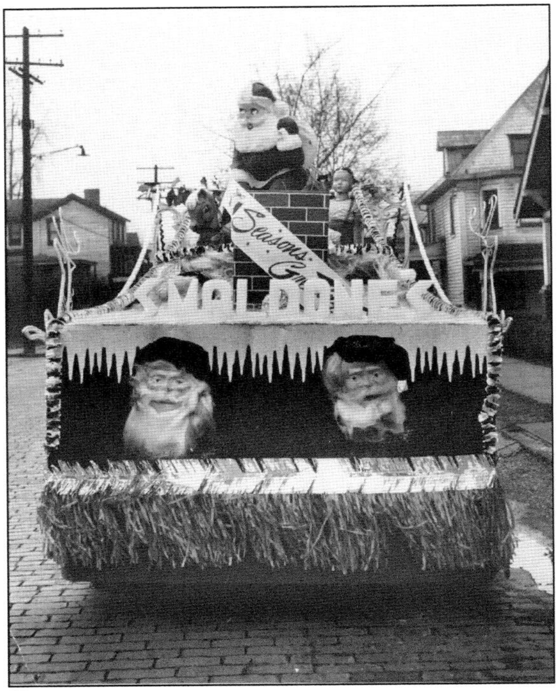

The Christmas parade in Monongahela was always a well-attended event in town. Merchants and organizations entered floats advertising their businesses, and community bands marched to the joyous songs of the season. Pictured here is Smaldone's Children Clothing Store's elaborate entry, with Santa coming down the chimney.

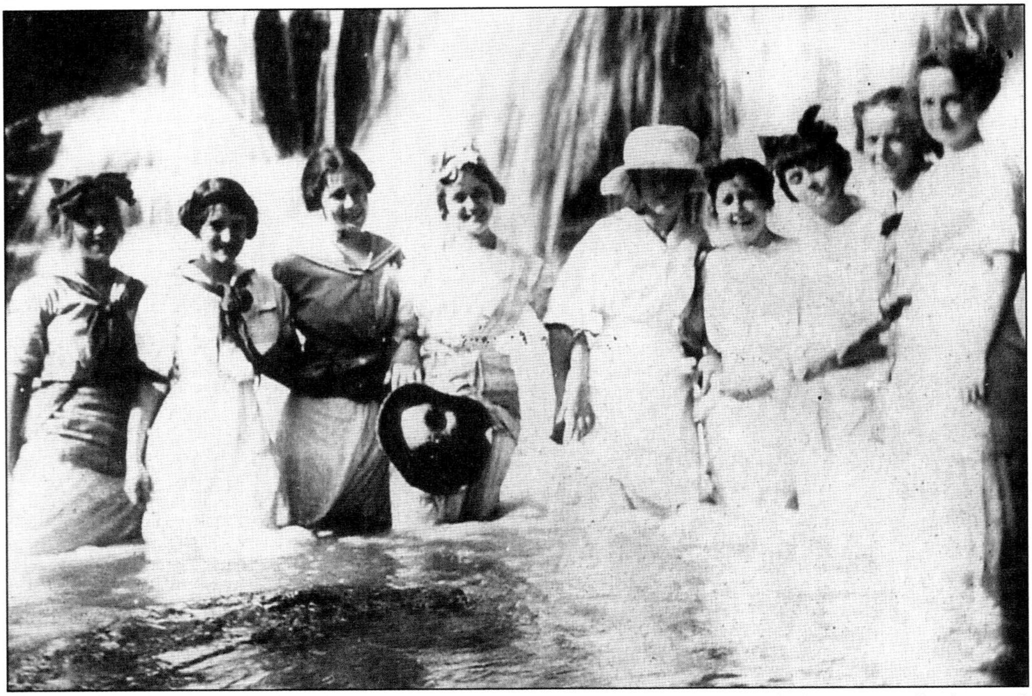

A 30-acre parcel of land purchased by the Sutzs family in the 1920s included Mingo Falls, located along Route 88. These Sutzs family friends and relatives are wading in the cool Mingo Falls water in summer. The Mingo Falls area was known for whiskey-making during the Whiskey Insurrection, and locals hid moonshine in Mingo Falls. In early days, a wagon trail connected Monongahela to Finleyville. In the 1920s, the trail was replaced by a streetcar line that eventually became Route 88.

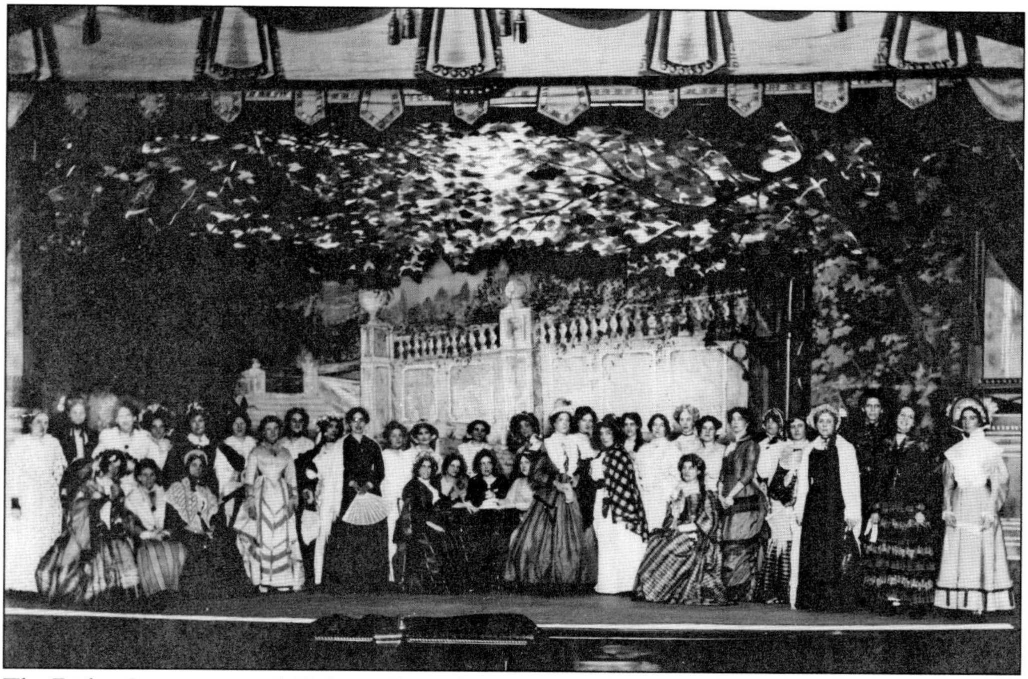

The Friday Conversational Club was formed in 1897. Here, members are holding a hospital benefit show at the Anton Theatre on Friday, February 13, 1914. The 1914 annual report of the Carnegie Institute shows that 30 members visited that year and the Carnegie Institute held a lecture for the group on January 30, 1914. As another testament to the group's interest in culture, history, and worthwhile projects, the Friday Conversational Club formed and chartered the Monongahela Area Historical Society in 1961. The president of the Friday Conversational Club was a vice president of the historical society until the Friday Conversational Club disbanded in 1975.

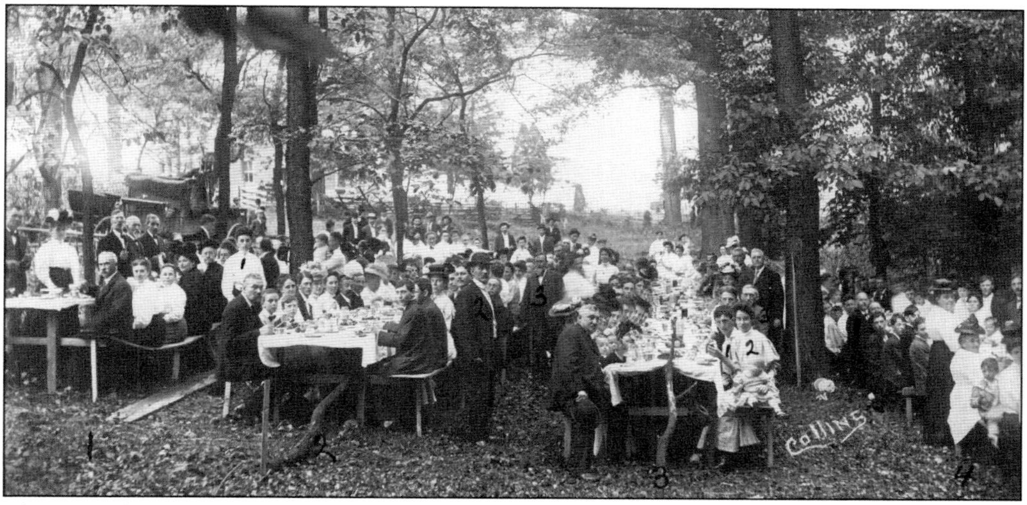

The second Yohe, Weygandt, and Stecher family reunion took place on September 16, 1907, at the Mount Zion Church at Ginger Hill, during Home Coming Week. The Stecher Historical Society invited descendants of Michael Yohe, Cornelius Weygandt, and Melchoir Stecher, pioneer settlers of Washington County who came in 1786. Yohe had served under George Washington and had been sent to squelch the Whiskey Insurrection. He had camped here years before on this very site.

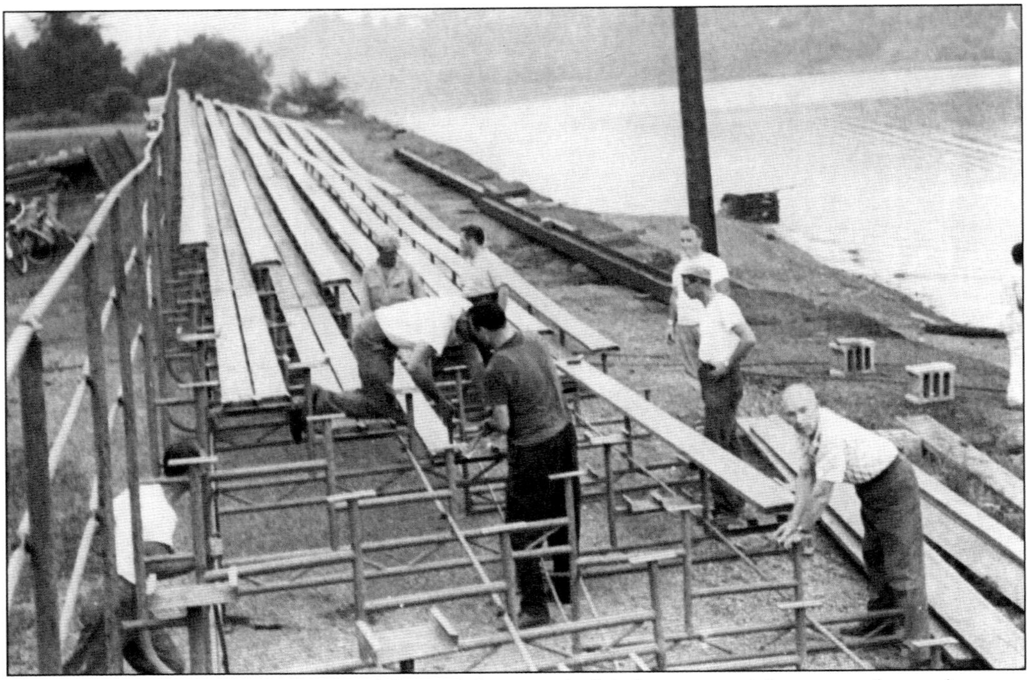

Early in 1969, the decision to celebrate Monongahela's bicentennial was made, and a new facility to stage the events was proposed by local contractor Frank Irey Jr. He suggested that a riverfront auditorium be constructed. This photograph shows the building of the Aquatorium. The facility included a huge stage, 65 feet deep by 200 feet wide, which extended out into the Monongahela River.

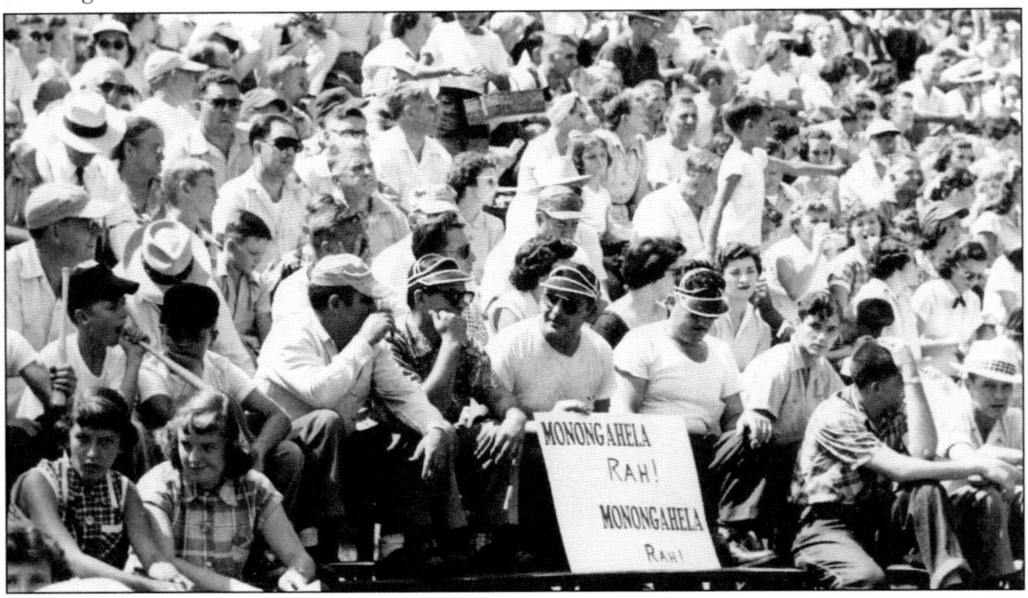

Hometown sports teams could always count on the fans of Monongahela to turn out in great numbers to cheer their teams on to victory. The sign says it all: "Monongahela Rah! Monongahela Rah!" The bleachers were full as fans watched the Pony League winners. Names like Stuyvesant, Wassel, Caldwell, Galiffa, Sasselli, DeRosa, Stattlander, Diaz, Sacane, McCall, Kikla, Voulker, Fabin, and Peters will be remembered forever.

Seven

WATER AND RAIL

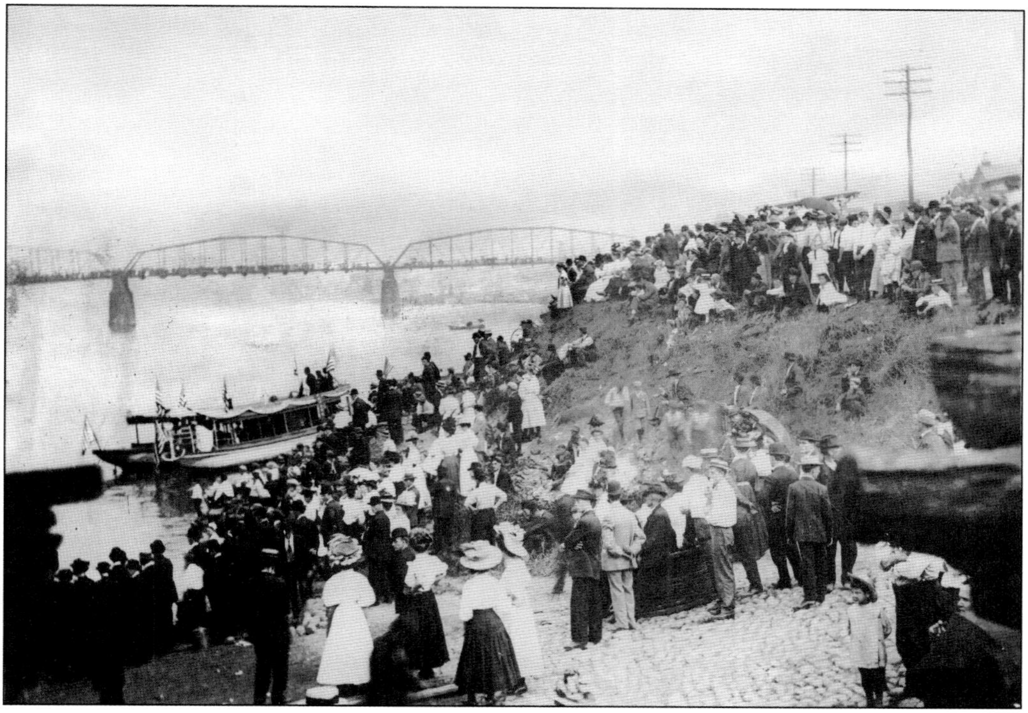

Traffic on the Monongahela River, one of the world's busiest, has always been a familiar sight. From coal-laden barges and steamboats to pleasure crafts, people have been enjoying it for many years. Pictured here are the boat races held during the Old Home Week celebrations of 1908. Throngs of town residents showed up for the event. (Courtesy scrapbook of Potente Zanardelli.)

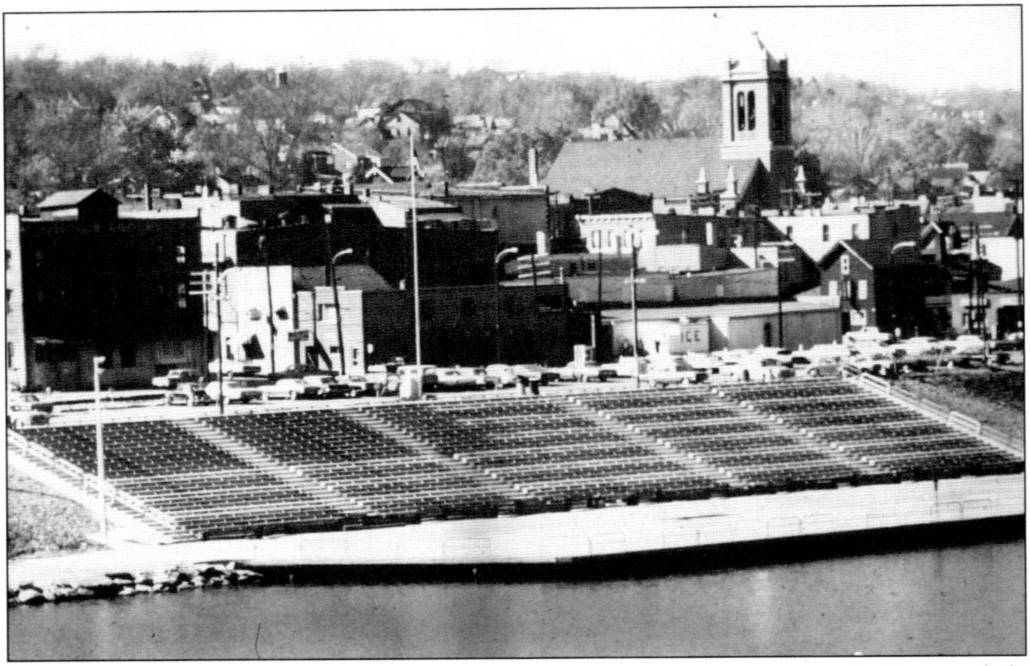

The Noble J. Dick Aquatorium was constructed by Frank Irey Jr. to commemorate the Monongahela area's 200th anniversary. It magnificently accepts the majestic and serene natural setting. The 3,500-seat arena has become a civic and cultural center hosting professional performances, religious services, amateur productions, and events of community interest. It is also populated with fishermen, water-sport enthusiasts, and relaxed casual observers.

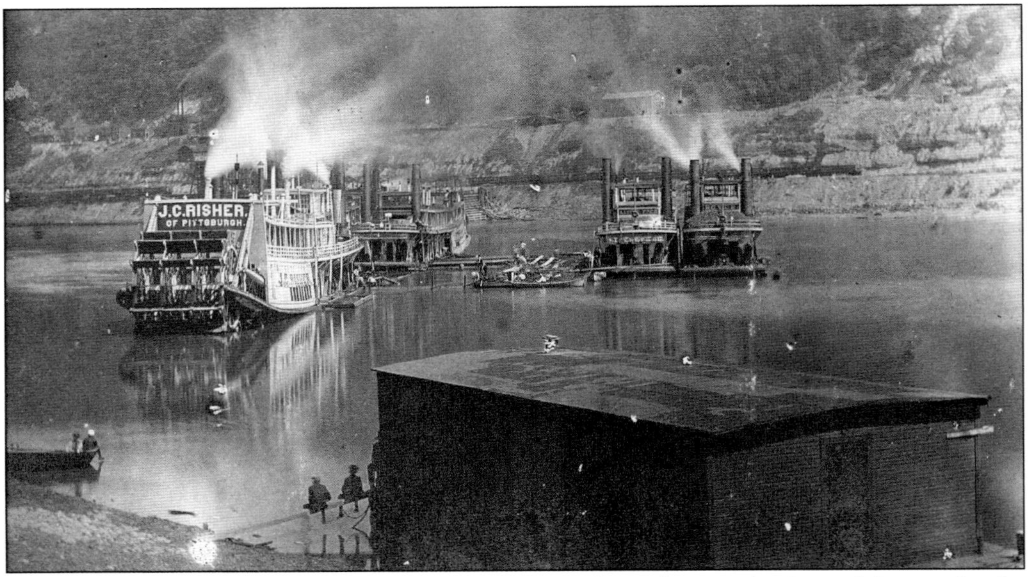

The Monongahela River was always a hub of activity. Shown here at the Second Street wharf is a series of paddle boats and steamboats, vital for commerce and recreation. The boats seen here are *J.C. Risher of Pittsburgh*, *Little Fred*, and *Rover*. Because it was a docking station, it is possible to see the men in the middle of the photograph who are securing the boats and using canoes to bring people to and from the boats. Smoke from the boats filled the air, and two young boys in the foreground are watching the activity.

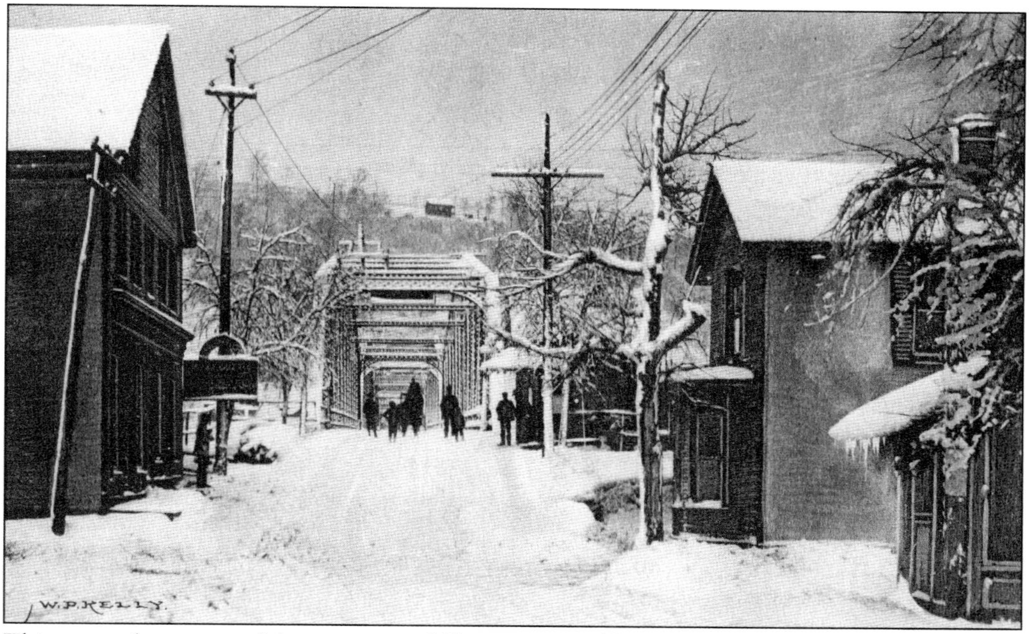

This scene shows one of the great snowfalls experienced by Monongahela. The entrance of the iron bridge was snow-covered and treacherous for traveling. It was located at Second Street when houses, no longer there, lined both sides. Perhaps the travelers should have stayed home and waited for the big thaw.

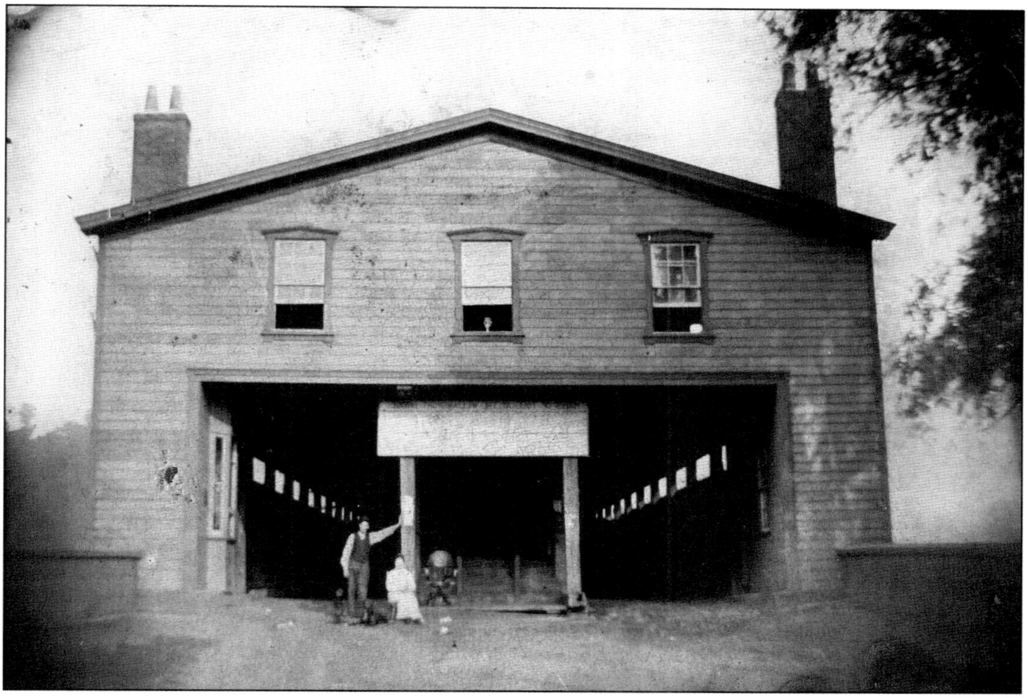

The old covered wooden bridge was built in 1838 by contractor Mr. Pagan. When the bridge was about half completed, a storm blew it down, and the workmen escaped just in time to save their lives. The bridge caught fire April 12, 1883. Allan Parkison said it took 27 minutes from the time the first blaze was discovered until the bridge dropped into the water.

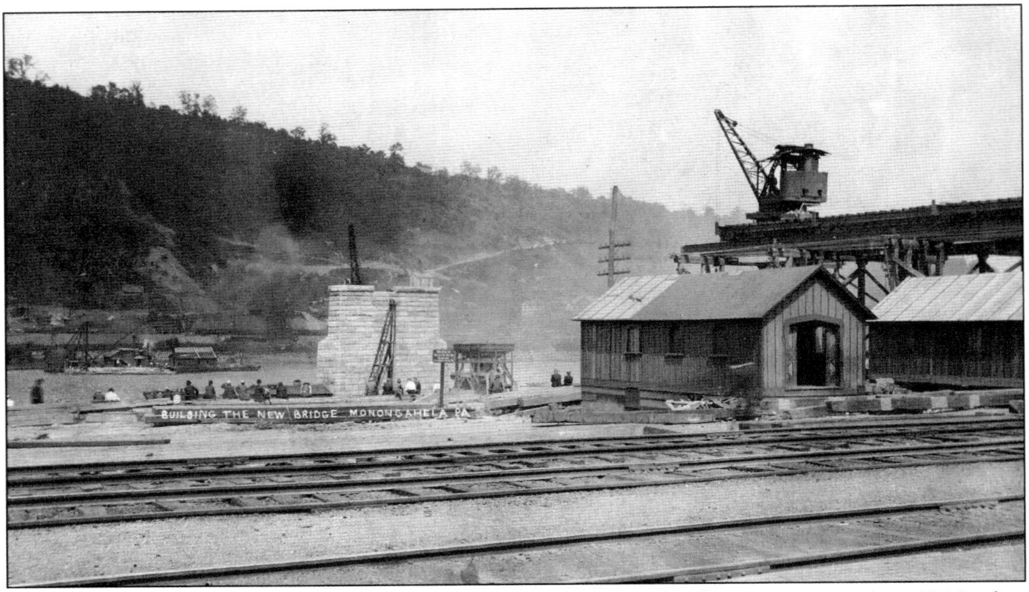

This photograph shows the building phase of the new iron bridge, constructed in 1909 after the wooden covered bridge had burned. The cost of the wooden bridge had been $125,000. In comparison, the new iron river bridge cost $225,000. Even though the iron one cost more, the taxpayers were counting on this one not burning. The bridge replacing this one in 1988 would come at a cost of $14.4 million.

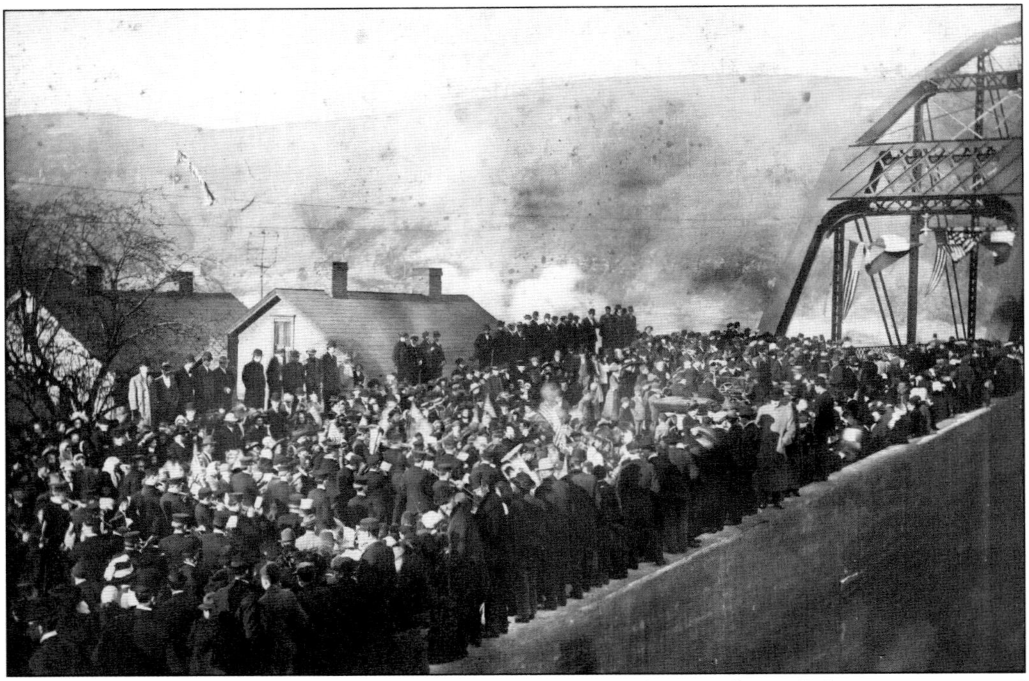

It was a huge day when the new bridge opened in 1909. People came from all directions to attend the ribbon cutting, as evidenced by the billowing smoke from the passenger boats docked on the river. Everyone dressed in their Sunday best and crowded in to be part of the festivities. Notice how many people were even willing to stand on the steep side walls with no railings, risking quite a fall to get a good view and make room for others. (Courtesy scrapbook of Potente Zanardelli.)

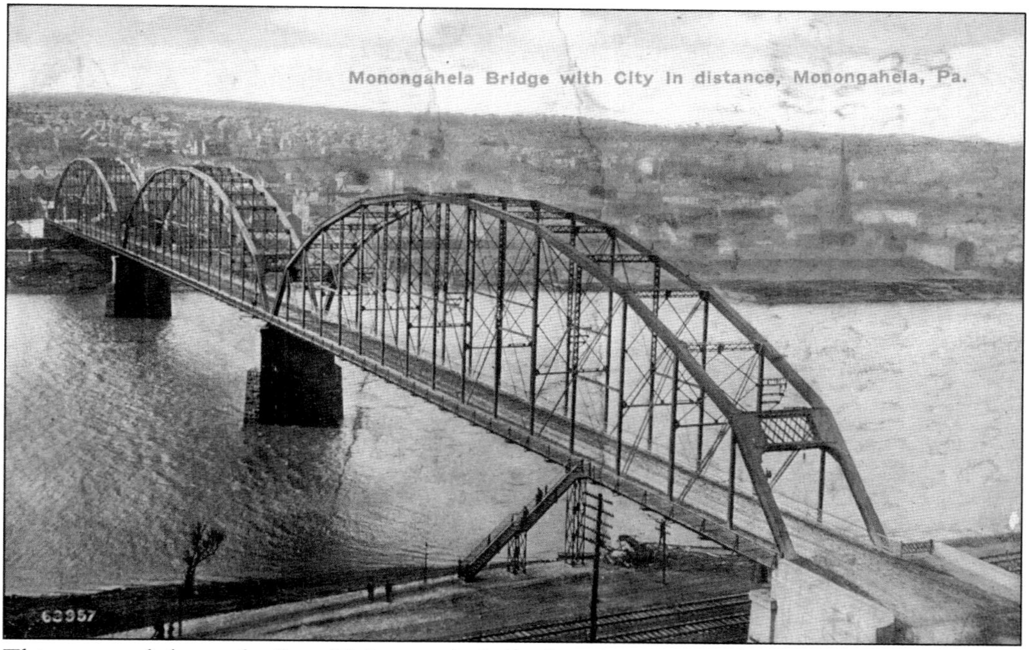

This postcard shows the "new" Monongahela Bridge after it opened in 1909. This view looks toward Monongahela from Forward Township and shows the metal through-truss of the three-span iron bridge. Note the pedestrian steps on the bridge. In the bridge's early days, it was more traveled by pedestrians than cars. This bridge served the entire region well for 80 years and was in service until the replacement bridge opened.

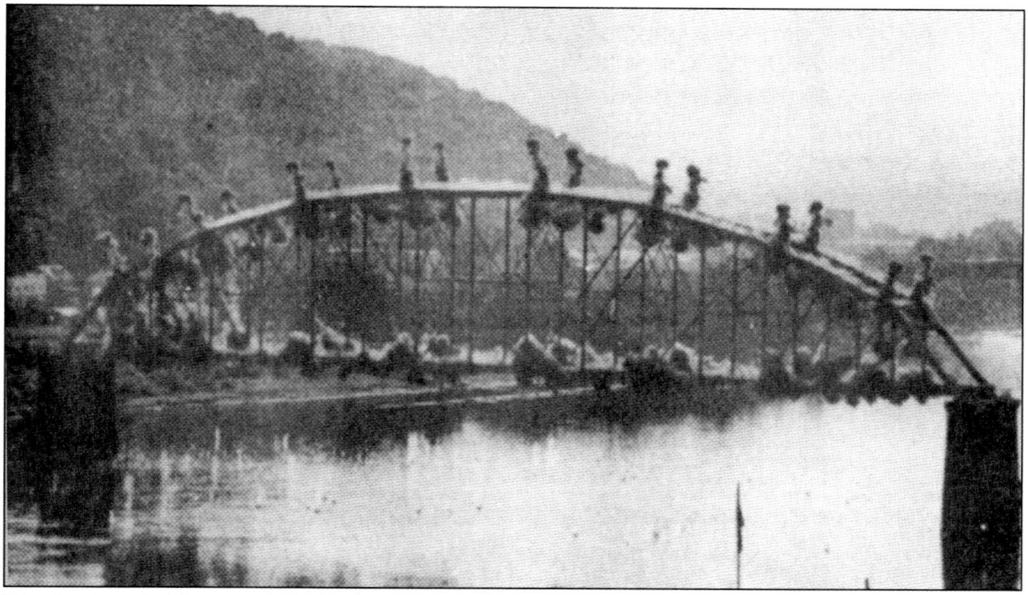

The landmark Monongahela bridge was razed on Tuesday, August 9, 1988. Two implosions were ordered (one at 7:00 a.m. and the other at 10:00 a.m.) to ensure additional protection for homes and businesses on both sides of the river. The replacement bridge was closed for 15 to 20 minutes during each implosion. Ribbon-cutting ceremonies were held for the replacement bridge on May 12, but it was closed again for some final work, and this bridge remained in service until May 26, 1988.

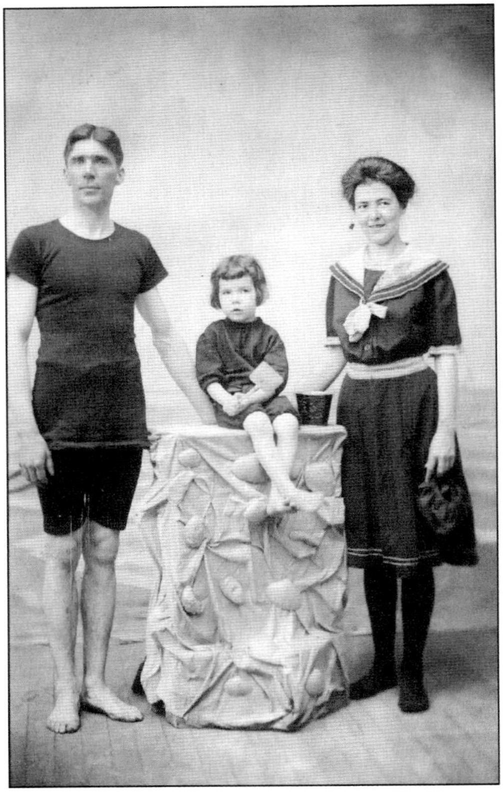

This is the Wall family's portrait from their Atlantic City vacation. Shown here are Dr. P.M. and Mrs. Wall with their little swimmer, Altha Wall. Note the modern bathing suits and the seashells decorating the photo set.

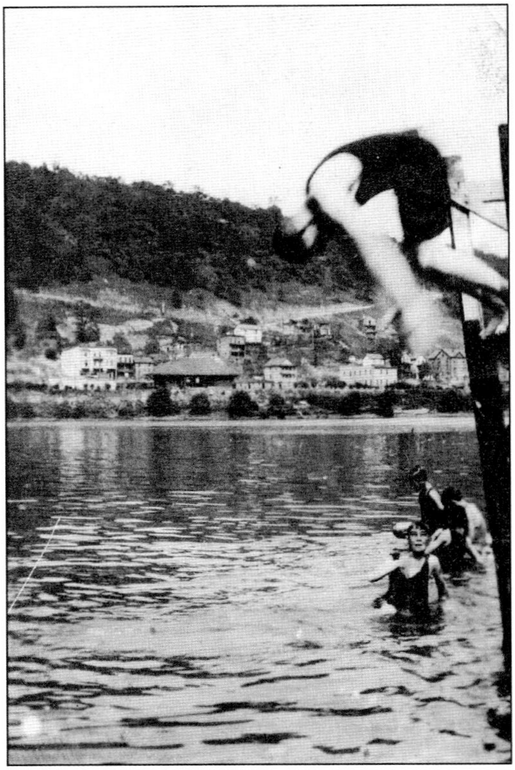

Ah, the days of summer and going to one of the many swimming holes and beaches along the riverbanks. Some youth ventured into the river without parental consent and may have risked facing consequences later, but many families enjoyed cooling off and picnicking by the river. Some favorite swimming spots were located at Fifth, Sixth, Eleventh, Twelfth Streets, the foot of Cemetery Hill by the Vaira house, and Rocky Beach, located between Factory and Jones Streets. Many also remember endless summer days at Wickerham Beach, located off Route 88 in the Fisher Heights area.

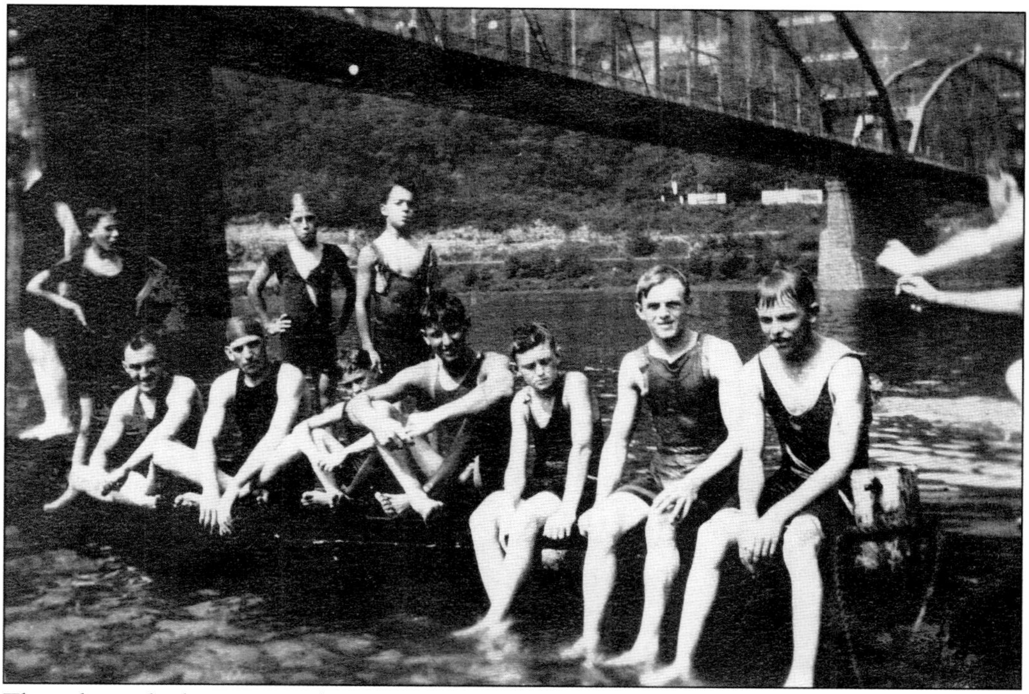

These dapper bathing suits and swimming caps were all the rage in their time. This swimming area was called "Cralls." People found great adventure by the river by holding parties and corn roasts, even letting their dogs take a dip. Some had the stamina to venture into the river, swimming from one river bank to the other and back. Some took delight swimming in the original wave pool, having the courage to swim out to greet passing barges. Other adventurers swam out to passing steam boats and caught rides south to Brownsville and then waited for a return ride home.

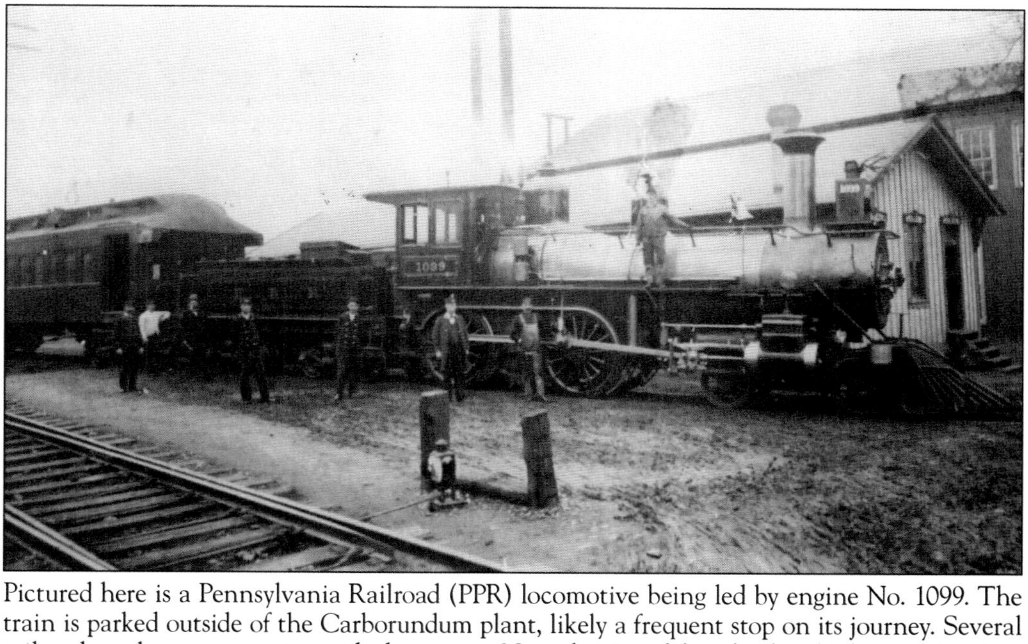

Pictured here is a Pennsylvania Railroad (PPR) locomotive being led by engine No. 1099. The train is parked outside of the Carborundum plant, likely a frequent stop on its journey. Several railroad employees are posing with the engine. Note the size of the wheels, which are taller than the men's shoulders.

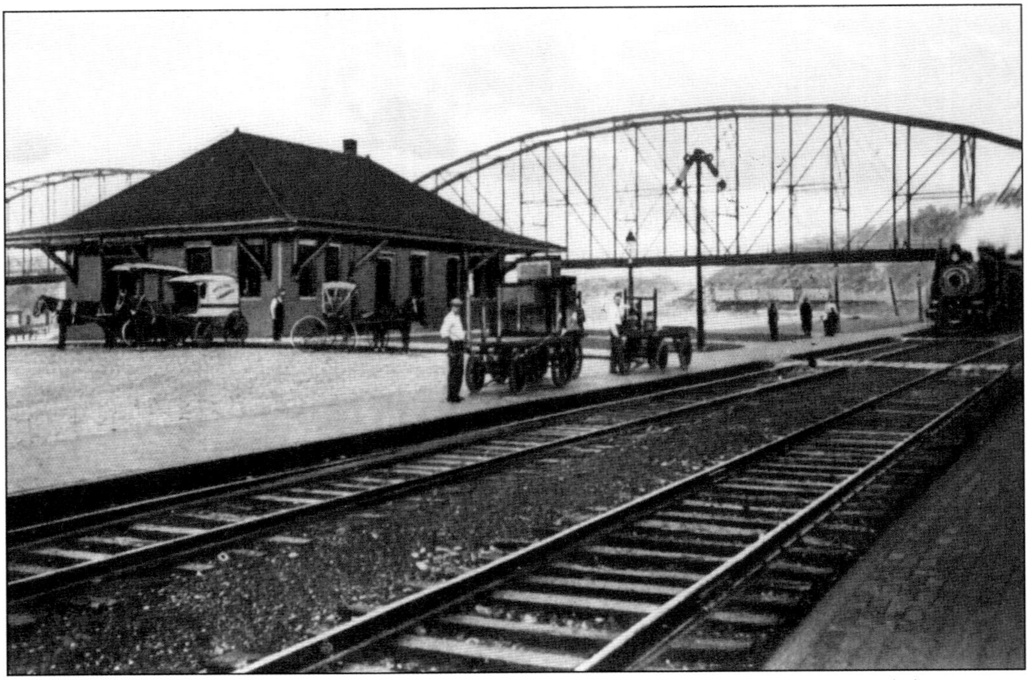

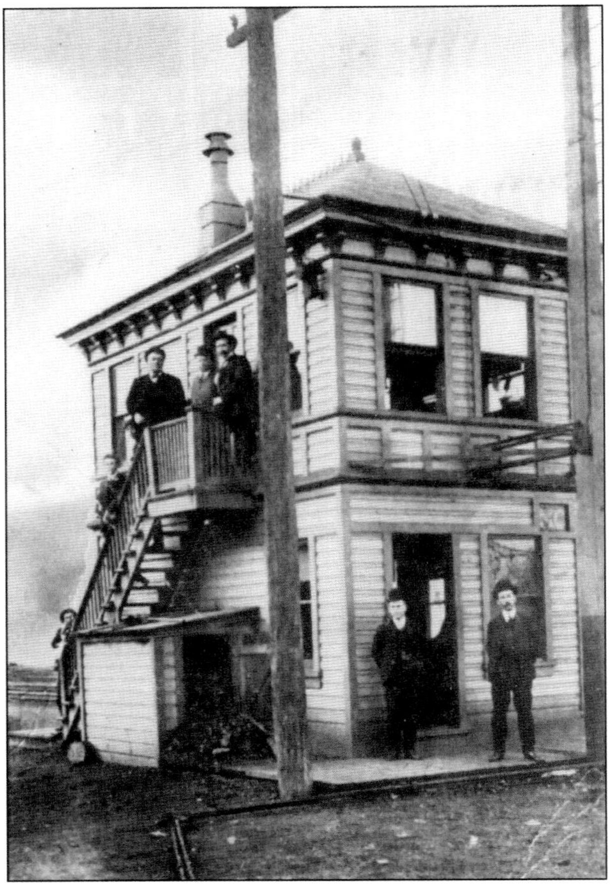

This is a tinted postcard showing some of the activity occurring by the river. The steam locomotive is entering from the south, and two men are waiting with empty carts, apparently to unload cargo. Pictured on the left are three sets of horses and buggies parked outside of the train station. A handful of people are standing along the tracks, waiting to either greet passengers or board a train themselves.

Shown here is the Pennsylvania Railroad Tower, the second signal tower in Monongahela. The Pennsylvania Railroad was founded in 1846 and was often referred to as the "Pennsy." Headquartered in Philadelphia, it was the largest railroad in the United States for the first half of the 20th century and at its peak controlled nearly 10,000 miles of rail.

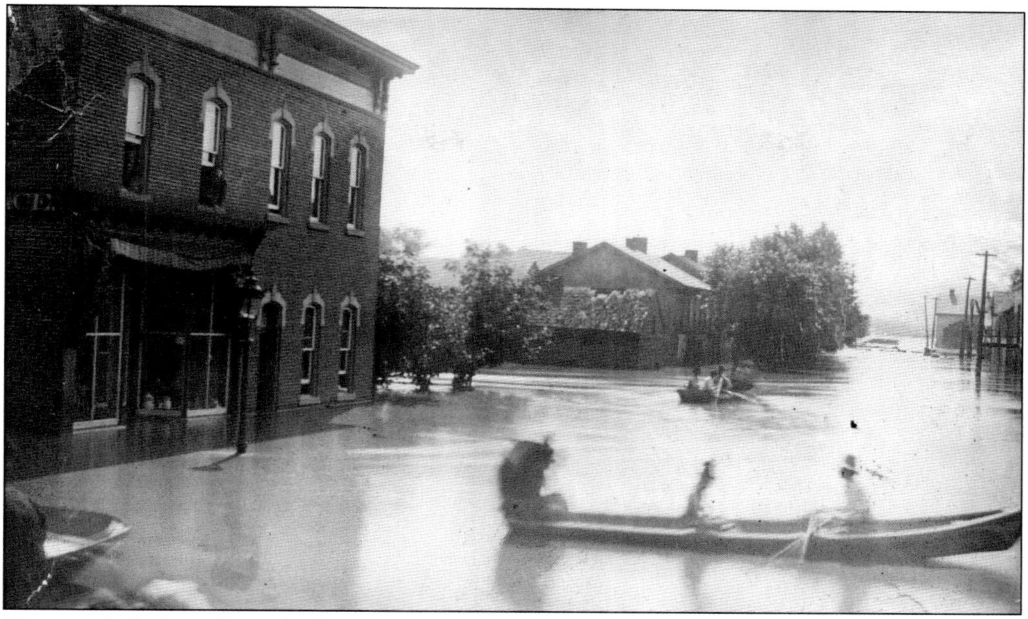

Monongahela has always had its share of flooding. This photograph shows one of the earliest ones, on July 10, 1885, near the corner of Park Avenue on First and Main Streets. An old log house stood where Hotel Main was later built. Rescuers in boats were coming to the aid of the trapped residents, like the man in the second-story window.

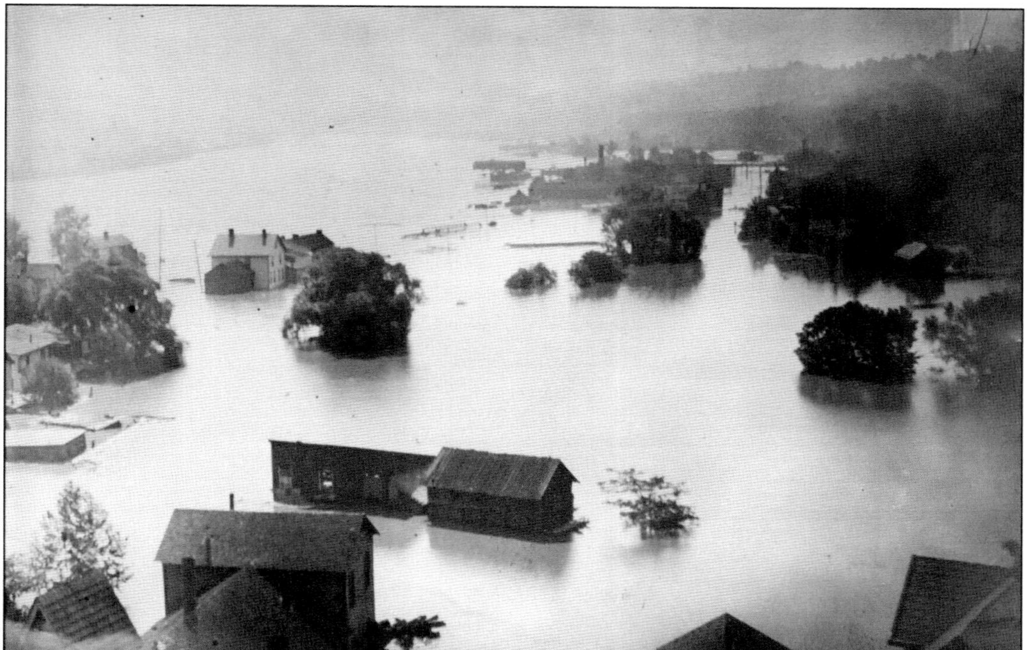

This is the flood of 1885. The photographer may have captured this panorama by standing on the bridge, taking a photograph looking toward the south. In the distance, only the top of the Pigeon Creek bridge and the old railroad bridge are visible.

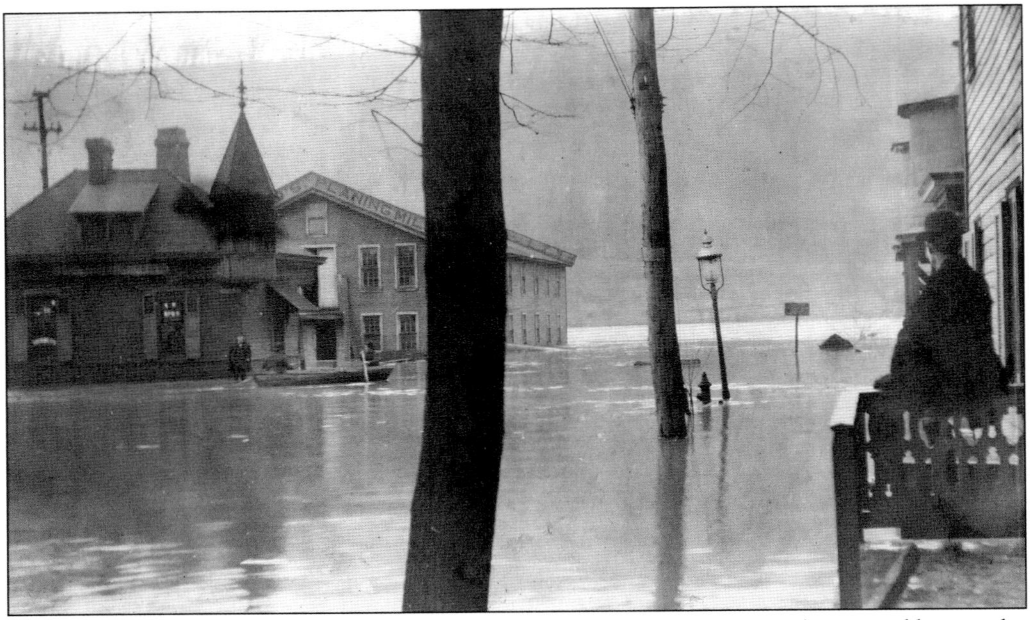

The flood of March 1907 was one of many devastating floods that occurred. Pictured here is the high water scene at Fourth and Railroad Streets. The man sitting on the porch on the right seems to be looking longingly toward the planing mill shown on the left hand side of the photograph, where two men in a canoe may be stopping to pick up a passenger. The water doesn't seem to be quite up to his knees.

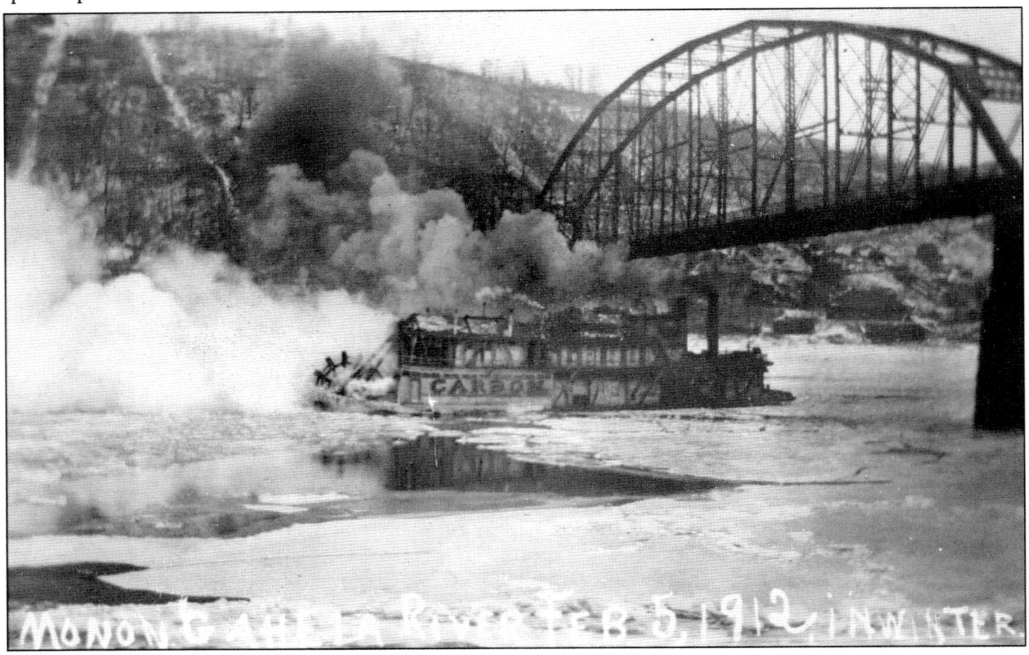

This photograph shows the steamboat *Carbon*, preparing to pass under the Monongahela bridge as it traverses an icy river on February 5, 1912. This boat was able to pass under the Monongahela bridge easily. The steam generated as the paddle wheel in the back of the boat moves through the water is clearly visible, as is the smoke billowing from the boat's stacks. It was always exciting when a boat passed by on the river.

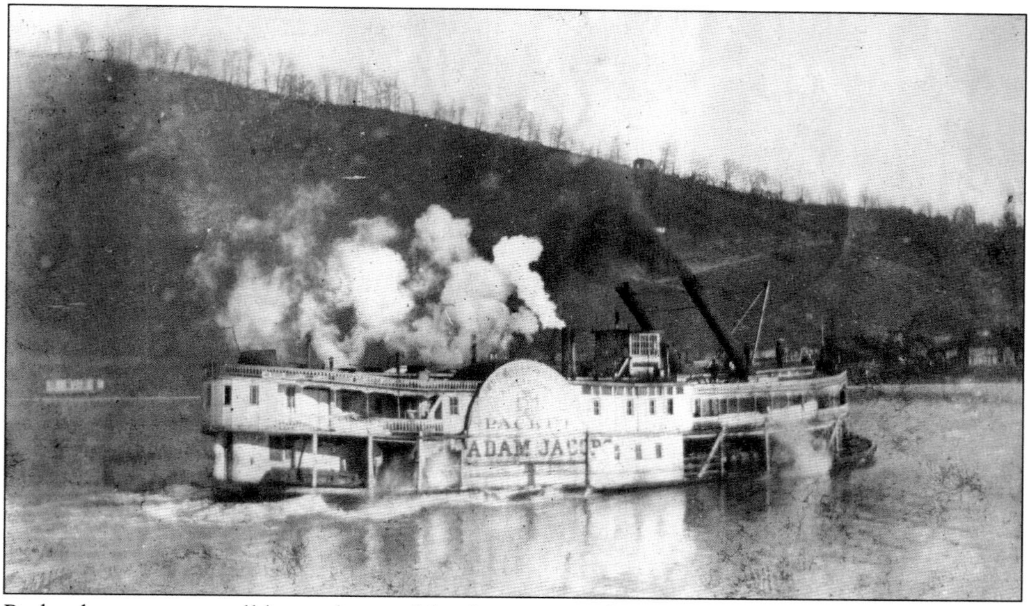

Packet boats were small boats designed for domestic mail, passenger, and freight transportation in the United States along rivers and canals. Packet boat No. 3, *Adam Jacobs*, is shown in 1900 traveling up the Monongahela River and preparing to pass under the bridge. This boat was an engineering marvel, as it was designed to let the crew lower the smokestacks to pass under the bridge. Capt. Adam Jacobs commanded several packets and built 125 steamboats.

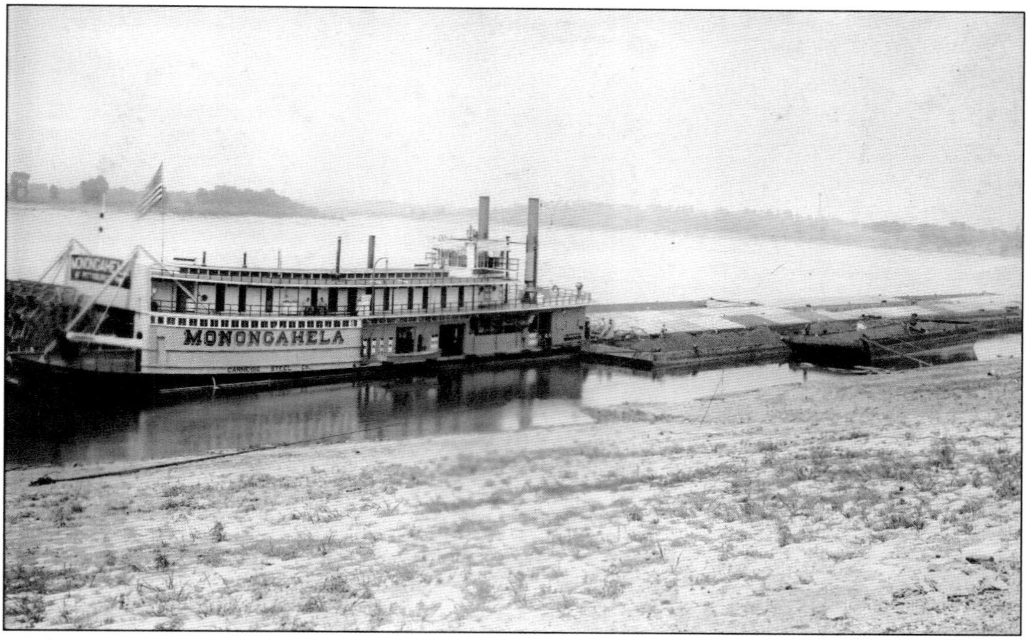

Towboats played an important role in the development of the communities along the Monongahela River, carrying resources along the rivers. Coal was needed first for home heating and then for industry, and due to the volume being shipped up and down the rivers, it was necessary to build locks and dams to make the rivers more navigable. Shown here is the towboat *Monongahela*, owned by Carnegie Steel, an Andrew Carnegie company. In the rear of the towboat, men with shovels and wheelbarrows are visible, apparently unloading the towboat.

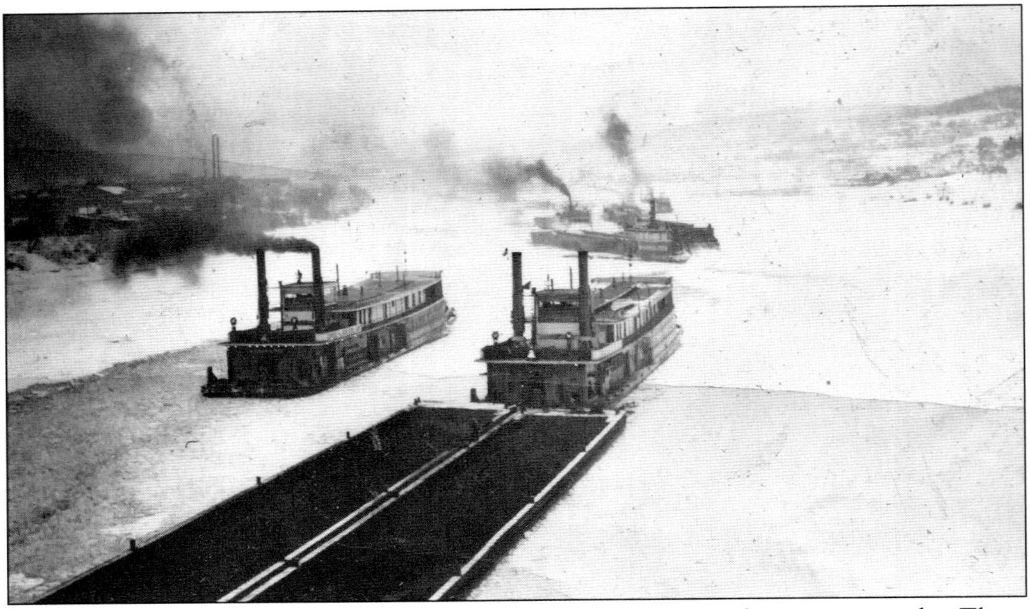

The Monongahela River could be extremely treacherous during the winter months. These excerpts were taken from a captain's journal describing the conditions, kept from December 22, 1909, to January 30, 1910: "The river froze so full of ice the boats are wearing their wheels out faster than we can repair them. Working all night, wetting resulted in death of Steve Howard. Ice broke up Monday, January 3, 1910 and the river was up twenty-two feet. Snow and drizzling rain all day Christmas."

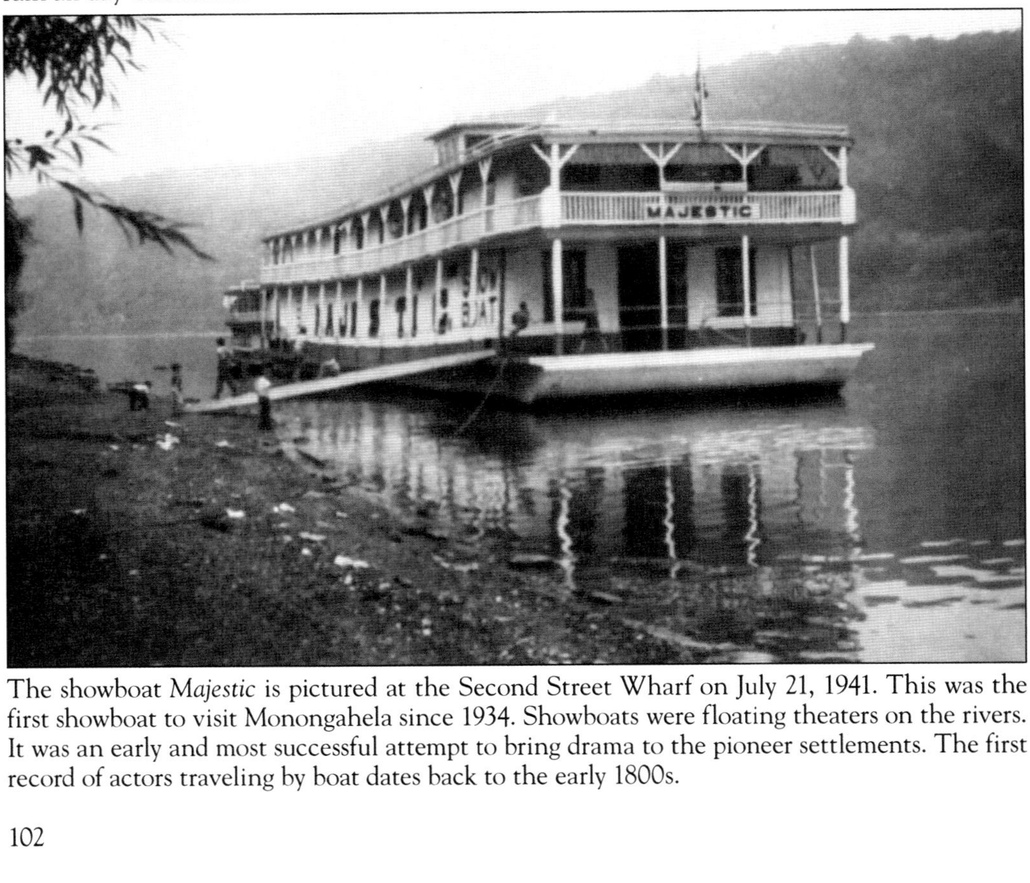

The showboat *Majestic* is pictured at the Second Street Wharf on July 21, 1941. This was the first showboat to visit Monongahela since 1934. Showboats were floating theaters on the rivers. It was an early and most successful attempt to bring drama to the pioneer settlements. The first record of actors traveling by boat dates back to the early 1800s.

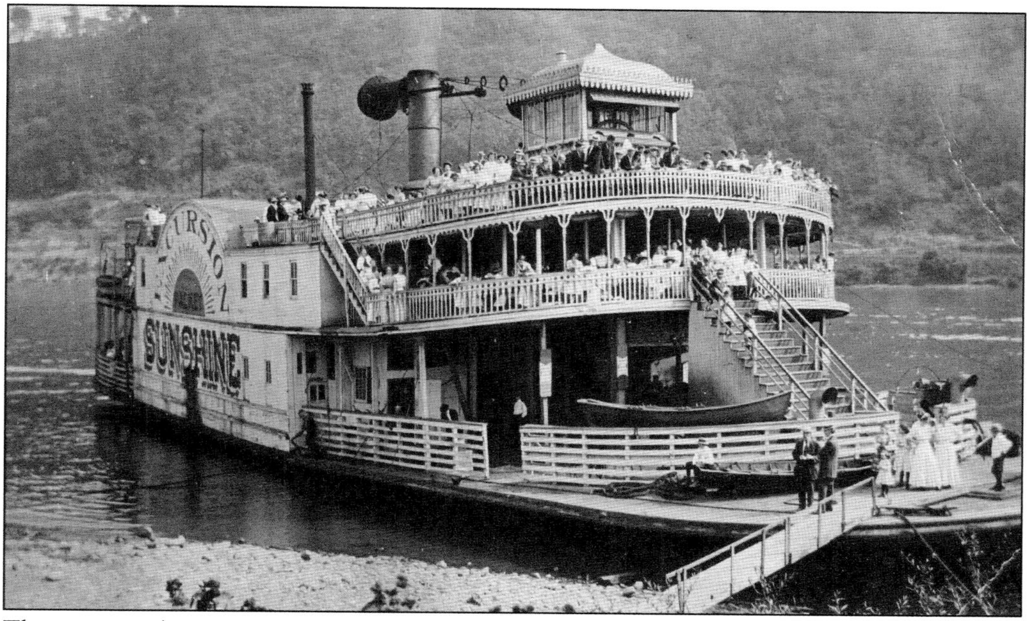

The excursion boat *Sunshine* is seen arriving at the Second Street Wharf. The boat was launched in 1888 in Jeffersonville, Indiana, by Howard Yard. In 1907–1908, the boat went to Pittsburgh on excursions up and down the surrounding rivers, such as the Monongahela.

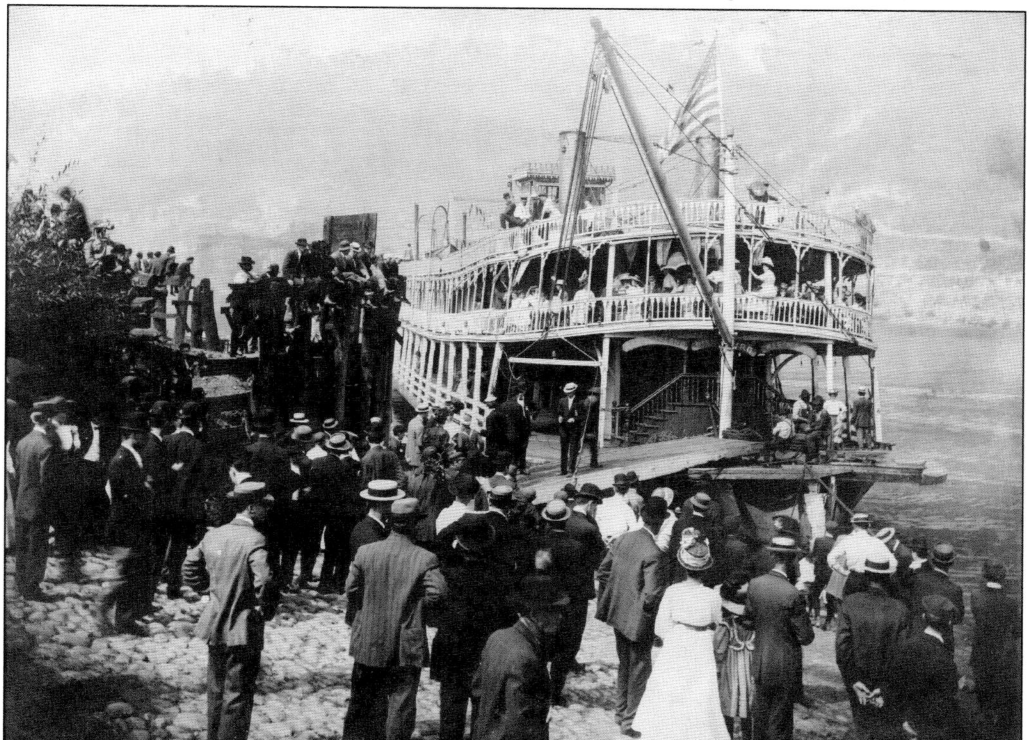

This photograph depicts an excursion boat docked at the Second Street Wharf during Old Home Week celebration, September 8–13, 1908. This type of excursion boat, which is a passenger boat, was popular during this time and a familiar sight traveling the river.

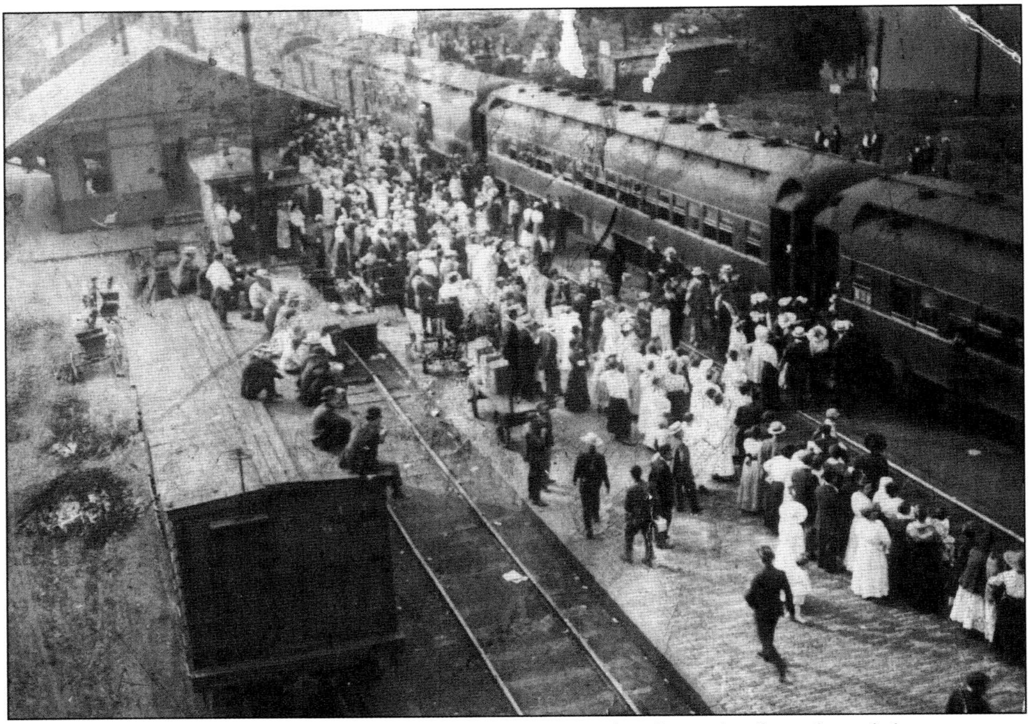

This scene depicts the farewell to World War I troops as they leave for duty aboard the passenger train at the Second Street railroad depot. This photograph was taken by a member of the Renk family. Mother Catherine is holding baby John Hearn Renk. They are near the center of the image. (Courtesy the Renk family.)

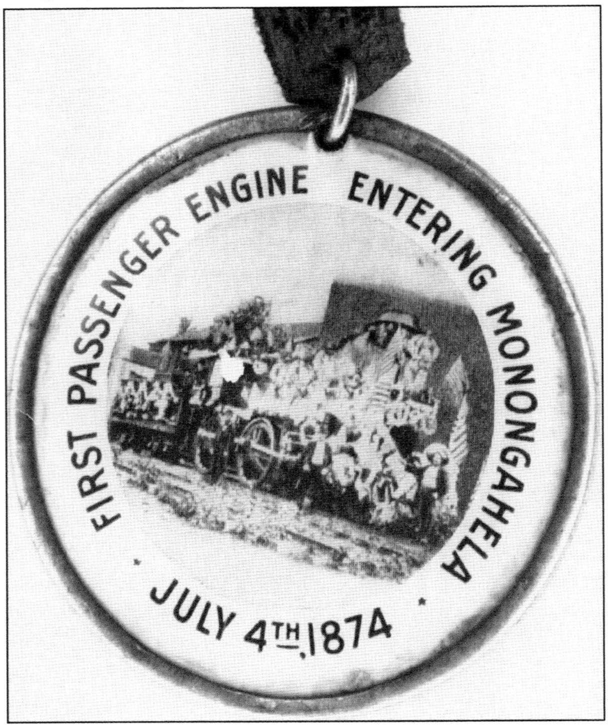

This medallion was handed out as a souvenir to commemorate the first passenger train entering Monongahela on July 4, 1874. This was a huge day in the city's history, and the engine and people riding it are decorated quite festively. The arrival of passenger trains really changed people's lives and made it possible for them to work in other places, visit friends and relatives who moved away, and travel on land to other parts of the country.

Eight

SALT OF THE EARTH

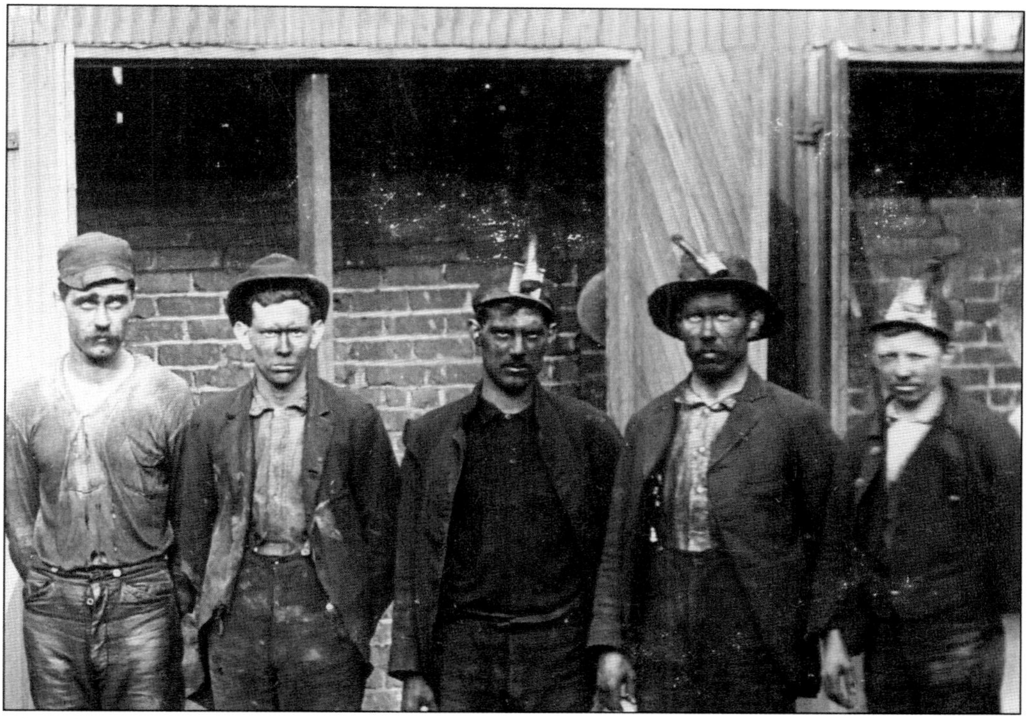

This photograph was taken at the rear section of Ella Mine of Sunnyside. The five miners are wearing Anton pit lamps, invented and manufactured by the Anton brothers of Monongahela. These lamps were sold worldwide and are collectibles today. Miners labored long hours and did exhausting work. Their contributions helped lead the country to its greatness and prosperity. (Courtesy scrapbook of Potente Zanardelli.)

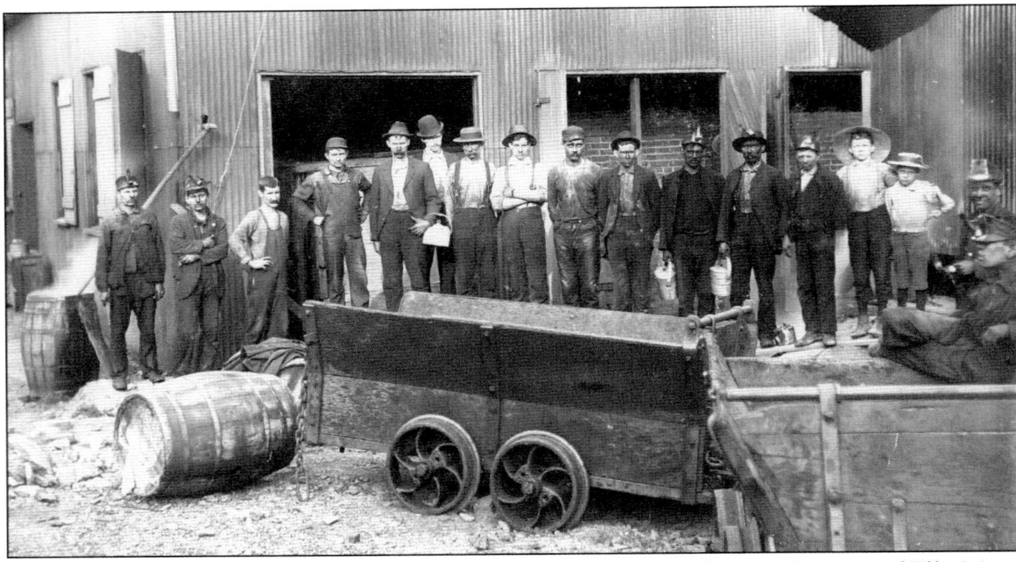

This photograph depicts a group of mine workers in 1898 standing at the rear of Ella Mine, which was across the river in Sunnyside. The mine was a division of Pennsylvania and Lake Erie Railroad in Allegheny County. The miners are listed as follows: Stricklin, T. Stricklin, Eicher, Morris, Hill, J. McMahon, Irwin, William McMahan, B. Gillingham, Mathews, Dyas, Wall, Rue boys, H. Gillingham, and Hamilton. (Courtesy scrapbook of Potente Zanardelli.)

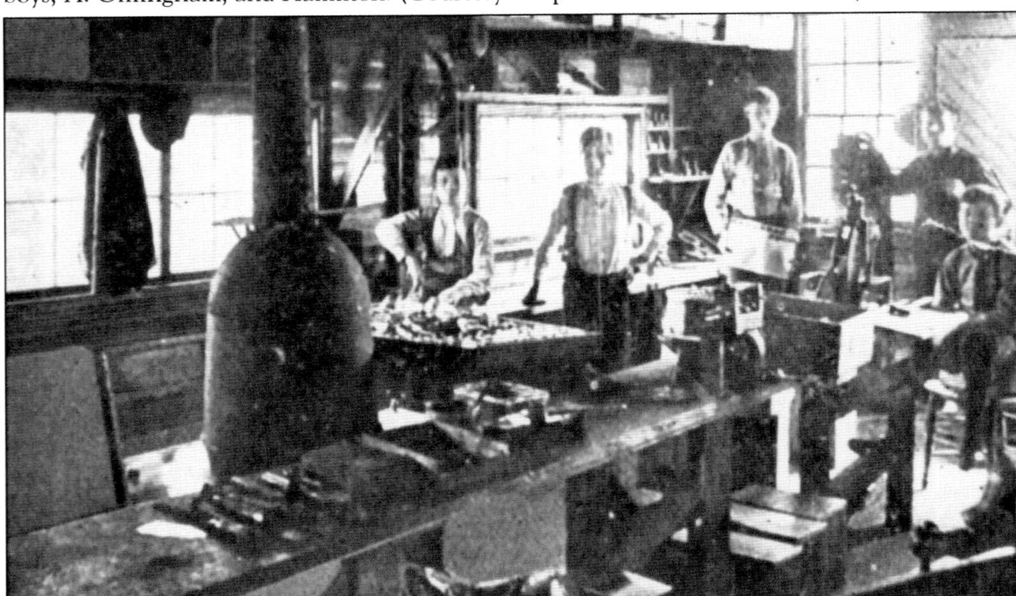

Edward Goodrich Acheson received the patent for Carborundum in 1893, and with funding from Mellon Bank, he established the Carborundum Company in Monongahela City in 1894. The interior of the plant is shown here, and it produced grinding wheels, whetstones, knife sharpeners, and powdered abrasives. The plant was located near the Monongahela River at Seventh Street. In 1926, the US Patent Office named Carborundum as one of the 22 patents most responsible for the industrial age. Later, it was said that without Carborundum, the mass production of precision-ground, interchangeable metal parts would be practically impossible.

Pictured is cemetery superintendent Adam Aughendobler during the late 1800s. Born in Germany in 1823, he came to America in 1852 after a voyage of seven weeks and landed in Baltimore, Maryland. After coming to Washington County, Adam worked for Maj. William S. Mellinger and James Stockdale. From 1865, shortly after coming to Monongahela, until a short time before his death, he served as superintendent of the cemetery.

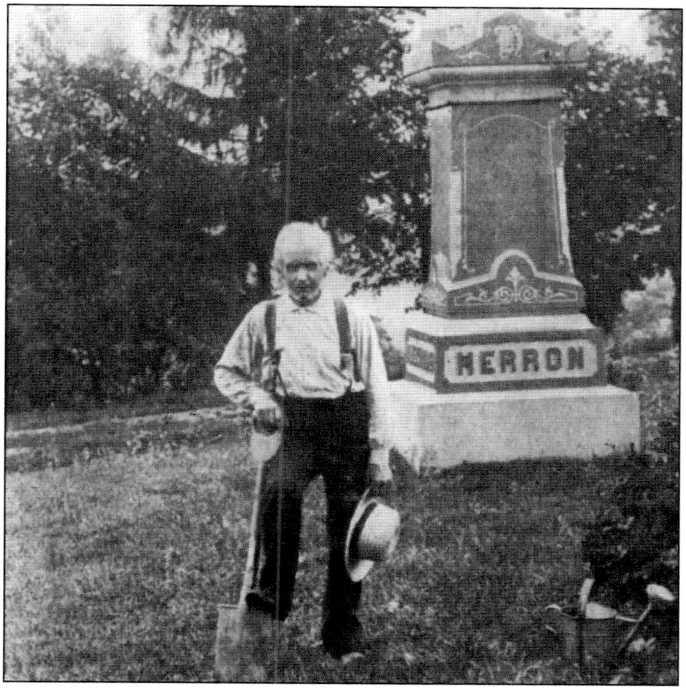

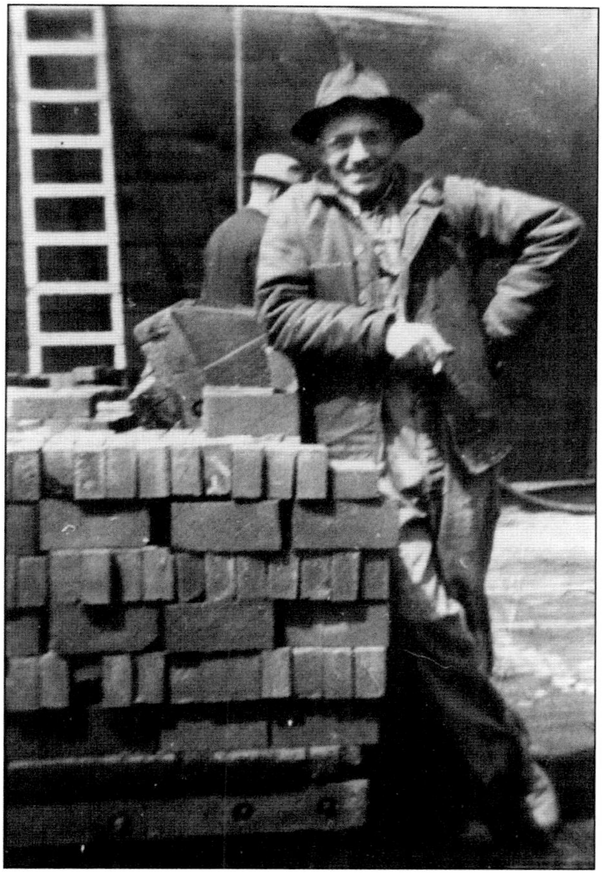

The brickyard worker in this photograph smiles as he takes a break from the very labor-intensive work involved with making red clay bricks; he had a very difficult job, making individual bricks and preparing each one to be fired. There are several steps involved, but a brick maker with an assistant might make 5,000 bricks a day. A modest home may require 20,000 bricks, and the grand homes being built in Monongahela would have required far more than that. The brickyard worker was obviously very busy.

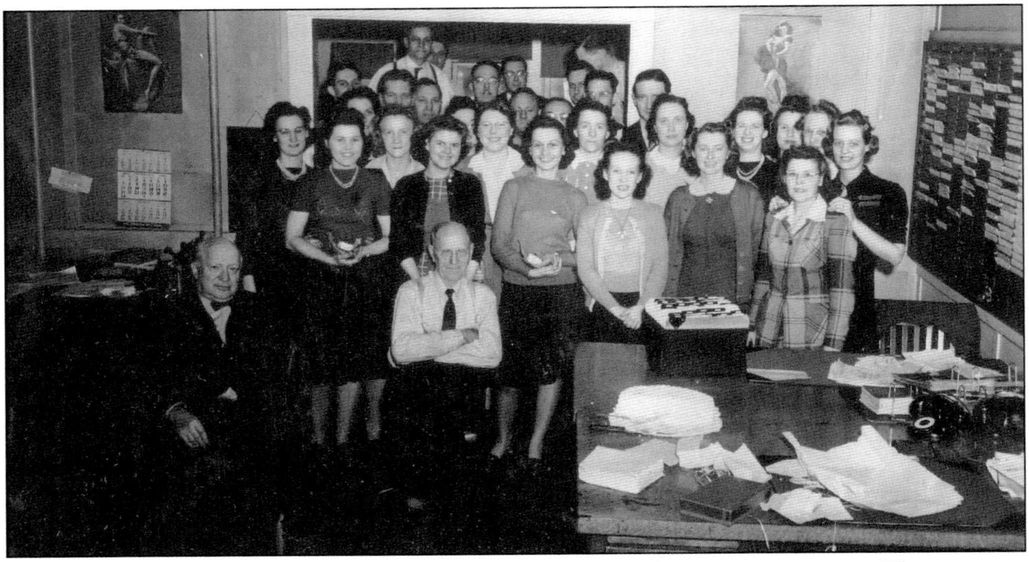

Pictured on February 12, 1943, are the office workers of Combustion Engineering. The two men sitting in front are J.S. Skelly (left) and J.E. Wagoner. The women include, in no particular order, Aline Santini, Helen Barkus, Harriet Williams, Jean Metzger, Marion Hagdern, Elizabeth Polaski, Hazel Myers, Dorothy Atkins, Thelma Rae, Dorothy Abbott, June Day, Helen Toth, Dolores Davis, Esther Leyda, and Francis Carson.

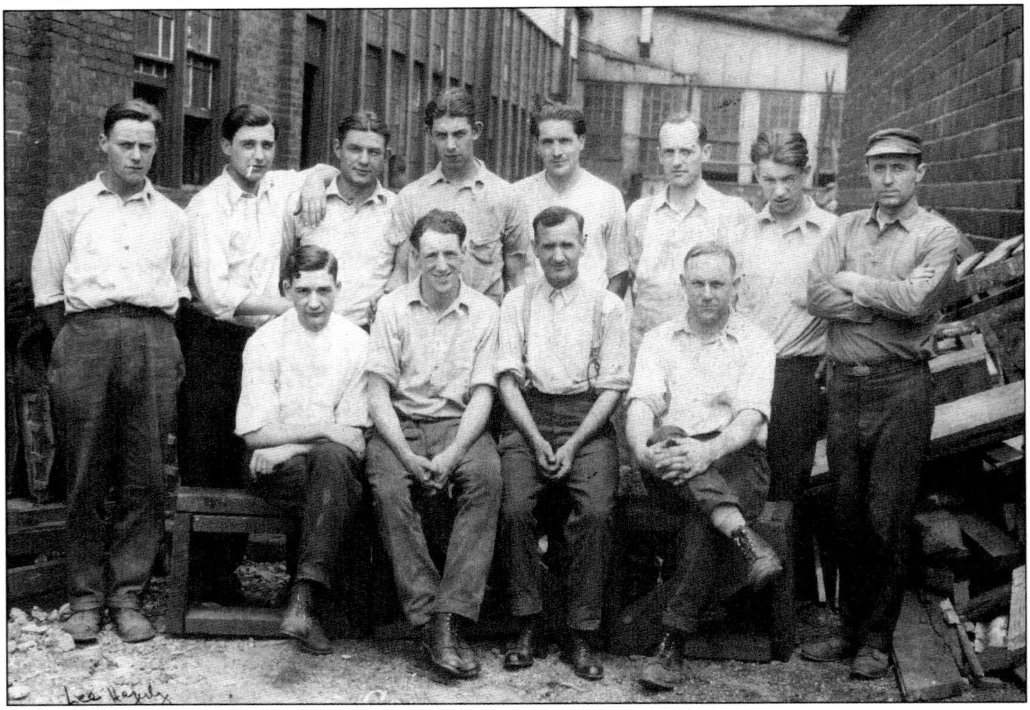

This photograph was taken of the pattern workers at the Coshocton Iron Works, which was once a part of the Liggett Spring and Axle Company that moved from Pittsburgh to an area across the river from Monongahela in 1903. It manufactured buggy springs and axles. With the shift to automobiles, the axle plant separated from the foundry and became Coshocton Iron Works, which manufactured parts for stoker furnaces. It later combined with Combustion Engineering.

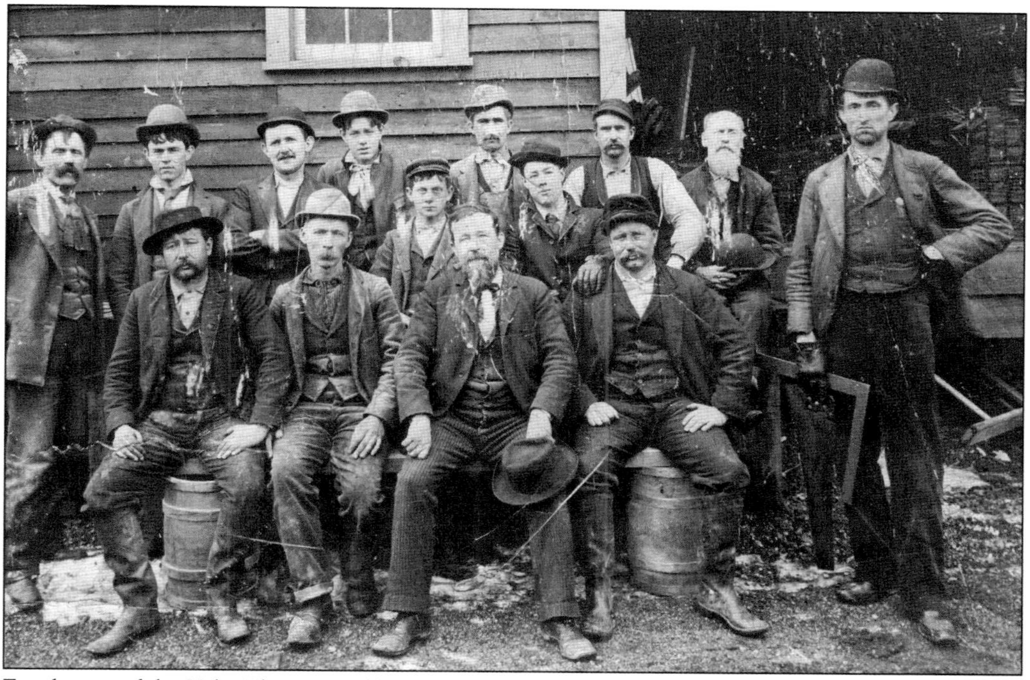

Employees of the Yohe Planing Mill are pictured in this 1893 photograph. The Yohe Planing Mill stood on the site where the first boats were built in Monongahela City. It was both a lumberyard and planing mill. The business was established in November 1880. The planing mill was two stories in height and filled with the latest types of machinery.

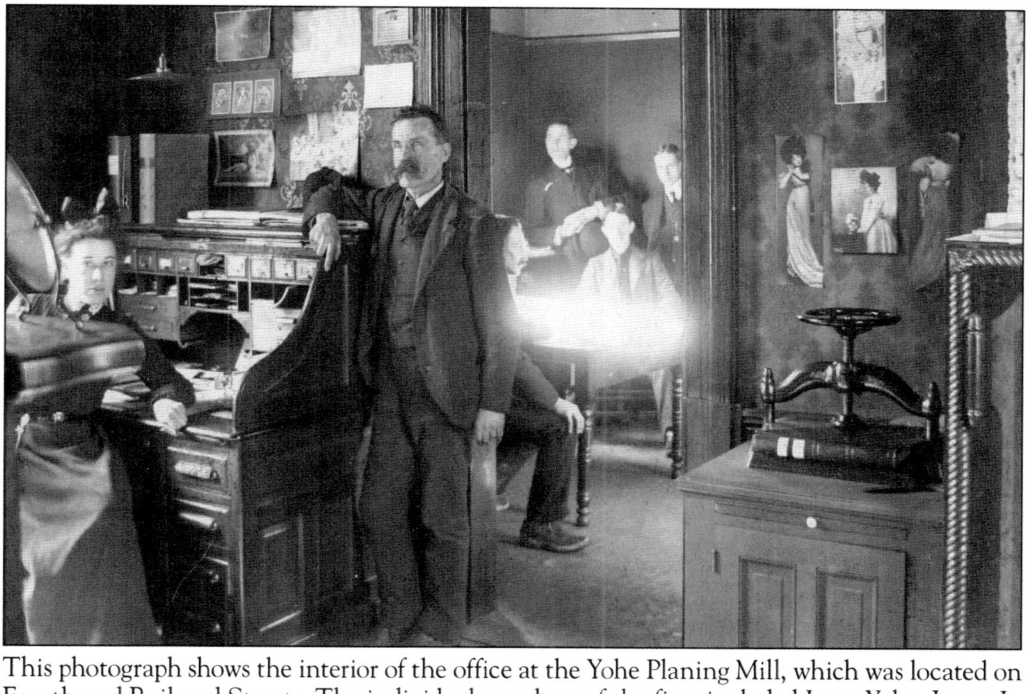

This photograph shows the interior of the office at the Yohe Planing Mill, which was located on Fourth and Railroad Streets. The individual members of the firm included Isaac Yohe, James L. Yohe, Lewis N. Yohe, and Edwin Corrin. The business was established in 1880 under the name of Yohe, Carson & Company.

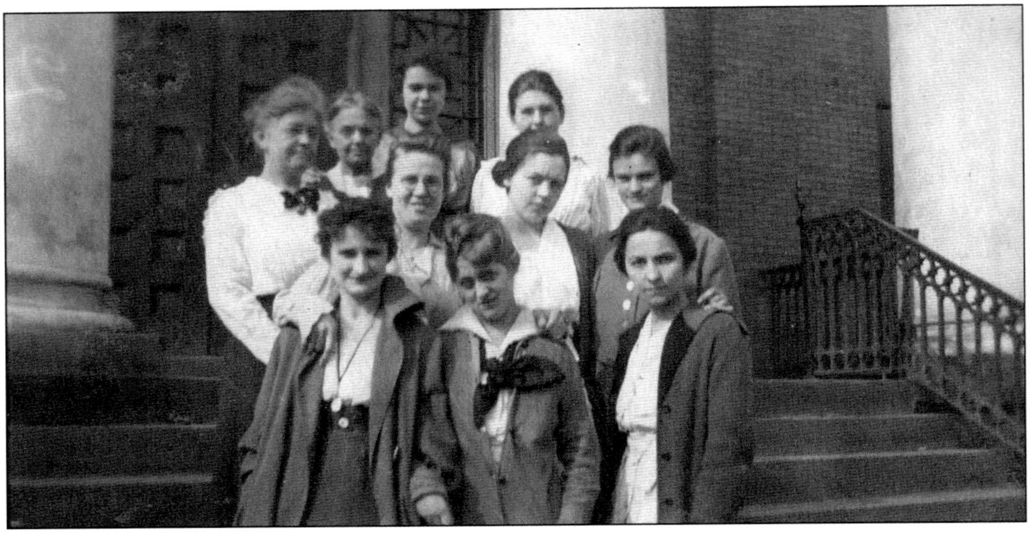

The First Ward school building was erected in 1896 on one of the most picturesque sites in Monongahela. It contained eight recitation rooms, an office, and a teacher's room. The school name was changed to Williams School in 1917. This photograph shows an early group of faculty. The success of the students can often be related to the caliber of teachers, and Monongahela always had excellent teachers in a public school system that leveled the playing field for everyone. Many of the teachers received their education at the California Normal School.

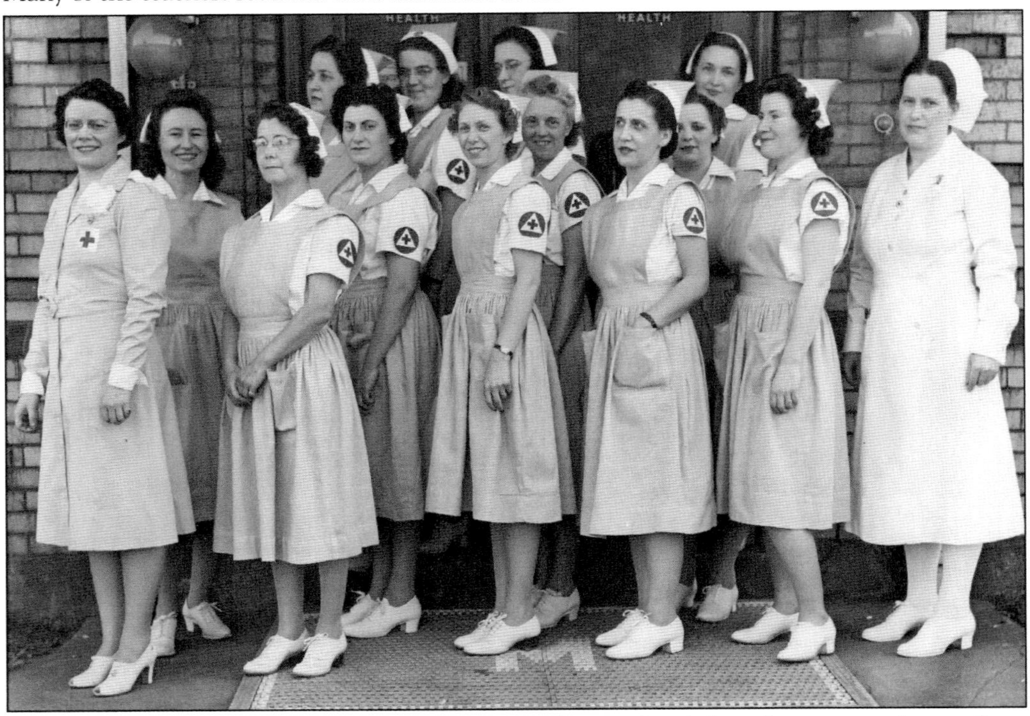

The uniformed ladies in the photograph were part of a nurse's aid class; they are standing in front of the Memorial Hospital in Monongahela on April 30, 1942. In the photograph are, from left to right, (first row) Anne Caldwell, Goldie Patterson, Mira Oppenheim, Ruth Van Dyke, Ellen Anders, and Agnes Zelenak; (second row) Margaret Jones, Toni Vaira, Dorali Rider, and Miriam Scott; (third row) two unidentified, Helen Langendorf, and Leah Tyson.

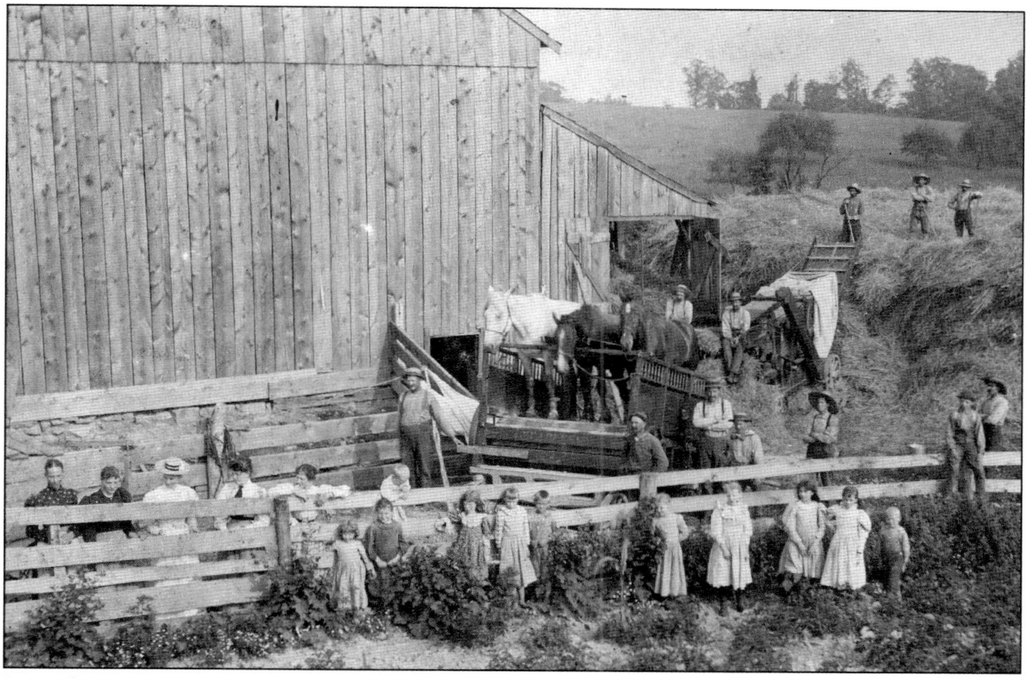

It was harvest time on the farm, and everyone was ready to work. This photograph was taken on the Jack Fisher farm in 1902. The entire area is now known as Fisher Heights in Monongahela. A three-horse treadmill is being used to furnish the power needed to run the thrashing machine. Men, women, and children all helped harvest the crops.

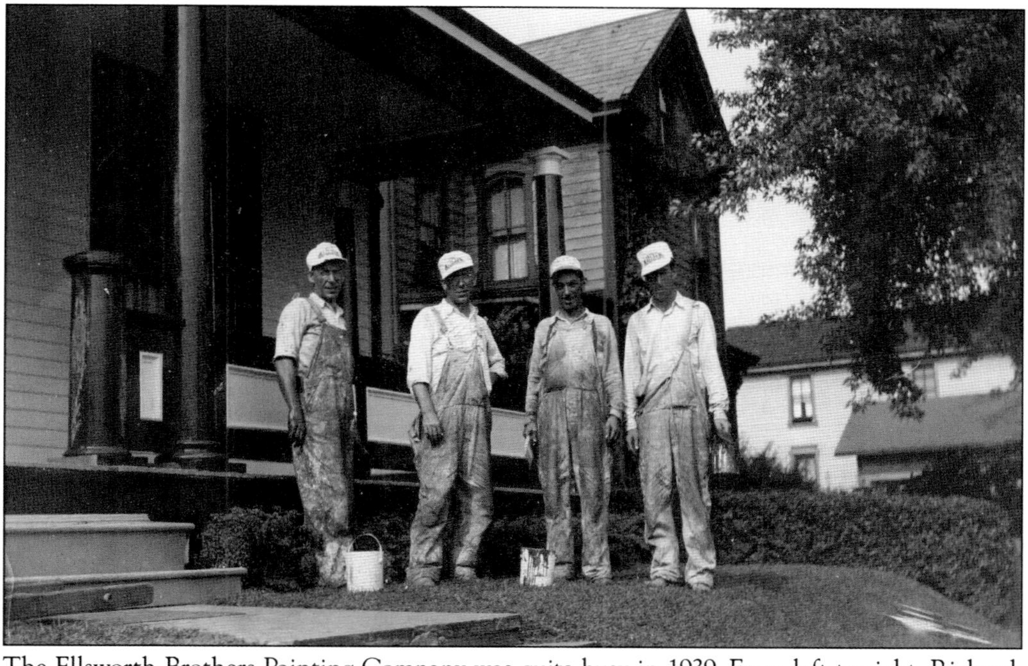

The Ellsworth Brothers Painting Company was quite busy in 1939. From left to right, Richard, James, Michael, and Edward take a break from painting at the home of William and Dora Turri, which was located on Fourth and Sherman Streets. Skilled laborers took great pride in their work and contributed to the growth and progress of the city. (Courtesy scrapbook of Potente Zanardelli.)

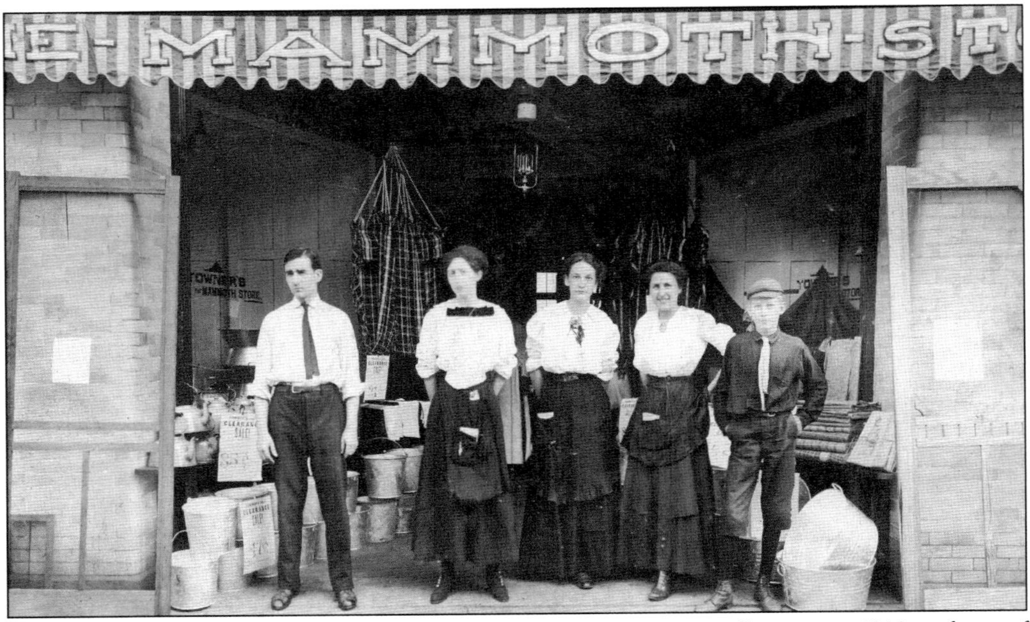

Workers from the Towners Department Store on Main Street proudly pose in 1910 in front of the store. The store was established in 1897 in the Towner Building in Monongahela. The store's advertisement stated that it had the largest stock of dry goods, carpets, wallpaper, millinery, ladies' ready-to-wear, and furnishings goods in the upper Monongahela Valley. It also boasted, "Towners Never Has Been Undersold!"

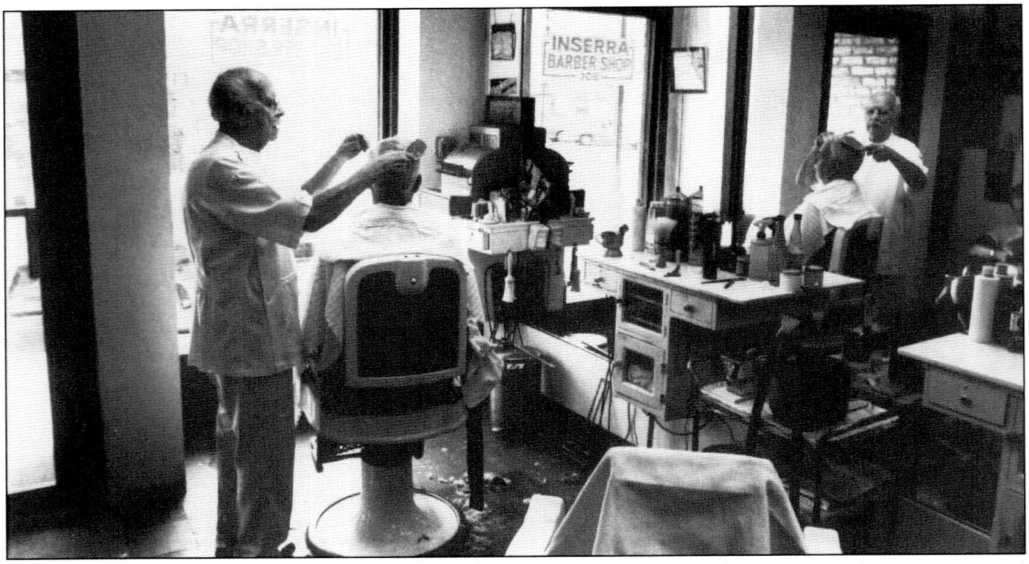

Shown here is Paul "Sho Sho" Inserra in his Main Street shop. Because of the exceptional quality of the photograph, the tools of his trade are exceptionally clear, and, with a reflection in the mirror, the shop name and street number are visible. It appears that Inserra has a mirror angled toward Main Street, perhaps so he can see what is happening outside. Over the manual cash register is a sign reading "Steelers Drive for Five," so the photograph was taken after 1980, when the Pittsburgh Steelers won their fourth Super Bowl trophy. One can only imagine how many sports conversations occurred in Sho Sho's shop. (Courtesy Patricia Inserra Allison and Paul Henry Inserra.)

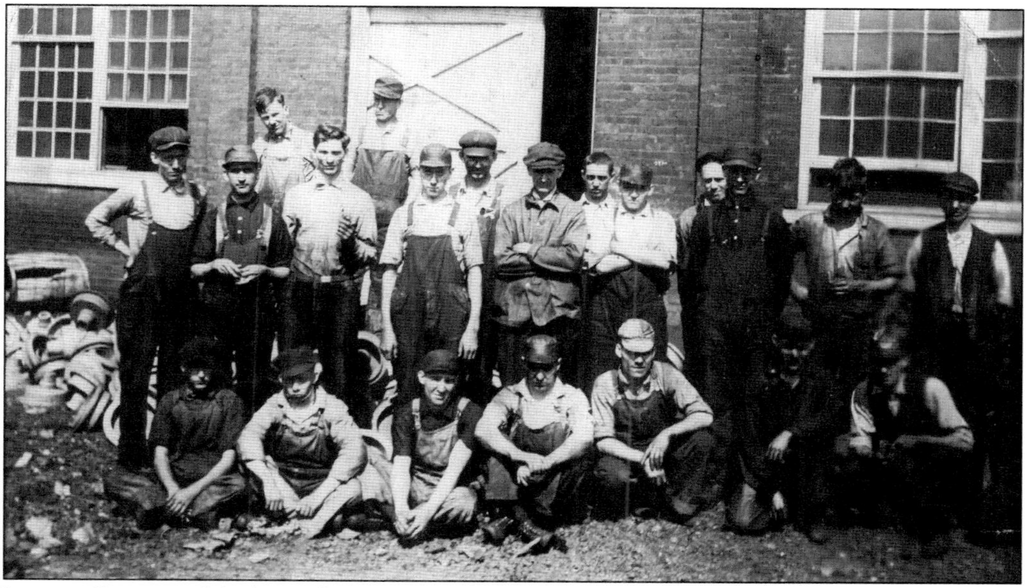

Liggetts Spring and Axle Works employees are pictured here. This plant was located in Axleton, in Allegheny County, across the Monongahela River. In 1903, it moved from Pittsburgh's North Side and built a factory to manufacture buggy springs and axles. To provide raw materials for the plant, the owners also constructed an adjoining foundry to supply castings. Many men from the surrounding towns were employed there until it burned.

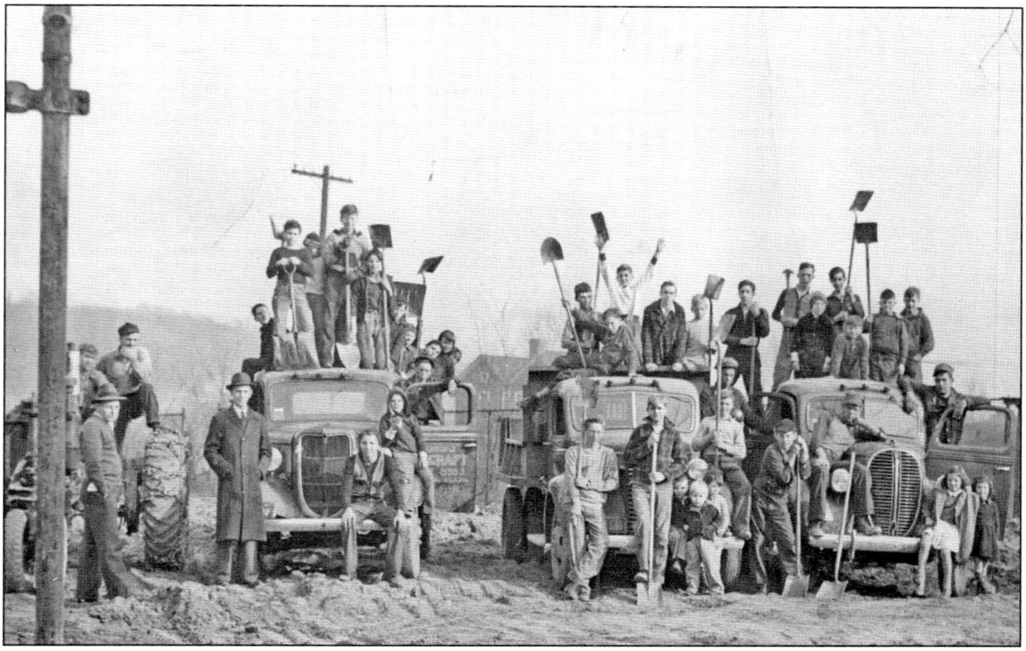

This photograph depicts what motivated people—mostly youth—can accomplish. A group of youth with the help of some adults picked up their shovels and went to work at the top of the hill between Third and Jackson Streets, where the old graveyard was located. This photograph was taken in November 1941, when the project to excavate an ice skating pond was started. The project was finished in 1949, likely due to the priorities of World War II. Harry J. Ashcraft and his trucks were on hand to haul away dirt. (Photograph by Floyd France.)

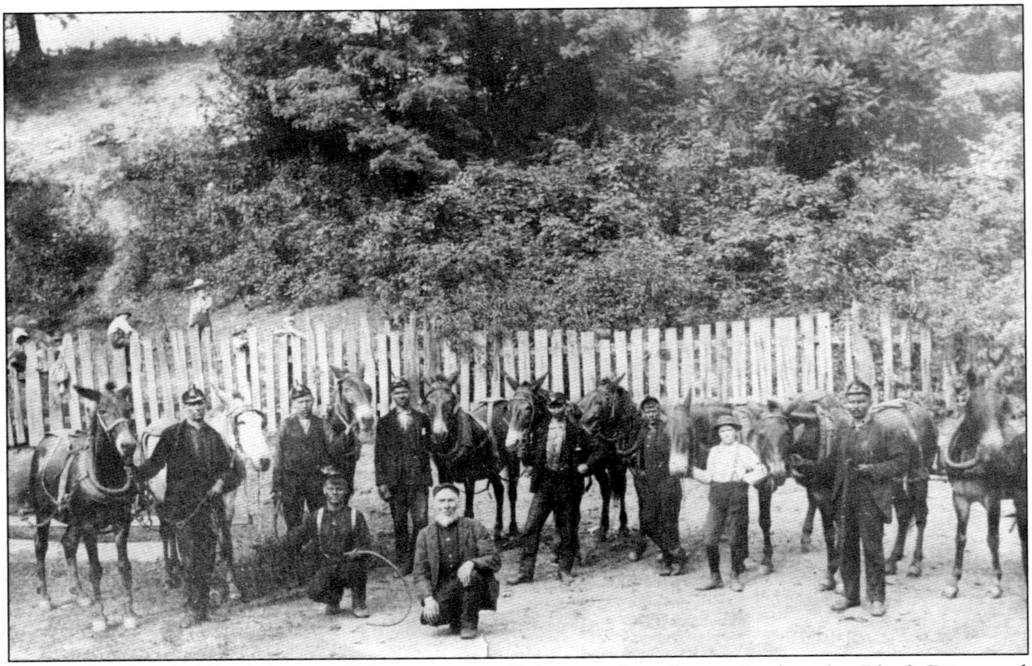

This photograph shows many of the miners and their mules who worked at the Black Diamond Mine in Monongahela. This picture was taken in 1889. The mine was started in 1869 by the first owner, the Black Diamond Coal and Mining Company. The mine was located in the coal-patch on the Pennsylvania Railroad along the Monongahela River.

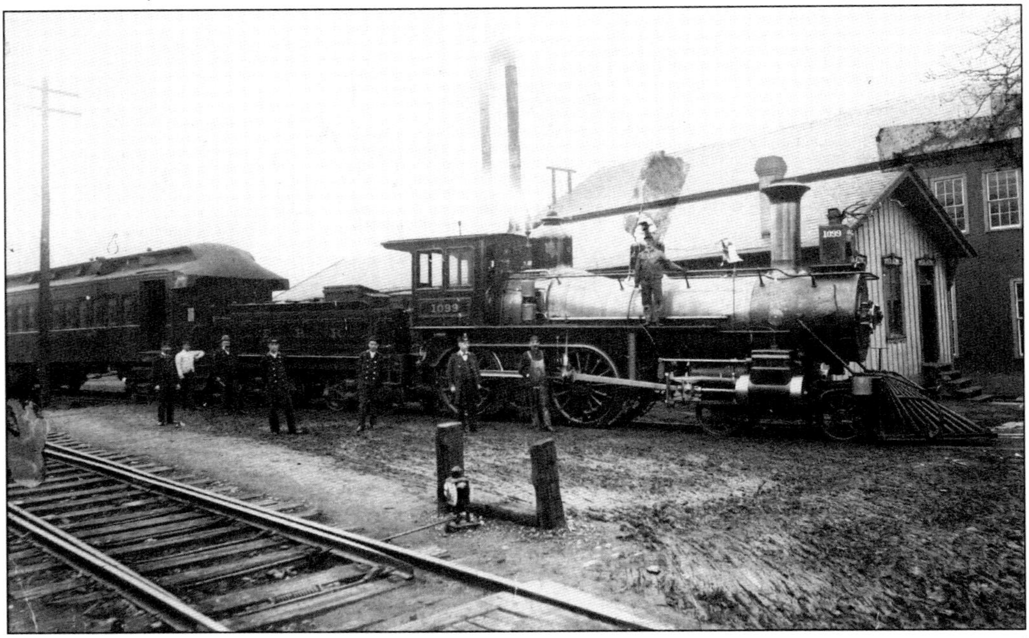

The railroad played an important part in Monongahela since its inception. Trains were used to not only transport coal, goods, and animals, but people as well. This photograph depicts the old passenger train and crew at Second Street. Edward G. Acheson's old Carborundum plant is visible in the background. Many town residents still remember riding the passenger train to Kennywood on Community Day.

Nine

For the Good of All

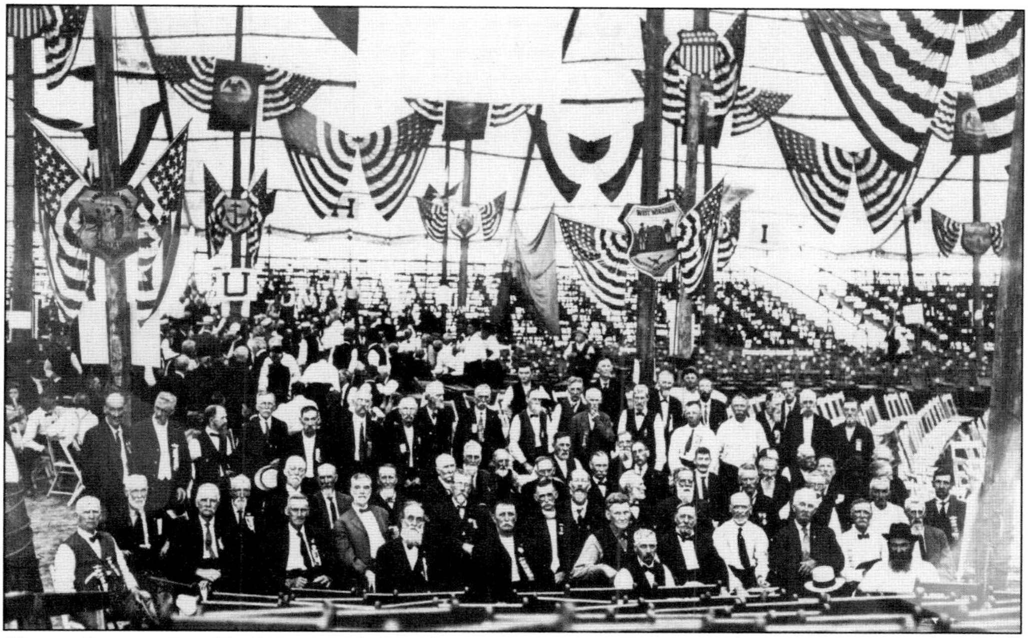

Shown here is the 22nd Ringgold Cavalry in a reunion photograph of the 50th anniversary of the battle of Gettysburg, which was held in 1913. Many members came from the Monongahela area. In a letter dated January 6, 1963, C.W. Griffith, principal of the Fallowfield School and a former Monongahela resident, suggested the newly merging Ringgold School District's name by taking the *R* from Carroll Township, the *I* from Union Township, the *N* from New Eagle, the G from Monongahela, the O from Nottingham Township, the *L* from Finleyville, and the *D* from Donora. A second G was added to match the cavalry's name.

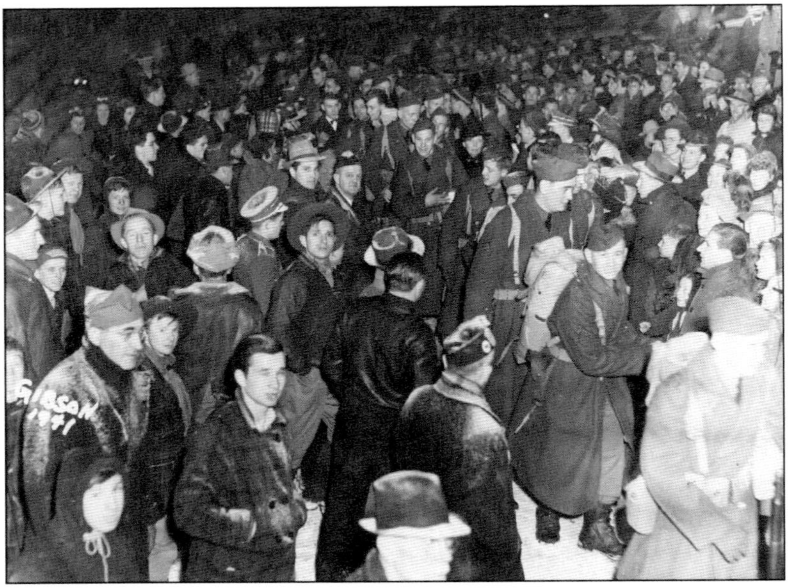

Company A is leaving for Indiantown Gap on February 27, 1941. The town turned out en masse at the Penn Railroad Station on a bitterly cold and snowy night to send the troops off knowing they had the full support and gratitude of their hometown.

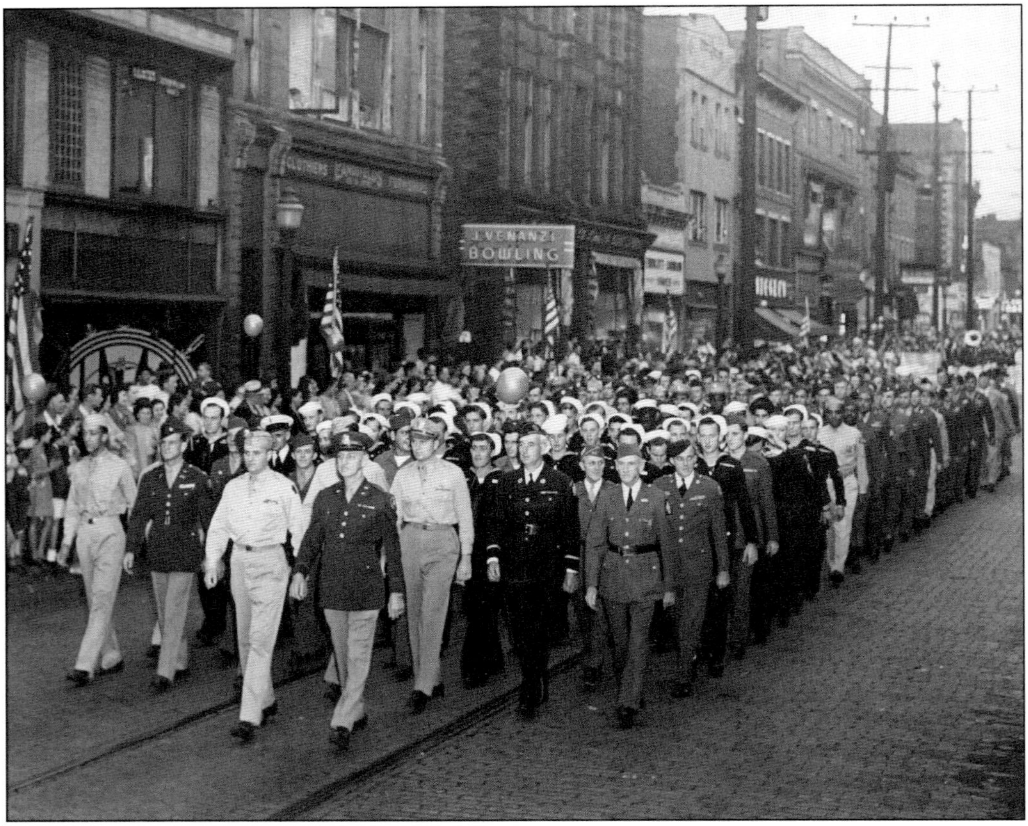

This parade was the first V-J Day parade in Monongahela, held in August 1946. V-J Day (Victory over Japan) was also known as Victory in the Pacific Day and was the name chosen for the day on which the surrender of Japan occurred, effectively ending World War II. The official US commemoration is September 2. Monongahela's pride was shown by the city's attendance to welcome home its heroes.

John Holland was the first mayor of Monongahela City in 1874. He also served as mayor in 1878, 1881, 1888, and 1891. He was a soldier of Company D of the original Ringgold Cavalry, postmaster, member of Post 60 GAR, and a burgess. As a resident, he was for the betterment of the community and worked tirelessly his whole life to make the town grow.

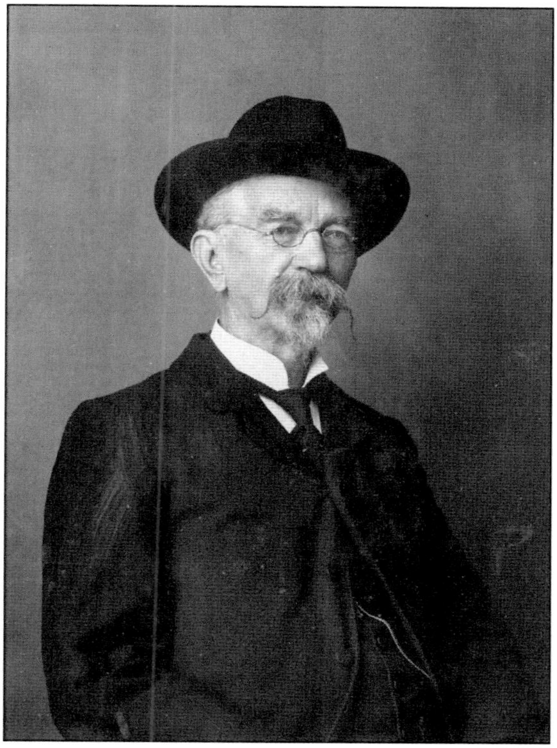

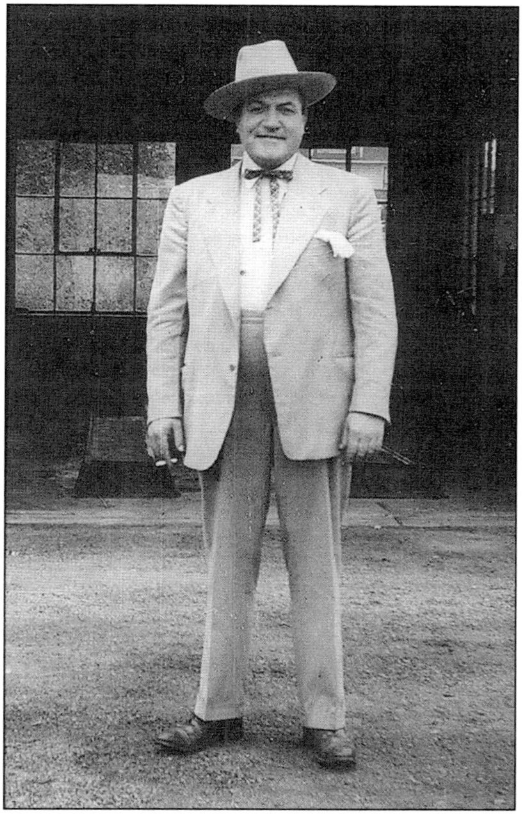

William B. Hill, a progressive mayor, was first elected in 1955. Mayor Hill was responsible for the municipal parking lot, street improvements, and the relocation of Route 88, which eliminated the dangerous conditions of Cemetery Hill. In the election of 1963, he suffered an upset in the primary. In November, his popularity was evident, and it was Hill who caused the upset, winning as a write-in candidate. His generosity and Stetson hat are long remembered.

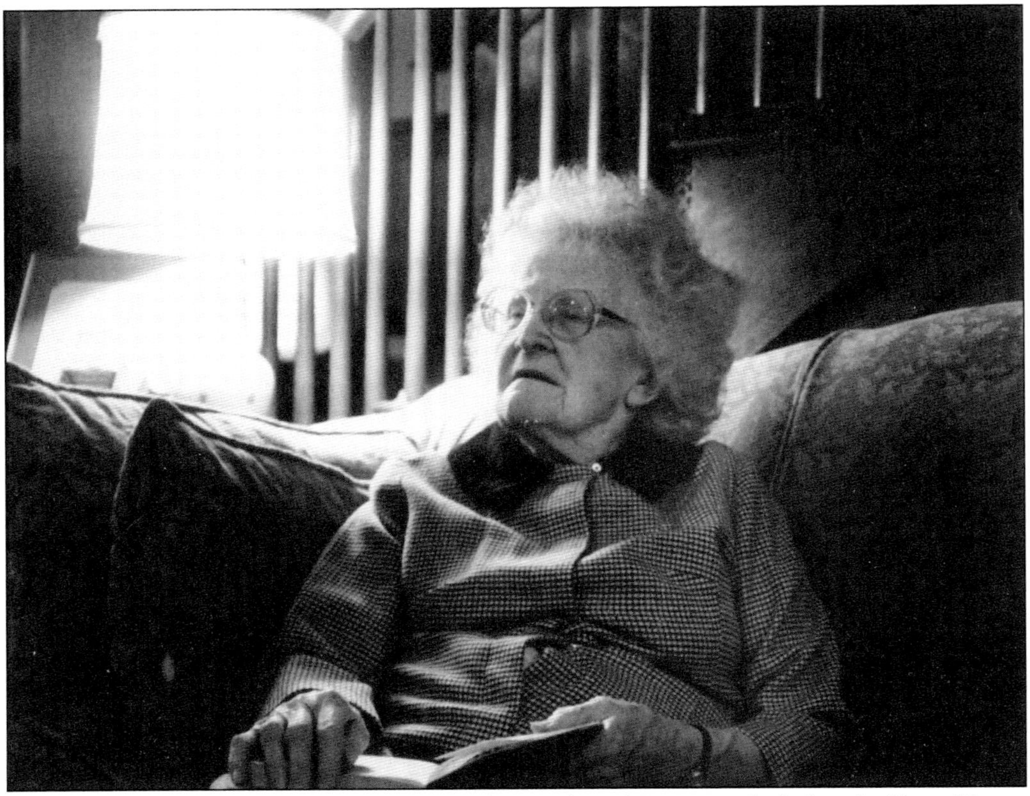

Dr. Josephine Stephens offered her services to the British Red Cross months before the United States plunged into war. She was one of 10 women doctors accepted in the United States. Dr. Stephens was made a contract surgeon and was one of three with the American forces in the European theater of operations, all first lieutenants. After the war, she returned home to Monongahela and for many years engaged in her career as a doctor. She truly was a pioneer for women.

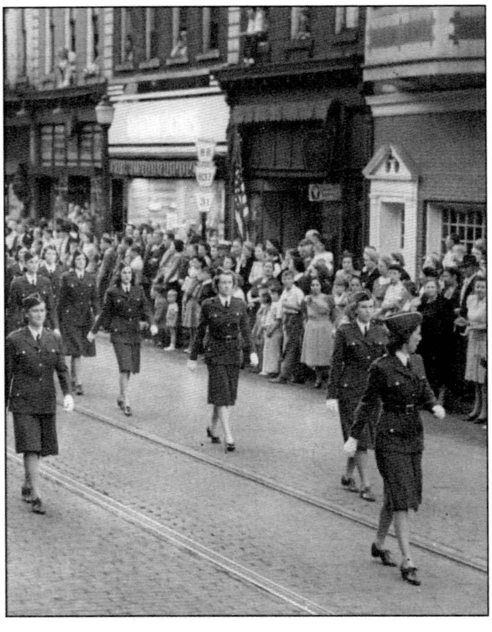

Military leaders were reluctant to integrate women into the military, believing a woman's place was in the home. With the attack on Pearl Harbor on December 7, 1941, the manpower crisis increased, and the military realized that incorporating women in some capacities could free men for combat. Thus the WAAC bill was passed in Congress on March 13, 1941. In step with the country's direction, the Women's Defense Corps of Monongahela was mobilized, and it marched in a parade on June 15, 1942, led by Capt. Marion "Murphy" Munce.

Giulio "Julio" Vazzana was a fixture at Western Pennsylvania National Bank, located at the corner of Fourth and Main Streets. A man-about-town, Julio proudly wore his World War I uniform. In this photograph, which hung in the bank for years, Julio is preparing to march in a local parade, honored to carry the American flag. It was not uncommon to see Julio on Main Street carrying a tray of milk shakes or sundaes from Miller's Drug Store for the bank tellers to enjoy on their break.

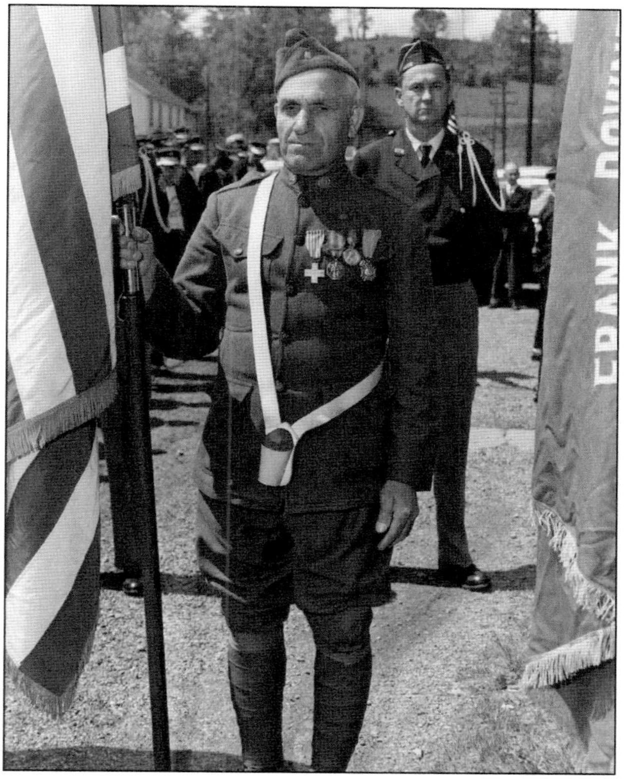

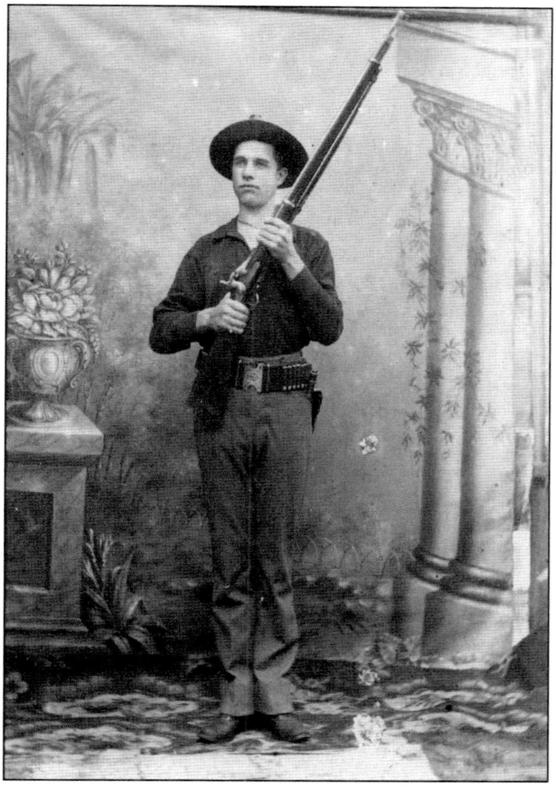

Frank M. Downer, a resident of Monongahela, was a Spanish-American War veteran who lost his life in World War I. He enrolled on April 27, 1898, mustered on May 11, 1899, and mustered out with Company A on August 22, 1899. The Frank M. Downer American Legion Post 302 was organized on September 13, 1919, and named for Sgt. Frank M. Downer.

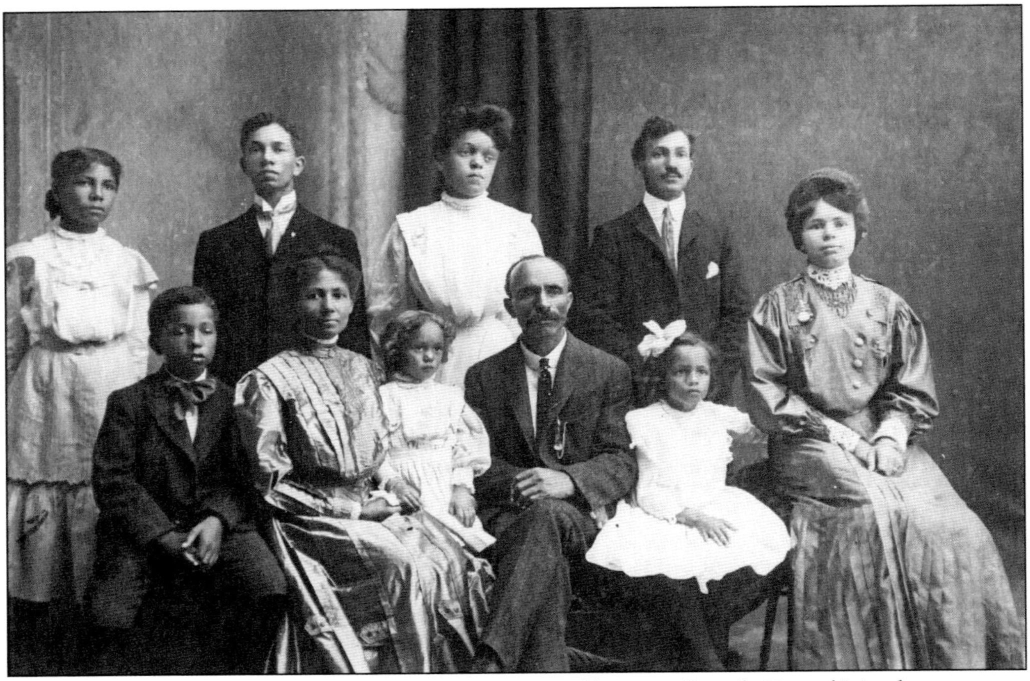

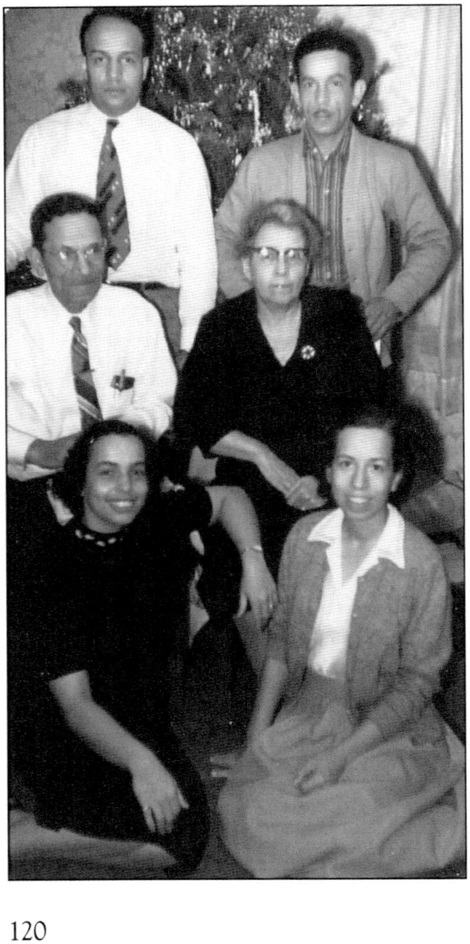

Pictured here are Joseph H. and Martha Simmons with their children. Mr. Simmons was elected to and served the Monongahela City Council in the late 1800s, representative of the positions of prominence to which all could aspire in Monongahela. The Simmonses were the grandparents of the Honorable Paul A. Simmons, a future federal judge. The Simmons family is, from left to right, (first row) Alden, Martha, Ruth, Joseph, Jeanne, and Alverda; (second row) Edith, Perry (father of Paul), Edna, and Frank.

Retired federal judge Paul A. Simmons is pictured with his parents and siblings; from left to right are (first row) Ruth and Eleanor; (second row) parent Perry and Lily; (third row) Paul and James. As a high school graduate, Judge Simmons suffered an industrial accident working on the railroad and lost part of his leg, and his mother prodded him to do his own legal research. He was successful in getting a settlement and went on to attend the University of Pittsburgh and Harvard Law School. Appointed by President Carter on April 7, 1978, Judge Simmons was the first federal judge to go through the merit selection process in Pennsylvania and the first African American judge appointed to the District Court of the Western District of Pennsylvania.

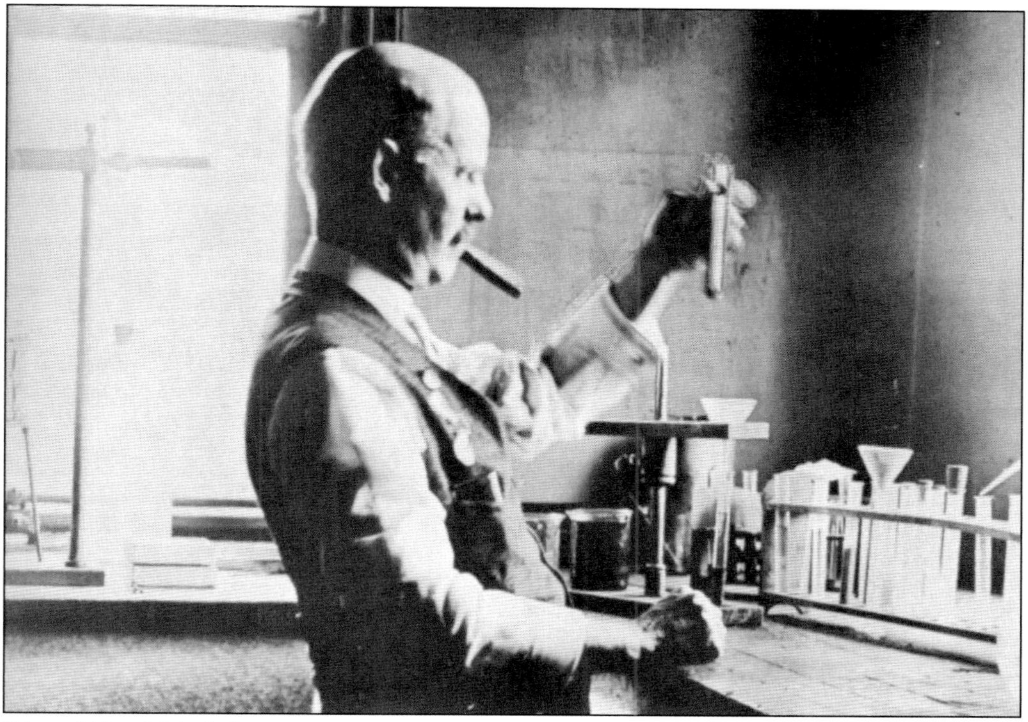

Edward Goodrich Acheson was an inventor, scientist, and industrialist. He is shown conducting experiments in his laboratory in Monongahela, where he invented Carborundum (silicon carbide) and started the Carborundum Company. For 50 years, Carborundum was the hardest known man-made substance. It is one of the patents most responsible for the industrial age. The Monongahela home where he lived from 1890 to 1895 is a National Historic Landmark.

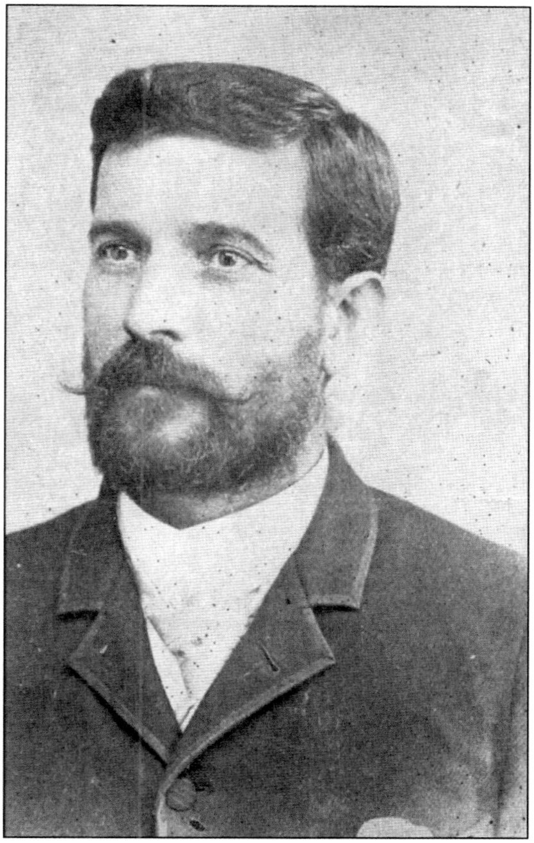

C.L. Anton and his brothers George and John were the premier wick lamp makers in the United States. Around 1874, the brothers each set up a workshop to manufacture wick lamps for local miners. Subsequently, George and John combined their operations, marketing their lamps worldwide under the George Anton name. The Star Lamp, first sold in 1898, was the bestselling mine lamp of its time.

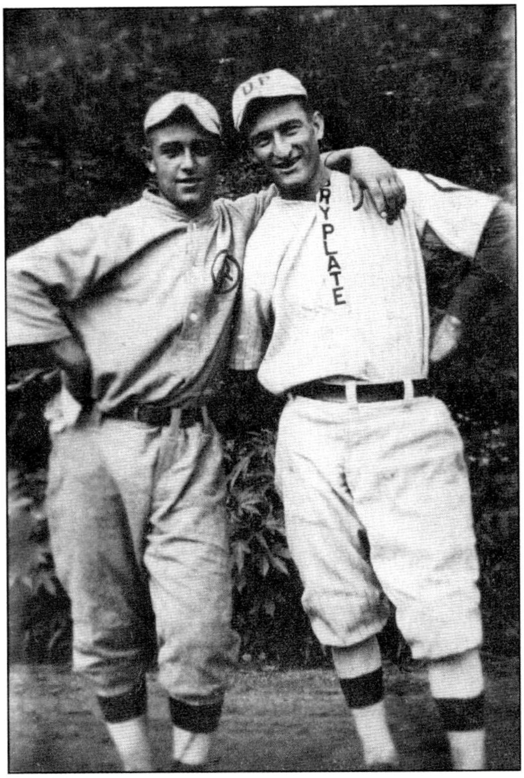

Pictured here are friends Vic Pezzoni (left) and Hook Montana (right), who enjoyed a game of baseball this day in 1919 in Axleton, just across the river from Monongahela. A true team player, Hook donated sports-themed photographs to Potente Zanardelli's scrapbook. Hook was known for his friendly nature and outstanding athletic abilities. One can only imagine the size of the smile in this photograph if Hook knew that one day his grandson "Joey" would arguably be the NFL's greatest quarterback—there's no need to argue that point in Monongahela. (Courtesy scrapbook of Potente Zanardelli)

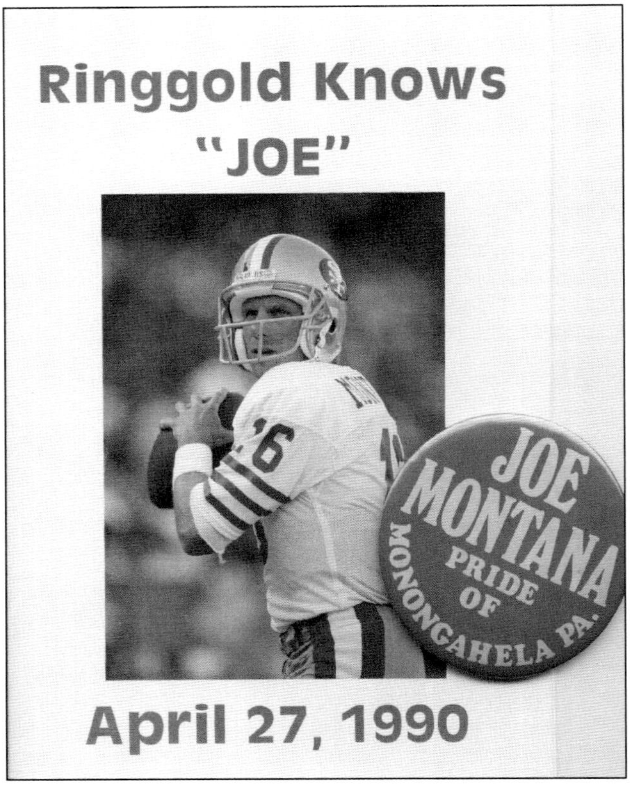

Joe Montana, son of Joseph and Theresa Montana, learned to throw a football through a tire swing in Bill and Emma Polonoli's yard on Park Avenue. Joe excelled in baseball, basketball, and football, graduating from Ringgold High School in 1974. One of the greatest quarterbacks ever, Joe won all four Super Bowls he played in as a San Francisco 49er and was inducted into the Pro Football Hall of Fame in 2000.

Judge Carl E. Gibson may be pardoning a frog he caught while on vacation. Graduating from Monongahela High School in 1891, Judge Gibson attended Pittsburg Law School and later served as Monongahela City solicitor. He was a partner in the Monongahela law firm of McIlvaine, Vance & Gibson and later became the president judge of the court of common pleas of Washington County. His son John F. Gibson wrote *The Judge's Stories*, recalling memories of his father. It was published in 1996.

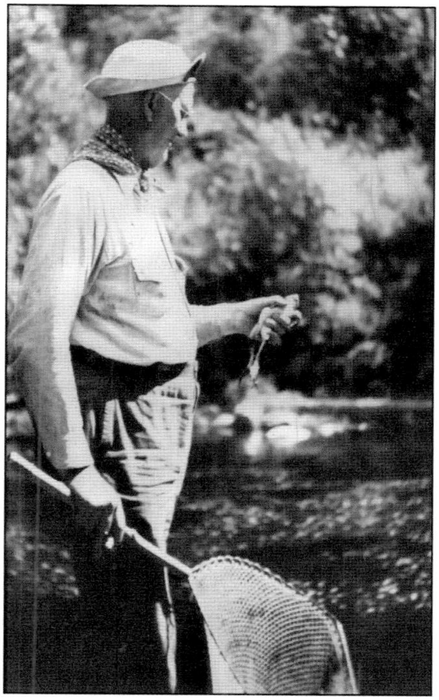

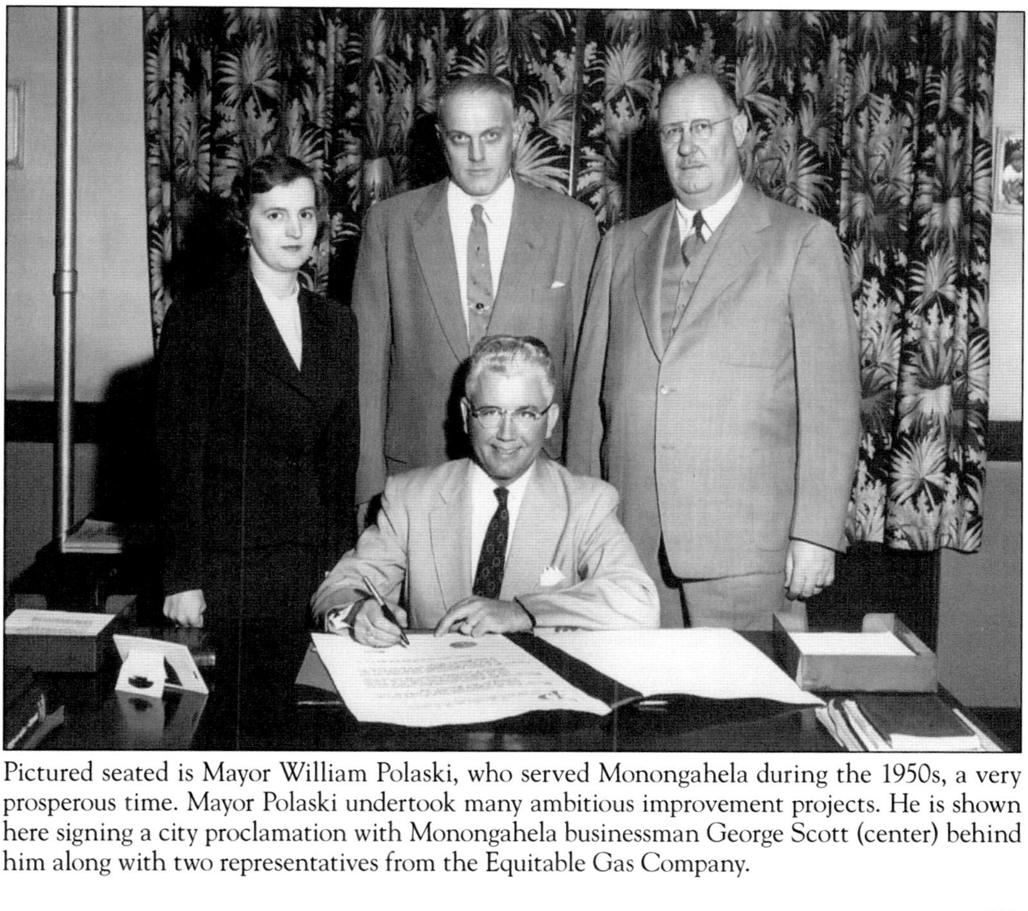

Pictured seated is Mayor William Polaski, who served Monongahela during the 1950s, a very prosperous time. Mayor Polaski undertook many ambitious improvement projects. He is shown here signing a city proclamation with Monongahela businessman George Scott (center) behind him along with two representatives from the Equitable Gas Company.

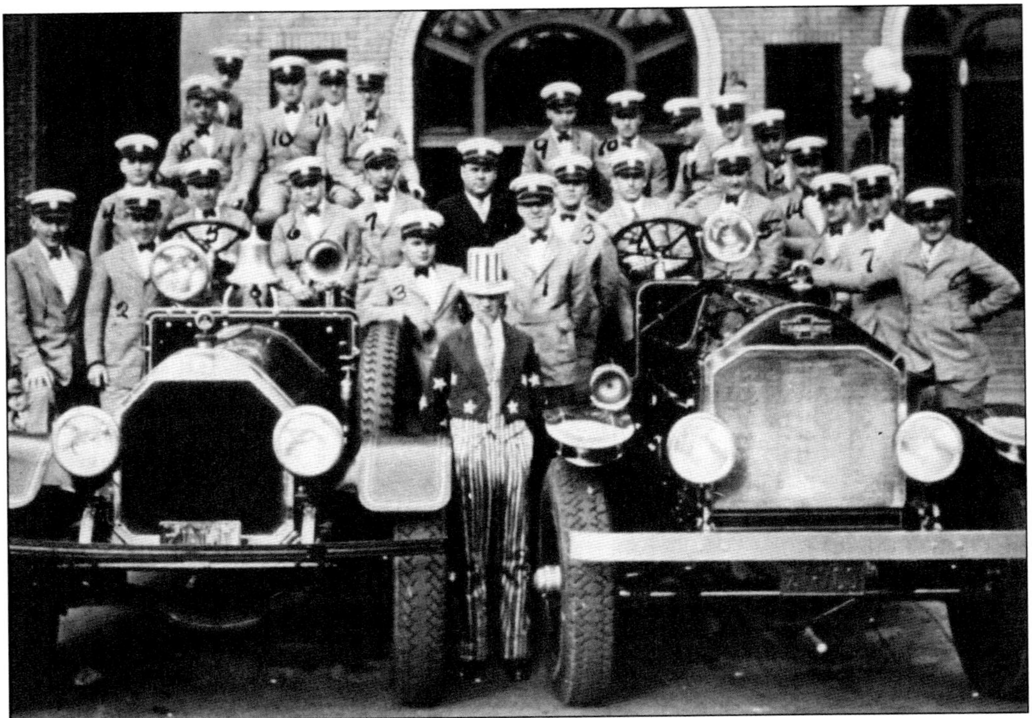

The Monongahela Volunteer Fire Department was organized in 1883 and has been faithfully responding in times of crisis, whether to offer fire protection, pump out flooded basements, or usher Santa Claus into Monongahela. Over the years, many of the volunteers have been business owners and residents, and when the alarm sounds, they have always dropped everything to come to the aid of the community.

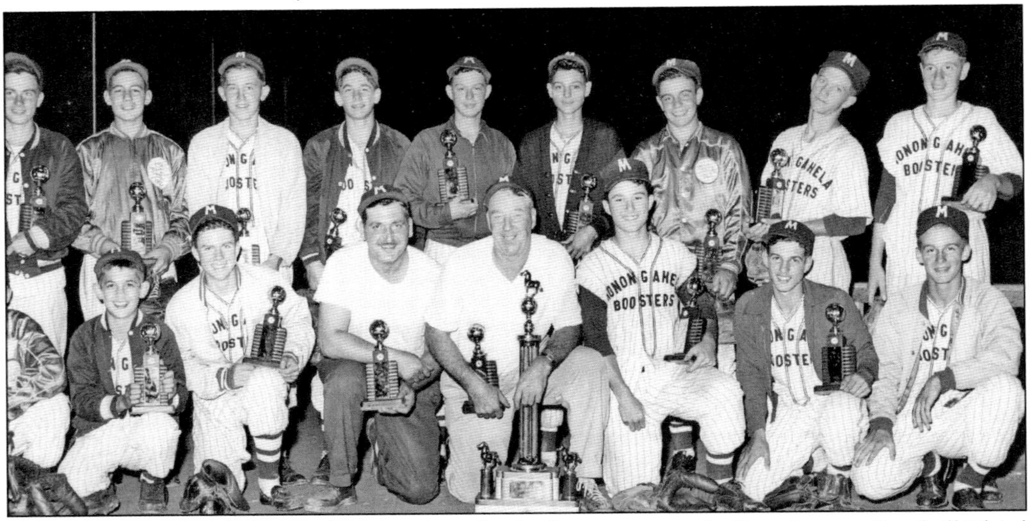

Monongahela prevailed over Chicago 8-2 in the final game to win the Pony League Baseball Third World Series championship, played at 8:30 p.m. on August 19, 1954, in Washington, Pennsylvania. Pictured from left to right are (first row) Gary Wassel, Frank DeRosa, Dave Caldwell, assistant manager Lou Revetta, manager Harry Sickels, Larry Sasselli, Ron Bertolini, and Ed Kikla; (second row) John Stuyvesant, Milton Diaz, Rich Sacane, Dave Stadtlander, Jim Voelkar, Dee Galiffa, George Peters, George Fabin, and Bill McCall. (Courtesy Martha Sickels Muniz.)

Cheerful Willoughby grew up in Monongahela City, the daughter of the opera house owner. This photograph was used as an advertisement for a local ice cream company. In May 1909, Cheerful was named "Miss Monongahela," winning the Monongahela Merchants Popularity Election. Merchant contest rules had promised the winner "a luxurious trip to the Bermuda Islands on the palatial ships of the Furness-Bermuda Company." Seemingly destined for big things, Cheerful eventually moved to Hollywood, where she became a silent film star.

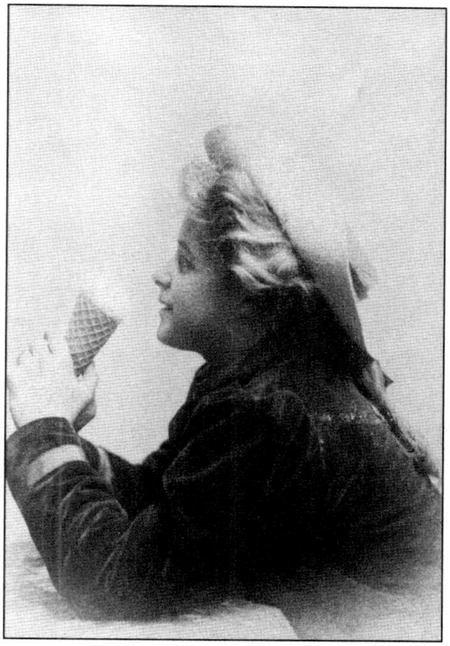

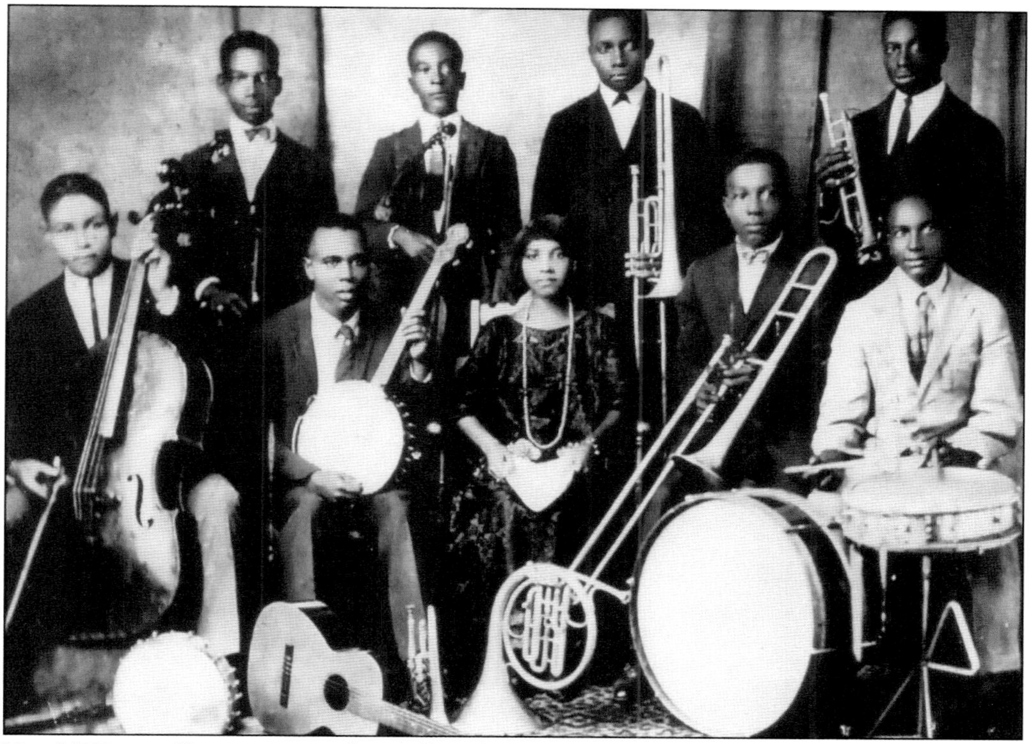

Harold Weaver (first row, second on left) is shown as a young musician with a banjo and guitar and his band, called the Weavers, during the Depression era. Born April 19, 1905, Weaver lived, played, and taught music in Monongahela throughout the course of his life. He was well known across southwestern Pennsylvania and taught music lessons to over 18,000, even when he was well into his 80s. From 1929 to 1935, his melodic voice was heard on the radio airwaves of WJAS and KDKA when he hosted radio programs.

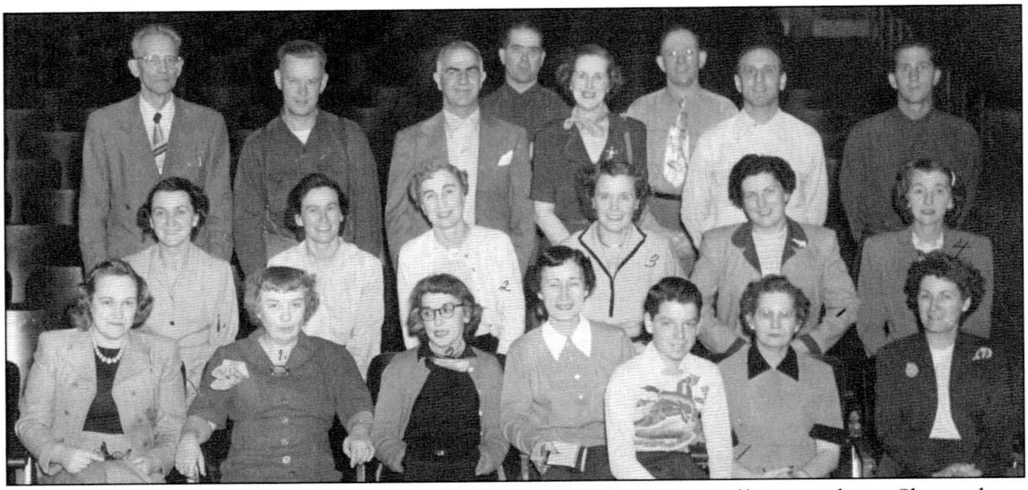

The Monongahela School District was long known for having excellent teachers. Shown here are some Waverly and High School teachers gathered in the high school auditorium. From left to right are (first row) Frances Duff, Louise Sanders, Blanche Parkinson, Suzanne Simms, an unidentified student, Ellen Styche, and Irene Robertson; (second row) Mary Vaira, Ruth Nevin, Harriet Moore, Anna Mae Wible, Anna Belle Sweeney, and Lois G. Woodward; (third row) Ernie Kahle, Hazen Neill, Tony Barbero, Kitty Bostleman, John Conte, and Harry Johnson; (fourth row) Mike Garry and unidentified.

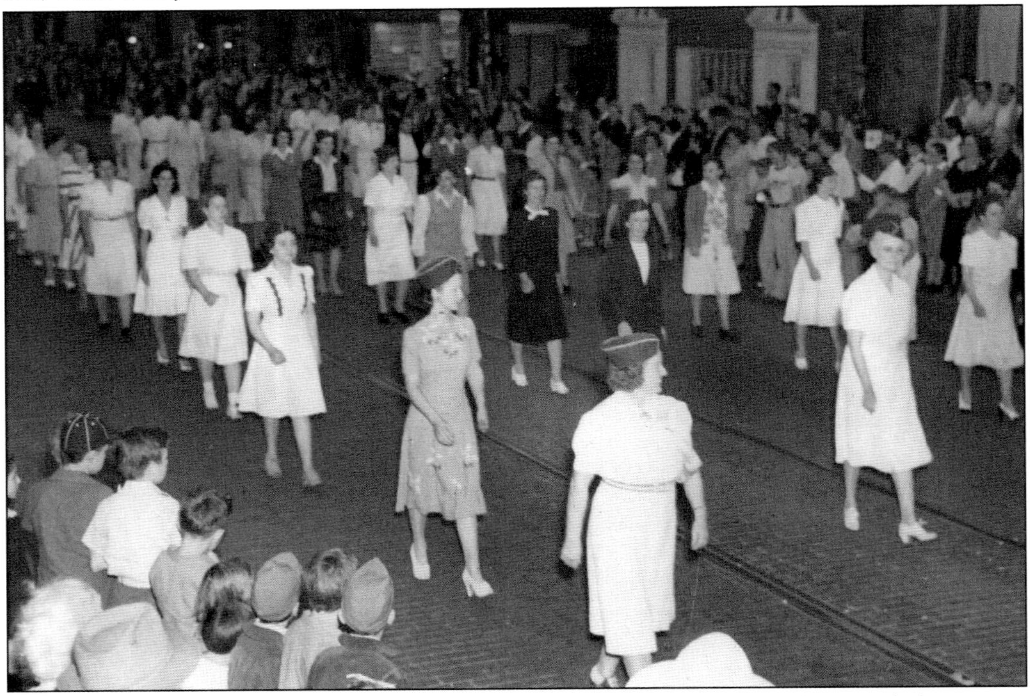

During World War II, women filled a variety of roles, including driving when needed. In many parts of the United States, Women's Motor Corps were formed, and Monongahela had its own. The women in the corps responded in a variety of ways. Sometimes, they used station wagons as ambulances to respond to emergencies. Sometimes, they were asked to pick up materials at industrials plants and drive them to where they were needed. In this photograph, the Women's Motor Corps is marching up Main Street on June 15, 1942.

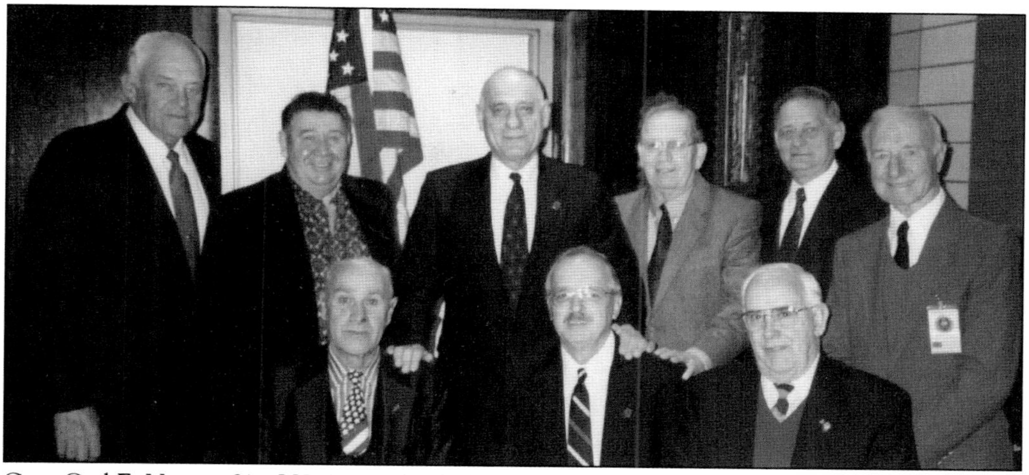

Gen. Carl E. Vuono, 31st US Army chief of staff, is a true hometown hero. General Vuono and his brother John are proud to be from Monongahela and equally proud to be born to a barber and neighborhood grocer, Carl and Rose De Santis Vuono. General Vuono is shown with local veterans, who rededicated the Veteran's Memorial in Chess Park in his honor in 1996. Shown are, from left to right, (first row) Art Doty, Til Necciai, and Tom Weygandt; (second row) Ken Cook, Fred Angerman, General Vuono, Mayor John Moreschi, Jack Coulter, and Bim Lodovici. (Courtesy Fred Angerman.)

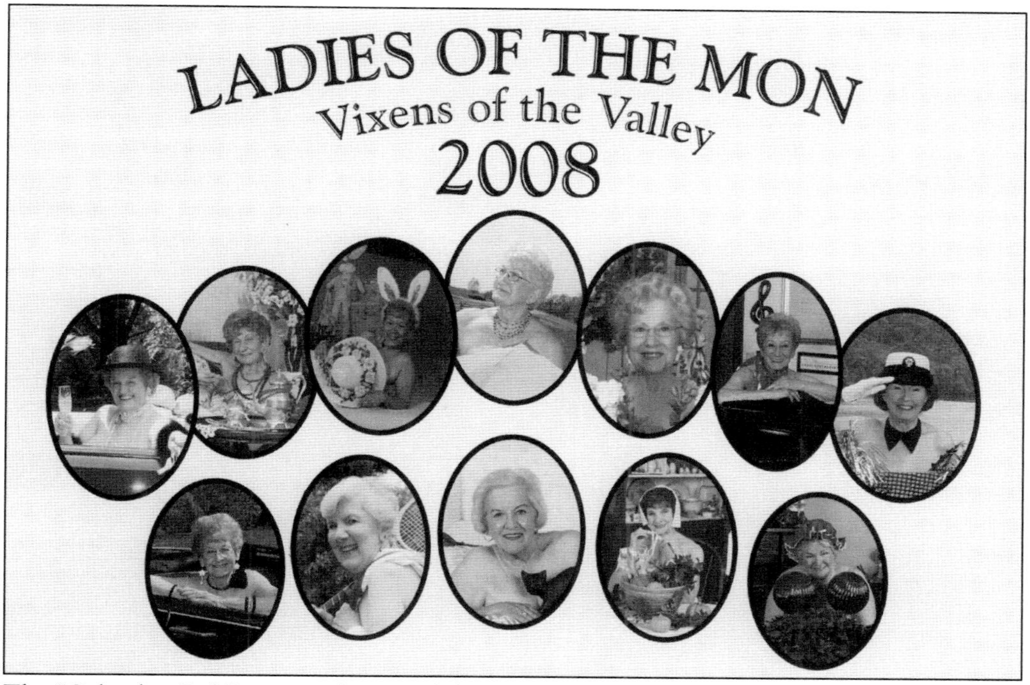

The "Calendar Girls" are true heroes of the Monongahela Area Historical Society. At a time when the doors were set to close, the calendar (brainchild of Lorys Crisafulli) was conceived and received worldwide attention. The heroes include Lorys, Fran Fusco, Dot Krol, Sally Stephenson, Wanda Magone, Lois Phillips, Esther Cox, Phoebe Barkey, Bebe Barantovich, Kathleen Bordini, Peggy Savadeck, Sondra Odelli Bordini, Chris Grilli for photography, and Claudia Willams for sales. Because of them, this story does not end; a new chapter has begun. This is the spirit of Monongahela. (Photograph by Chris Grilli.)